Wild Parsley

Waldron Caldwell

Special thanks to Margaret Moore for the hours of memories and laughter, Nancy Waldron Blaisdell for reading every word written, and Tyler Caldwell for his artistically abstract talent.

Table of Contents

Waldron Caldwell hopes your reading experience is a pleasant one.

6

The Broken Circle

We stood in the hospital room unable to move. We knew that people didn't live forever in this world, but Mamie wasn't supposed to die. She was our rock. She was the one that we compared everyone to in order to judge their worthiness. She was our matriarch. She couldn't just die and leave us alone. Part of me wanted to be angry, but the bigger part of me just wanted her to open her eyes and tell me that everything was going to be all right just as she did when I skinned my knee as a child. But we weren't children any more. We were grown women who now had to accept that Mamie was gone and our bond with her was now broken. Incomplete. And would never be the same.

I began to cry. My sisters huddled around me and we all, except for one, cried together. Julia never cried. Not because she didn't love Mamie, but she knew that she would be the one who would hold the rest of us together. She didn't have the luxury to have her broken heart show. She would have to express her grief in solitude while she laid on her pillow. Even though she wasn't the oldest of us, she knew that Mamie had groomed her to take the reign of the family if anything happened to her.

The hospital let us stay in the room with Mamie's body until we were ready to leave. She died with Julia holding one hand and Gertie holding the other. Elisabeth, Ava, and I stood at the foot of her bed. We watched her take her last breath and all of our worlds stopped turning. The last breath was long, but not labored. When she exhaled for the last time, she was in peace.

How do you let go of something that had always been there in your life? Suffered every broken heart with you? Guided you, taught you how to read, and taught you about God? How do you accept that the mainstay of your life as you knew it, just left you alone? We had never awakened to a day when Mamie wasn't breathing the same air as we were. It was surreal.

"She look mo' like momma now, don' she Gertie?" asked Elisabeth.

Those words made my heart skip a beat. I was only two when momma had died. I never knew her. I couldn't remember her face or how she looked. I only had one picture of her and I kept it in my bedroom in a shiny brass frame. I never failed to tell her good night. I envied the sisters who knew our momma and got to hold her and tell her they loved her. Now Mamie was gone, too.

There was a light tap on the hospital door. Pastor Washington from our church stuck his head in and asked, "I-I-I-I was j-j-just wonderin' if you l-l-l-ladies might w-w-want to have a p-p-prayer?"

"What you goin' do, Pas'er? Resurrect 'er?" Elisabeth asked.

"Elisabeth!" Gertie scolded, "The pastor just wants to offer comfort to the family."

"Well, she done gone ova yonda, sista. He can't pray her to get no betta now."

Pastor Washington looked at Gertie and said, "B-b-be happy to s-s-sing a s-s-s-ong of p-praise with all of y-y-y'all."

8

"W-w-well, I says no thank y-y-ya!" Elisabeth said to Pastor Washington, mocking him.

Julia finally stepped in with, "We all thank ya for stoppin' by pastor, but we are finishin' up here. There is a lots to take in and a lots more for us to take care of."

"Certainly, J-J-Julia. J-J-Just let me know if I-I-I can b-b-be of service. D-d-don't forget the p-p-play coming s-s-soon."

With that, Pastor Washington left the room and we actually felt better after the interruption. It allowed us to break the shock and rebound our emotions.

"I am so glad tha' man left. Ever Sunday after preachin', I start to stutterin', too. Afta two or three hours of him, I jus' wants to slap 'im up side his head to help 'im get the words out. Don' know why he would go inta preachin' no way," Elisabeth said.

"Elisabeth, Pastor Washington is a man of the Lord. You shouldn't be so critical of him," Gertie said to Elisabeth and gave her a deep frown.

"I ain't bein' critical. I jus' bein' honest."

9

"Okay, that's goin' be enough. Like I told the pastor, we gots a lot on our plate now. We need to be gettin' back to it. It's what Mamie woulda wanted us to do," Julia told us all firmly.

We gathered ourselves and the things we could carry out of the room. With bowed heads, we touched Mamie's hand that was still warm, but frail in appearance. We opened the door of the hospital room where Mamie had died, but did not suffer long. The hallway was full of our friends who had tears welling in their eyes. I can hardly remember all of the faces of the people sharing warm embraces that lined our pathway to exit the hospital. Mamie was such a beloved woman. She would have been proud.

She had touched all of their lives in one way or another. Mamie nursed the ailing with chicken soup and homemade biscuits. Always looking for the good in people. It bothered her that so many youths found themselves outside the law and helped them with legal aid. Then, she would do what she could to help the families incorporate the children back into their fold. She would always say, "The best thing you can give a child is love".

It took almost an hour for us to make our way through the crowd. By the exit door stood Judge Holcombe, a dear friend of Mamie's. There was a single tear rolling down his cheek. He took out his handkerchief and wiped his face. His heart was broken, too.

I remembered back to the first time I had ever seen Judge Holcombe. I was just a little girl sitting in his courtroom. He was sitting way up high on the bench. At least at the time, it appeared that way to me. He wore a black robe and a large pitcher of iced water sat to his left. I remember it so clearly. He slowly poured the water into a tall, clear glass until it overflowed. A law clerk cleaned up the spilled water with a white bar towel. He hit his gavel to let everyone there that day know that court would begin.

I remember being there where my oldest sister, then herself the mother of four children, threatened to pull out her razor and cut the throat of her now dead husband. Elisabeth didn't cut him that day. Well, not with her razor. Mamie had counseled her before court started to watch her temper. After Leroy had accused Elisabeth of being an unfit mother while she did without new shoes or clothes to make sure her children had their needs met, we all held our breath and kept an eye on her purse where we all knew she kept a well sharpened straight blade razor just in case she needed it. When the judge asked her if she understood the charges being brought against her that day and she told his honor that she didn't, we all knew to be prepared to jump to the floor and pray. Sure enough, when the judge explained to Elisabeth that Leroy was saying that she was a bad mother, we all hit the floor. We had all seen Elisabeth with her razor before after Leroy had pulled some of his shenanigans. If Mamie had not talked to Elisabeth before court had begun, we would all have been attending Leroy's last rites. But Mamie had control. Elisabeth did pick up her purse and after the judge asked her how she felt about the charges, Elisabeth walked over to Leroy and beat all the hell out of that man that the judge would allow. About five minutes worth before he called the bailiff to rescue Leroy. Mamie smiled at the judge and all went well and the charges were dropped. Judge Holcombe knew Mamie well, and he knew that Elisabeth worked two jobs and still took in odd jobs to do the best she could for her children. Judge Holcombe also knew Elisabeth was less than well educated, but knew her to be a good mother.

Leroy rubbed his head and asked the judge if he planned to do anything about the beating he just took from Elisabeth. Judge Holcombe took a long drink and sat down his glass of ice water and told Leroy he was a fortunate man to have a wife as good as Elisabeth and even more fortunate that he didn't call a lunch recess and let her finish bashing his head in. After that day

11

in court, Leroy knew well enough not to accuse Elisabeth of anything. Especially when she had her purse.

Today, Judge Holcombe was grief stricken. He waved Julia to come to him. Where once he sat majestically up on his bench, he now leaned on a walking stick to keep his balance. It steadied him and allowed him to walk. He reached into his suit and withdrew an envelope. It was thick and had something written on the front of it that I couldn't quite make out.

"Here, I want you to have this," Judge Holcombe said to Julia.

"What is it, judge?"

"Just something to help keep things running smoothly. Mamie told me only months ago that you would be keeping the farm and baked goods going. I wanted to help, if you know what I mean."

"Yes, the farm will still be up and running as usual and thank you for your thoughtfulness."

Julia slipped the envelope inside her jacket pocket and rejoined us.

She looked at all of us and said, "The funeral home is on their way to pick up Mamie's body. We are goin' to have to get her burial clothes ready. Let's go and get all of this taken care of."

The words, "burial clothes", gave me a slight tingling up my spine. I wasn't sure I would be able to look at Mamie in a coffin. I knew she had already handled the arrangements and that was probably what the judge had given Julia. She always told us that she had everything done so we would not have to worry about picking out a casket or anything else. Mamie knew how difficult something like that would be for us.

Julia drove the truck home and Ava and I rode with her. Elisabeth drove her car with Gertie beside her. I noticed the envelope poking its way out of Julia's pocket.

"Julia, what did the judge give you in that envelope?"

"A donation," she responded.

"You mean, he knows about…"

She quickly shut me up with, "Yes, he knows."

"So, he is a client?"

"Has been for a litta ova a year. Now no more about this now."

Ava looked on and didn't say a word. My mind, however, was racing. But I knew that Julia would give me the details later.

The rest of the ride home was quiet. I turned to look back at Elisabeth and Gertie in Elisabeth's car. They were both looking straight ahead. Very much out of their norm. They were chatterboxes, especially when they were together. I turned back, closed my eyes, and thought of Mamie.

I knew the paper would call her a saint. Cookham is a small town in South Carolina and most likely, everyone by now would know of Mamie's passing. No one in Cookham could break wind without someone else ready to analyze what they had eaten. Mamie abhorred gossip, and she didn't mind taking down a switch to one of us that she caught telling some off-handed hearsay, especially about someone who attended the local A.M.E. Church to which she was a member. We all belonged to it faithfully. All seven of us. Now just five.

Mamie had assumed responsibility of our caretaking when our mother passed away when I was just a little girl. I was never told what my mother had died from and I had always been afraid to ask, but considering what Mamie raised on the farm, I suspected my momma died from cancer. That was years ago and there were not as many medical advances as there are today. That, plus the fact my mother was black. I remember Mamie speaking of the colored waiting rooms at the doctor's office even for me when I was young. I never understood why I had to be the last one Dr. Shipley saw after he treated all the white children. I thought it only as an adult issue. One day they would grow out of it.

I did decipher from Mamie's comments that she had not cared too much for my father. She labeled him a deadbeat. At age three, I had not a clue what

14

that meant. But from the tone in Mamie's voice, I knew it wasn't a good thing. I, also, knew better than to ask about him. Mamie wasn't a violent tempered woman, but there was something about my father that could cause Mamie to say words that I never knew existed. "Son-of-a-bitch" was never on my vocabulary lists from school. When I heard that we had another bitch in heat, I always looked around for my father. He was never there and was not likely to be. We didn't need him. We had each other and Mamie had taught us to take care of our own and take on a few of someone else's if need be. The entire town of Cookham would miss Mamie Nesbit even more than they would ever know.

My thoughts stopped when the truck did. Julia didn't hesitate to jump out and get ready to go inside. I was a little reluctant. My chest felt vacant and the house looked empty.

The three story house stood majestic on its thirty acre farm surrounding it. Pecan and walnut trees scattered the landscape of the freshly mowed two acre lawn and grew tall against the house's yellow paint. It had just been reroofed and the shingles gleaned in the sunlight.

Yellow was Mamie's favorite color. A prime color she always called it. She often dressed in yellow and had pale yellow roses on each side of the house. Purple flowers of every kind sprinkled the recently mulched beds between the rosebushes. Wild or purchased, Mamie loved flowers. She had a gardener's green thumb and talked to her plants as though they were the best friends she had ever had. She respected them as much as she did people, maybe more. Mamie said that flowers were God's paint on canvas. When the world got too dismal to take, Mamie always went to the barn and potted seedlings. She taught us a lot about planting. And harvesting. And we learned. Oh, how we learned.

15

The Prodigal Sister Returns

"Yes, of course. Do you want me to have her call you back or I can give you her work number. Gertie, I am so, so sorry for your loss. Please, express my sympathies to the entire family."

"Thank you, Patrick. You are such a wonderful man. Patience must be so glad to have found you. If you wouldn't mind, please tell Patience about Mamie's passing and she can call us if she wants or needs to. We will all be here at the farm until dark. She's got the number."

"Of course. And, again, I am so sorry for your loss."

"Thank you, darling. We appreciate your kind words."

We elected Gertie to be the one to call Patience and tell her about Mamie. Since we were black, we often referred to Patience as the white sheep of the family. Julia paced the floor.

"Well," Julia said nervously, "is she gonna be comin' down here or not?"

"I don't know, Julia," Gertie responded. "Patrick is going to give her the news and the rest is up to Patience. So, we will just have to wait and see."

A number of hours passed and we had not heard from our sister, Patience. She had not been back to the farm in many years. Probably fifteen years or so. We thought she would surely call, but she was one that we were not particularly close with.

"Won' be right if Patience not be at her own grand mama's fun'rel," Elisabeth said.

"It would be fine with me," Julia said. "I've never liked her, and she hasn't even come back and be with Mamie and she knowed she was sick. Besides all that, I gotta be in North Carolina in the mornin'. I gotta keep the farm runnin'. I made promises to Mamie. Got no time for waitin' for Patience to call or sho'. I'm gonna be headed to bed. Goodnight to all y'all."

We felt the tension between Julia and Patience without the presence of Patience actually in the room. We knew the animosity between them. What we didn't know was that Patience and Patrick were on their way from Washington headed to Cookham, South Carolina. Would that have changed the way Julia felt? No. But, coming home she was.

Patience looked over at Patrick and asked, "How long did you rent the car?"

"Two weeks. Why?"

"I was hoping we could be back by the end of the week. We have a large case getting ready to go to court."

"Oh, yeah, which one?"

"Another case on drug trafficking. I can't talk much about it."

"Well, I'm sorry, Patience, but you yourself have told me how long your family's funerals can last. And, besides, you get to see the family that you haven't seen in years."

"Patrick, I am looking as forward to that as I am the funeral itself. I would rather be working. I just want to be there for the reading of the will."

Patrick rolled his eyes and shook his head.

"You have no idea how fortunate you are to have family. It's lonely being an only child. I have always wanted to have siblings."

"Well, take mine and we will call it even."

"Why do you hate them so much, Patience?"

"It's not them so much as who they are."

"Oh, you mean they didn't grow up to be well-to-do, filthy rich, and honest like all of the wonderful trust fund babies who run D.C.? That's who you want to be a product of?"

"I hardly even remember my momma and I wouldn't know my daddy if he were in the car with us right now."

"What about Mamie?"

"Mamie was my world until I left that hick town."

"Well, there you go. You have to be feeling some kind of grief after having lost someone who meant so much to you, right?"

"Don't start to psychoanalyze me, Patrick. If I need a shrink, I'll call one."

"Okay, okay. I know you're upset."

"I am doing what is expected of me."

"Never do what I expect of you," Patrick said under his breath.

"What did you say?"

"I asked you what it was like growing up in South Carolina."

"I think we have already had this conversation. I grew up on a small farm. One house. Three bedrooms. One outhouse. One washtub for bathing. One cow and two horses. Mamie. Five sisters. And a truck."

"Wow! You had a truck?" Patrick said jovially trying to humor Patience.

"I'm not laughing, Patrick."

"Look, Patience, you talked to Mamie every Sunday, at least, and she told you things were going really well on the farm. Small family farms have a tough time in this economy. You should be proud of your family."

"Yeah, well, if they are doing well, maybe you can ask them for a job when we get there. And, in the hot summer, you can get yourself a shower with the garden hose and dish soap."

"Ooh. I bet that dish soap really made your hair brittle, didn't it? Mamie probably couldn't give you those expensive salon treatments you get now, could she?"

"Just drive, Patrick. Keep your eyes on the road and just head south. The sooner we get there, the sooner we can leave. And, as I recall, you had a lot of frizz going on with your head when I first met you, too. Did your voodoo momma put some kind of hex on you?"

"She sure did, and its name was 'Patience'."

"Your momma was a damn voodoo priestess. Chickens hanging from a clothesline in her apartment. What kind of crazy shit is that?"

"Well, she didn't like you. Maybe she did cast a spell on you."

"Crazy woman kept trying to touch my hair. Thought I was actually going to eat anything she put in front of me."

"Patience, you threatened her."

"I didn't do nary a thing. I just told her that there was nothin' she could put on me that a good ole fashioned ass whoopin' wouldn't cure. The dinner was over."

"Sure was. She hated you even more after that. You just need to learn to go with the flow sometimes. Let things roll off of your shoulder. That temper you have always seems to make enemies for you. You know it's true."

"I know nothing of the sort. But I do know that I'm tired and I am going to catch some sleep. We still have a long drive in front of us."

"Yeah, I thought you could take a couple of hours of the driving so I could get some sleep, too."

"You shouldn't be tired. It's not like you're exhausted from working. I have been pulling in all of the money."

"Right, Patience, right. You should just go to sleep. I'm thinking about stopping by my mother's house on the way to get some herbs and things for your attitude."

"Uh-huh. Then you and your momma both can get a good ass whoopin'."

Patience turned away from Patrick and went to sleep with dead chickens on her mind. She slept for two hours and Patrick found some peaceful calmness in the silence. He thought of his mother and her crazy ways. He, also, thought of what it would have been like living and growing up on a farm like Patience and her family had done. He thought he might have liked that.

Two hours turned into three and Patience still slept. Patrick heard the ding of the gas tank telling him it was hungry. He would have to stop and fill up the tank. He was getting hungry himself. He exited I-95 and pulled into the nearest gas station he saw. He left Patience asleep in the car. He went inside to find something for his own tank. Not much to choose from so he stocked up on junk food. He started to open the honeybun before he reached the counter to pay. He held the barcode for the clerk to scan and popped all that was left of the honeybun in his mouth. After spending seventy-five dollars on gas and the junk food, he returned to the rented car and found Patience in the driver's seat.

"Oh, did you decide to wake up?" he asked her.

"Yeah, but I am still really tired, but I thought you'd need a break. Get in and let's find a hotel for the night."

"Patience, we can get a little farther south than this. It took us two hours to get out of D.C. We have almost the entire way left to go."

"The farm isn't going anywhere, and they will all still be there tomorrow. I'll drive about an hour and find a place to stay."

They drove only forty-five minutes and Patience turned into the first hotel she saw. A small mom and pops inn that gave Patrick the creeps.

"Hmm, I wonder if they have room service here," Patrick said a little nervous about the place. "Hey, in the movies, isn't this the type of place people check into and hardly ever check out?"

"It looks a little shabby, but the rooms are clean. They have a diner and the food is not bad."

"And, how exactly do you know all of this?"

"Because I have stayed here before."

"Yeah? When?"

"Get my gray bags out of the car, will you? Oh, and don't forget the overnight case."

"All of your bags are gray. You want all of your bags out to spend one night in this place?"

"Yes, and I stayed here last winter when it was snowing so badly, we couldn't make it into D.C."

"Okay, but if anyone named Norman checks us in, my ass is out of here."

"Don't be such a baby, Patrick. I'm going to check in."

"Okay, but I hope you don't plan to stop at a motel every three hours. We should have just kept on driving."

He watched as Patience walked into the office and registered for a room. Then, he saw her hug the desk clerk and watched as they held hands and smiled at one another. He struggled with all of Patience's luggage and entered the office.

"Oh, hey there, young man. I'm Alfred and who would you be?"

"Alfred? Alfred who?"

"Alfred Wilson."

"Oh, okay. I'm Patrick. I am Patience's husband. I would shake your hand, but I would probably never get all of these bags picked back up if I dropped them."

"Not to worry. You folks are checked in. You have cottage eight. The room right beside the diner. Better step it up though, Vera said she was closing at nine sharp tonight."

"No problem, Alfred. We will be on our way right now," Patience said with a smile.

"A great woman you have there, Patrick."

"Oh, yes sir, Alfred. She sure is. And did you see how she took some of her luggage from me to help carry it all? Got me a true gem in that one."

"Yep," Alfred said, "a great girl."

Patience was already in the room a few minutes before Patrick arrived with all of the bags.

"Where have you been?"

Patrick, weighted down with luggage, gave her a frowned look and dropped all of the bags in the center of the floor.

"Well, we better get to the diner. Vera closes at nine tonight."

Patience whisked past Patrick and was already out the door. Patrick walked over the mound of luggage and followed her to the restaurant. The seating was self-serve. They chose a corner booth and sat opposite of each other. Patrick picked up a menu and started to scan his options for dinner.

"You should try the hamburger steak," Patience said gleefully.

"Hamburger steak? Is that an oxymoron?"

"No, it's a tender hamburger covered in dark gravy. I think it comes with mashed potatoes and green beans."

"Then why not get a hamburger and French fries? Doesn't sound much different."

"Order what you want. I am getting the hamburger steak."

The waitress approached the table with an order pad in her hand. When she glanced up, she screeched in excitement, "Patience!"

Patience stood up and hugged Vera. Patrick was impressed with the interaction between the two women.

"Girl, you look as pretty as ever. What brings you down this way? I know you don't like leaving Washington."

"I had to get down here and taste your fine cooking, Vera. This is my husband, Patrick."

"Well, hello there, Patrick. It is so nice to meet you."

"The pleasure is all mine, Vera."

"I am just so glad you got here before we closed tonight. You must be starving. What can I get for you?"

"Girl, you know what I want. Your famous hamburger steak with the fixings."

Vera gave out a hardy laugh and started writing on her pad.

"You want plain black coffee with that, too, don't you, hon?" You don't think I would forget what my favorite customers drink, now do you? What can I get for you, Patrick?"

Patience blurted out, "Oh, he just wants a hamburger and fries."

"Actually, Vera, I would like to try the hamburger steak, too. Patience has told me so much about it that I feel that I must try it, too."

"Well, all right then. I will get right to work on this. Patrick, what can I get you to drink?"

"I would like to have some hot tea, if you have it."

"Sure thing. Coming right up."

They handed the menus back to Vera and watched as she walked away.

"Patience, what was that I just saw?"

"What did you see?"

"You had a kind interaction with someone. I'm not sure I have witnessed that very often."

"I don't know what you are taking about, Patrick."

"Patience, in the last few minutes, I have seen you converse with two people that you didn't pass judgment on as soon as they turned their back on you. What gives? Not to mention, they were white people, and you don't like white people."

"I like some of them. I just don't like the crackers."

The table fell silent while Vera delivered the drinks and the conversation resumed after Vera left.

"Well, excuse me, but I have never seen you behave in a considerate way to white people."

"Patrick, I just think that people get back what they give."

"And, don't you forget it, Patience."

"What exactly does that mean?"

"Nothing, Patience. It doesn't mean anything."

The table went silent again. Vera came back shortly with two large plates of food. The smell was overwhelming and Patrick took in a deep breath to take it all in.

"Mmm, that smells wonderful! I detect onions and a slight hint of green bell pepper."

Vera said, "Why that's correct, Patrick. I can see who does the cooking in your house."

"You know I'm not much in the kitchen, Vera," Patience added to bring herself back to the center of the conversation.

"Well, you probably don't have time with your job and all. You have to handle all of those court cases and defend the country from criminals!" Vera said emphatically. Vera, then turned to Patrick and explained, "Patience told us all about her work and what she did in her job with the government. She didn't give up any secrets though. Just that she does her best to keep all those illegal drugs off the streets. We had such a nice visit this past winter during that big snowfall."

"Yeah, it sounds like you really got a big snow job, all right," Patrick responded and gave Patience a questioning look.

"Thanks, Vera. I can't wait to bite into this," Patience said with a smile.

Vera left the couple alone to eat. Patrick was impressed and enjoyed the food. So did Patience. She ate as though she was tasting part of her heritage. Food she was raised eating.

"So," Patrick asked between bites, "would you like to tell me what all of that was about?"

"All of what?"

"Come on, Patience. What exactly did you tell these people that you did for a living? What is all of the crime you have been fighting?"

"I only told them that I was an attorney with the U.S. Department of Justice."

"I am finding that hard to believe. From the tone of Vera's voice, you sounded like J. Edgar Hoover. You have never first chaired a case in your life. You are more of a law clerk."

"Do you always need to put me down, Patrick?"

"No, but I have never felt the need to put you on a pedestal either. I think I am beginning to see why you stopped off here. You needed some ego boosting and character building, so you dropped in to let Alfred and Vera tell you how wonderful you are. Always a catch when you act nice."

"I'm full and I am going to go to the room," Patience said abruptly.

"Me, too."

Patience picked up her jacket and purse and put a twenty dollar tip on the table for Vera. She glared at Patrick as she did it.

Patrick smirked at Patience. "I would compliment you, too, for a twenty."

"You don't do anything good enough for a twenty."

Patrick laughed and they both went to their single room with separate double beds.

Welcomings and Windshields

In the early morning before dawn even thought of awakening, Julia was up
and dressed. She had on her work clothes which consisted of bibbed overalls,
boots, a long-sleeved shirt that was rolled up to her elbows, and our
granddad's old fedora; her bargaining hat. The night had been a long one. She
woke up twice in a sweat and had gotten up to adjust the thermostat. She
finally set it down to seventy degrees and tried to sleep.

She grabbed her keys from the key rack and noticed that Gertie and Elisabeth
had spent the night at the farm. She smelled coffee brewing, but resisted the
urge to have a cup. Gertie must have set the timer on the pot so they could
wake up to the aroma of the coffee. Julia also noticed that some cleaning had
been done and some furniture had been rearranged. She and Elisabeth must
have done that to accommodate their restless spirits and to busy their grief
with work. We knew, too, that Mamie's funeral would be a major event. They
must have worked hard to the very early morning. Elisabeth's snoring would
put a freight train to shame, but it told the tale of someone who suffered
from exhaustion.

Julia found herself relieved to find that Patience had not arrived after she had
gone to bed. She was hopeful she would not show at all. She would be
disappointed.

Patrick and Patience had awoken half an hour before Julia did in their hotel
room and decided to get on the road. Their sleep was restless, too. They both
showered. Separately, of course. Sharing a shower would be too intimate for
Patience. She went first and Patrick went second to enjoy a cold stream of

water. One of the many cold showers he had experienced in their marriage. Certainly nothing he wasn't accustomed to.

Patrick loaded the car with all of Patience's luggage. She had used only one of them. He, then, went in the office to surprisingly find Alfred at four o'clock in the morning.

Patrick asked, "Do you ever sleep?"

"Not much," Alfred said with a chuckle.

Patrick pulled out his wallet and put a credit card on the desk indicating for Alfred to use it to pay for their stay. Alfred waved his hand and told Patrick there would be no fee for the room.

Patrick looked surprised again.

"Patience explained why and where you are going. The room is the least I can do. Please, your money is no good here. Godspeed."

"Thank you, Alfred. We are indebted to you for your kindness."

With that and a firm handshake, Patience and Patrick were headed again to Cookham, South Carolina. Due south.

After Julia had gathered all of the merchandise she needed from the kitchen down in the barn, she, too, started her vehicle and headed to North Carolina. The state line was only about thirty minutes from Cookham, but her destination was about one and a half hours away. She would steal away in darkness and try to be back by the time her sisters were getting up and preparing for breakfast. There were things to be done that day. They had to take Mamie's burial clothes to the funeral home. Julia knew that Gertie and I would have most of that prepared. Julia put her foot to the accelerator and found herself heading due north.

Leaving the comforts of her normal environment always made Julia a little nervous. But she would never let that show. She always minded the speed limit and did little to bring any attention to herself. She would conduct her business and she would then return home. She always seemed to have a sixth sense about things. Mamie had that, too. They always knew when things did not quite seem right and they were rarely ever wrong. Julia had that feeling driving to North Carolina. Her inclination was to turn around, but she knew people were depending on her to supply what they needed. Crossing state lines always made Mamie nervous, too. But who would suspect a woman carrying baked goods, jellies, and farm produce to a farmer's market?

It was still dark and the blue lights reflecting in the truck's rearview mirror were very bright. Julia immediately checked her speed and knew she wasn't speeding. Her mind and heart were racing, but her exterior was as cool as the cucumbers she had packed in the truck bed. She pulled over but left the truck running.

An officer approached her. "Morning, Miss," the patrolman said, "where you headed to this early in the morning?"

"Mornin', Officer," Julia responded. I thought I'd head up to the farmer's market in Tucker. Crops are good this year."

"Yeah, seems that is true. Must be. I don't see many traveling up from South Carolina selling baked goods, though."

The officer shined his flashlight into the extended cab of the truck and then aimed the light onto Julia's face. She squinted her eyes and shielded her face from the bright light.

"Think you could show me your driver's license and registration? Going to need to see some proof of insurance, too."

Julia reached above her and pulled down the sun visor.

"Here ya go."

"You just sit right here for a minute and turn off the engine. I'll be right back."

"Sho' thing."

Julia rubbed her hands together and then rubbed her shoulders. Even in this heat, she felt cold.

The officer walked back up to the truck and asked, "You cold in this heat?"

"Yeah, must be hormonal. My periods do that to me. I ain't never been reg'lar. Ter'ble thing, goin' through the change and all. You know."

She had made the officer blush and that threw him off his game.

"Yeah, well, this all checks out, but you need to get that tail light fixed."

"Oh, I got a light out?"

"Yeah, driver's side."

"I'll see it gets tended to."

"I'll let this pass this time. You drive safe now."

"'Preciate that and I will, Officer."

Julia started the truck and the officer watched her drive off. What he couldn't see was the towel she used to wipe the sweat from her face. Cold sweat. She rolled up her window and turned on the heat regardless of the warm spring morning. She wasn't actually sure herself if she was truly cold or if she just got the chills from being pulled over while carrying well over ten pounds of marijuana baked in cookies, cakes, and pies.

She turned on the radio and said aloud to herself, "I am jus' getting' too damn old for this shit."

Daylight was breaking and she had never been happier to pass the Tucker town sign. She knew the route and knew her contact well. He might not be expecting her since he was aware that Mamie had passed. She took a sharp right and then a left and pulled the truck up to a large retirement home that doubled as an assisted living facility for mainly elderly people who were in the last stages of life. Most of them due to cancer.

She waited for the front entrance light to come on before she turned off the truck's engine. The light flashed on and off twice and that was her signal that it was safe to exit the truck and start unloading. Her contact came out the front door to help her.

"You're a little late today, Julia."

"Sorry 'bout that. Got pulled over for a burned out tail light."

"Ooh, that could get scary."

"Dr. Reid, you jus' don't know."

"You want to come in and have some coffee?"

"Don' have no time fo' that today, but thanks for offerin'. Got ta get this stuff unloaded. Need ta show you some of this."

"Julia, I was grief stricken when I heard about Mamie. We are certainly going to miss her."

"Thanks, Doc."

"Are things still going to run as usual?"

"As far as me and my sisters be concerned, we will. 'Course got one sister from up north. She don' know nothin' 'bout this though."

"You mean, there's one besides Elisabeth who doesn't know?"

"Yep, that's what I mean. Now come over here and look at this. Well, on second thought, let's get in yonder. I'll explain in the kitchen."

Julia and Dr. Reid moved stacks of boxes filled with baked goods into the kitchen. It took three trips with both of them using hand trucks to get all of the boxes inside. The last thing Julia picked up was a large ice chest and they went into the kitchen and closed the door.

"This here is what I need ta show ya. Ya already probably know that I am goin' to be busy for a while with Mamie's fun'rel and all. Here's what I need ya to do. Freeze all the baked goods. You know, in one of them hazard waste holders. Nobody'll go near that. Tell 'em it's blood or somethin' that you are sendin' off for testin'. The boxes are marked 'cordin' to strength of the strain I put in each. And each one is named for what it can do. See here this one? It's got a belly drawn upside down."

"And that would be for upset stomach?"

"That's right. It's also good for eatin' more. Gainin' weight, you know. Made extra of that causin' of Mr. Crawford. And this one here with the knife stuck in the head, that for..."

"...headache?" Dr. Reid interjected.

"That's right. Now you look over the boxes and see if you got questions. Probably goin' ta be a month or so afore I be getting' back this way. Here, I made a list of which strain is in what. Tried to mix it up so evabody wouldn't be eatin' the same thin' all the time, you know."

"I see. You have really put a lot of time and thought into this, Julia."

42

"People dependin' on me. They need the medicine, Doc."

"They sure do, Julia. Even though, what we are doing would be considered unethical and I could lose my license over it, I have seen huge improvements in so many of my patients' health, so I will continue to do it as long as I have a means. And, by the way, I have something for you. A donation. The Crawford family is greatly appreciative for what you have done for them."

Dr. Reid handed Julia a very large envelope. It was stuffed with cash and it contained a sympathy card from the Crawford's.

"They didn't know your name, Julia, just that you lost someone close to you."

"That was real kind of 'em. Makes what I do all the more worth it."

"They want to meet you one day, Julia."

"You know that can't happen, Doc. Not as long as I'm growin' weed."

"They understand. They appreciate you, too."

"Oh, afore, I forget. I figgered ya might run outta somethin'. Look ova here."

Julia opened the ice chest to reveal two large tubs of butter.

"Wow!" Dr. Reid exclaimed. Is that what I think it is? Your secret recipe?"

"Nah, they ain't no such thin' as a secret recipe. It's all in the bud. Growin' it right is the secret. So, listen, jus' use this when you need a little extra of somethin' or you run outta somethin'. Goes on anythin' ya can use butter for. Now you keep a hazard sticker on this here ice chest, ya hear? Wrong person gets inta this and it would rock they world."

"I know it would. It will be safe with me, Julia. I promise."

"Doc, you think weed will ever go legal?"

"I really don't know the answer to that, Julia. As long as it is classified as a Schedule One drug, I don't think it ever will."

"What does Sched'le One mean?"

"Basically, it means that people can abuse it. You know someone could use more of it than they should and by doing that it could make them sick or they could die from it. Really silly, if you ask me."

"That really is silly. I mean, damn, too much water could kill ya."

"I agree, and the people here who use it only do so to keep them alive. But prescription use is too expensive for most. Sure, some could afford it, but it could do damage to a life's savings in a hurry. But, as long as it is classified the way it is, health insurance, even Medicare, will not cover the cost of it even if a person has a prescription for it."

"Okay, then. I gotta be getting' to the farmer's market and drop off this truck load of produce. I'll be seein' ya soon. Just heat up what you need after ya freeze it."

"Will do and thanks, Julia."

They exchanged a quick embrace and Julia was off again. She dropped the farm produce off at the farmer's market just as she said she would. It was approaching eight a.m. and Julia frowned at being behind her schedule. She was now heading back home to Cookham. The radio was the only company she had and being alone would normally never have bothered her, but her bold exterior was catching up with her interior heartbreak that needed to come out. Her heart was like a swollen appendix and was getting ready to rupture.

She leaned over and pulled out a box of tissues that Mamie had always kept in the glove box. With tears streaming down her face, she completely allowed herself to let go of all the emotion she had been holding inside. She wanted to scream. She wanted to ask God why death had to hurt so much and why He needed for Mamie to die. It wasn't fair. Good people shouldn't have to die. He should fix them up and let them live forever. She rationally dealt with irrational emotions for about fifteen minutes and suddenly, it began to rain.

Patrick looked over at Patience and asked, "Do you want to pull over and get some breakfast?"

She thought for a second and them responded, "Let's just go to a drive thru and eat while we still drive."

"Yeah, that sounds good. Let's grab a biscuit and keep going. We are over half way there."

"Yeah," Patience said nervously.

"Are you okay?"

"Yeah, I'm fine. Just feels like all of my emotions are arguing in my stomach."

"It's been a long time since you've been back, Patience. You have to be on edge about a lot of things."

"You have no idea."

The sky was turning dark and large drops of rain started hitting the windshield. Patrick was startled to see the sudden change in the weather.

Patience noticed his wonderment. "It's just the southern springs. Storms pop up like all the time. We will probably drive right out of it."

Julia's tears stopped falling as quickly as they had started. She felt like a new person. It was as though she had let poison out of a snake bite and her soul was ten pounds lighter. She was almost happy. She took a deep breath and decided to drop in at the local automotive store and get them to replace that broken tail light. Jonathon was working and things were looking up.

Julia and Jonathon had dated for over a year. Everyone thought he would be the one she would finally settle down with and marry, but they split up. They never advertised what happened between them, but they did remain friends and got along famously well.

"Hey," Julia said as she stood looking over at Jonathon stooped below the counter. I am here ta see a guy about a broke tail light."

"Then I guess I would be the man you'd wanna see," Jonathon said without looking up already knowing who was in the store.

He stood up and reached across the counter and hugged Julia. His arms were strong and he felt good in her arms. She rubbed her hands across his back.

"Mmm, that feels right nice."

"Sure do. I don't think I wanna let go," Jonathon said jokingly.

"Then don't. Just keep holdin' me."

"But what about that broke tail light?"

"What broke light?"

"The one you came in to talk me inta fixin' for ya."

"Oh yeah, that one. I would have gotten Elisabeth to fix it, but I was jus' passin' by and thought of you."

Jonathon walked from around the counter and pulled Julia closer to him. This time he kissed her. She would have typically pushed him away, but she kissed him back. She needed him to want her.

"You know, I think that ole truck of yours might need ta be put up on the rack so we can fully check it out."

"You sure you want to check out the truck or me?" Julia said flirtingly.

"Maybe both."

"How 'bout you get Jason to check out the truck and you drive me home in your big ole truck?"

"That sounds like a plan."

Jonathon called for Jason over the intercom. When he approached, Jonathon told him that he would be gone for a couple of hours and to replace the broken tail light on Julia's truck. He obliged without question.

"I really miss you, Julia."

"When we pull in down at the farm, you can show me jus' how much."

Jonathon hit the gas pedal and sped his way to the farm.

Patrick and Patience finally made it to Cookham. Patience marveled at how much different it was to still be so much the same. The courthouse was still the same. The post office was still right next to it, but she noticed that the Cookham textile mill had shut down. She recalled the so many years that Elisabeth worked there. She ended up being the only colored person to run a maintenance department in that mill.

"What are you staring at that old worn down building for?"

"My sister, Elisabeth, used to work there. Retired from there. She was the only black woman to ever do work only reserved for white folk back in the day. She could fix anything. She could work on anything mechanical from engines and looms to cooling towers. She was amazing. Couldn't hardly read a sentence, but if you told her what you needed something to do, she could make it happen."

"Wow, that's really impressive," Patrick said.

"It really was. All because of air conditioning."

"Come again?"

"Textile mills were known to have extremely hot working conditions. When more jobs became available with air conditioning, the white folks flocked to them leaving more jobs open to blacks. With the skills Elisabeth had, she was a natural mechanic and got moved from what was considered a colored job of cleaning toilets to a maintenance position. Best mechanic they ever had."

"You sound proud of her."

"I guess I am. She retired from that mill and had benefits. Her husband could never hold down a job, so Elisabeth took charge and raised her family. She and Gertie even bought a two family mill house on the hill. Gertie lives on one side and Elisabeth in the other half. Although they probably have a door that connects the sides. They are always together."

"That's kind of nice that they have each other."

"Yeah, I guess so."

"What did Gertie do?"

"Gertie always loved to cook. And read. She worked and retired from the school district. She ran the cafeteria. Mamie told me she spent a lot of time on the farm now. Planting and cooking. She and Julia were raised in a barn."

"Yeah, a lot of small towns have suffered from this economy. Some of the small shops seem to be holding their own here, though."

"Oh, my God," Patience uttered, "I cannot believe that girl has opened a fashion store."

"What girl? What store?"

"Amy Rogers, a witch I went to high school with. I don't know what she thinks she knows about fashion."

Patience peered at the shop's window and noticed a pair of shoes that she thought were actually quite nice. But she turned quickly away when she saw Amy exit the store still swaying her long blonde hair and still exhibiting a rather nice figure.

"The GPS is telling me to turn in about three miles."

"Uh-huh, you are going to make a left at the next dirt road."

When they turned on Mamie's road, Patience noticed that areas once full of tall pine trees were now cultivated farmlands.

"Oh, wow, somebody has bought this land and turned it into a farm. This used to be nothing but trees."

"Hey, look! Is that your house?" Patrick asked with excitement. It's nothing like you described it."

"That's because it's nothing like I remember it. The house has been added on to. They have two barns. And are those heat pumps I saw on the side of the house?"

"Yeah, and look at this manicured lawn. This is absolutely beautiful, Patience. I am almost in disbelief."

"You? I think I might stroke out."

There were already several cars in the yard. Family in town for the funeral. Patience and Patrick approached the side door. The front door which led into the parlor was rarely used. It had been so long since Patience had been to her childhood home. She wrestled as to whether to knock or just walk in like she was one of them. Patrick turned the knob and pushed the door open and then pushed Patience inside.

Elisabeth was the first to notice her. "Well, look at what the cat's done drug in here."

Gertie grabbed Patience and hugged her tightly. You could see that Patience was uncomfortable.

"Hello, Patience," said a soft voice.

"Hello, Ava," Patience responded and still felt the tingling of jealousy over how beautiful Ava still was.

"How about me?" I asked and stood before Patience.

She threw her arms around me and I felt a tear hit my shoulder.

"We are so glad you came home, Patience," Gertie said to her.

"And look at that good lookin' man she bringed with 'er," said Elisabeth.

"Y'all hungry?" Come over and sit down at the table," Gertie insisted.

"We have been in the car for so many hours. Would you ladies mind if I just walk around a bit?" Patrick asked.

"Not at all, but you can walk and eat, can't you?"

"Well, yes, ma'am. I guess I could at that."

Before he could take a step, Gertie had a fried apple pie in his hand and was pouring him a glass of tea.

"Patience, what can I get for you, darling?"

"Oh, Gertie, nothing for me right now, but maybe if you could show us our room."

"Sure thing, sweetie. The house is a little different since you left here. But just go upstairs, and it's the last bedroom on the right. Do you want me to help you with your things? Be glad to."

"No, Gertie, Patrick will get those. But I do appreciate the offer."

Patience observed the house still in disbelief. She walked up the same stairway that she had climbed thousands of times when she was young. She rubbed her hand along the banister she slid down as a child. She paused on the landing and had to smile when she remembered Julia pushing her down the steps in a heavy cardboard egg box. She could hear the childlike giggles and Mamie yelling at them to stop before they got hurt. They didn't care. They were invincible.

She walked into her designated bedroom and found it to be much like the one she shared with Ava and me when we were younger. Except the three twin beds that had crowded the room had been replaced with only one queen sized bed. She loved the lavender painted walls and the welcoming quilt that Mamie must have made that covered the bed. She wondered if Mamie had put it together hoping she would have returned to visit. She had a sudden pang of guilt and wandered over to the back window and looked across the lawn at the huge tobacco barn. So much had changed.

She was disrupted by Patrick entering the room and then they both stood and admired the view of the farm.

"This room is really nice. Isn't it, Patience?"

"Yes, it sure is."

"Look, we have a private bath connected to the bedroom. We don't have that in our apartment at home."

"Did you come up here for a reason, Patrick?"

"Everybody was just wondering where you disappeared to."

"By everybody, do you mean Julia?"

"No. Julia isn't here. She delivered some produce to North Carolina this morning and hasn't gotten back yet."

"That's one piece of good news."

"You have a house full of family that want to spend time with you, Patience."

"I know. Let's go down now. We are going to need to bring the luggage in."

"By we, do you mean, me?"

"Yeah, I kinda did."

They walked downstairs together and the sisters who were present sat in the parlor. They caught up on a lot of things. They had not seen Patience in so long, they had a lot to share. Patience asked about the house and all of the remodeling and each sister took their turn in telling about all the things that had happened in their lives. Ava kept it short and simple and hadn't much to say, but she was glad that Patience had come home. Before they knew it, two hours had passed. Their family reunion came to an abrupt end when they heard a loud crash outside.

Patrick and Patience covered their heads out of instinct and the others ran over to the window to check out the disturbance.

"What in the world was that?" Patience asked alarmed.

"Sounds like Julia done hooked up with Jonathon," Gertie said nonchalantly.

"What do you mean?" Patrick asked.

"Oh, yep, she sho' did. That's her foot stickin' through the win'shiel'," Elisabeth said while she stared out of the window.

"Why would her foot be through the windshield?" Patience asked and was now looking out the window herself.

"I 'magine they got too much inta one of life's pleasures, if you knowin' what I mean," Elisabeth explained.

Patience left the window and found a seat in a far corner away from the window.

Elisabeth asked, "Ya mean to be tellin' me you ain't never had sex in ya car befo'?"

"No," Patience said with a look of disgust.

"Did she break that boy's windshield again?" asked Gertie.

"She sho' did. Her foot is stickin' clear through the glass."

"How many does that make this year, about five?" I asked.

"Five 'bout right," Elisabeth responded.

"I'm surprised they don't drop his car insurance," Patrick said as he looked on in excitement.

Patience leaned back in her chair while the others watched.

"Look at 'em. They still at it!" Elisabeth exclaimed.

"She won't let him stop. Nothing like tension sex," Gertie said.

"Are all of you going to continue to watch her demean herself by staring out of the window?" Patience asked.

"Damn straight I is. Glad to see som'body getting' happy. I ain't been that happy in 'bout fo'ty years." Elisabeth told Patience.

"I hope she hasn't cut her leg. She had a bad cut the last time," Gertie said sounding concerned.

Patrick, glued to the window, said, "I don't think she is worried about her foot or her leg."

"Patrick!" cried Patience, "Get your ass away from that window!"

"She's a comin' in!" yelled Elisabeth as she began to push her way through the crowd of people who had gathered at the window to gawk.

Everybody scurried away, bumping into each other to find a seat.

Everyone, except for Patience, fought over a piece of the newspaper so they could hide their face and not look at Julia when she came inside. Gertie and Elisabeth looked at the same page and pretended to read.

Julia came into the parlor and noticed that everyone was reading. She leaned over to Elisabeth and Gertie and said," It would prob'ly help if ya didn't read that upside down."

Most of us, including Patrick, broke out in laughter. Patience sat with a stolid face. But no one cared. It was just another day in our never boring lives. But it was in that moment, I felt the need for my past to pay a visit into my memory and I thought of Momma.

Momma

After our momma died, Mamie gave each of us a part of her. Nature did the same. I got a photograph and her eyes. Julia got her hair and a pair of her favorite shoes. When I needed to be close to her, I would hold her photograph and dig into Julia's closet and get out the pink box where Julia kept her shoes. Then I would talk to her like she was sitting beside me.

"We lost Mamie, Momma. You might already know that, but I thought I would tell you anyway. Maybe I just thought I needed to say it out loud to my best friend because you are sometimes the only one who understands me."

"She didn't suffer like you did, Momma. Julia saw to that. She went peacefully like you should have been able to. She didn't have to wait to be the last one seen or wait in a colored waiting room. She had doctors that you didn't have and medicine that wasn't available when you suffered so much. And we were with her. We wouldn't let her die alone just like we promised her. Just like we were there when you died. I only wish I knew you better, Momma. I wish I could hold you and you could hold me and we would never have to let go."

"Mamie did good by us, Momma. She taught us all the things that you would have. About working hard to get the things you need and harder to get the things you wanted. She taught us how to talk to God and how to pray. And that believing was more than just saying the words, but feeling them deep in your soul. And she taught us about love and how true love never runs smooth. She loved us like she loved you. We were you to her."

"I'm so sorry you suffered, Momma. I'm sorry that you were born in a time when the color of your skin meant more than the beauty in your heart. I wish you could lay beside me now and we could talk for hours so you could know about everything you missed. I need you here now."

I held her photograph tightly to my chest and rocked back and forth wiping the tears from my face as I sobbed. I needed the release of all the pain that was building up inside of me. I had to let it go and shed it from my heart.

I had no idea how to let go of the only constant I had ever had in my life. It didn't matter that death was a natural occurrence or that it was life's way of coming full circle. The only thing I knew was that I hurt like I had never hurt before. Even though I knew I had sisters who had been around me all of my life and who would continue to be, I felt more alone in their presence than I did alone in my room with my photograph and Momma's red shoes.

Julia couldn't fix this hurt with magical brownies or cupcakes. I wondered if I was suffering what Gertie had felt when she had turned inside herself. I hoped not. I would have to find a way to shake this.

I fell back onto my pillows, still holding the photograph and the aging shoes and found myself in the clouds. The tears had dried to my face and the salt from them tightened my skin. The sleep felt so welcoming and I gratefully gave in to it. Slumber took me away and my exhausted body found peace in it.

A storm had crept onto the farm and a jolt of thunder awakened me. Startled, I sat straight up in my bed feeling like a child in school being caught talking in class. I looked around and caught my bearings and glanced at the clock to find that I had been asleep for only twenty minutes. It felt as though I had slept for hours. I heard the kitchen chairs being pulled out and chattering going on below me. I was saddened that the entire world hadn't felt the need to stop and grieve with me, but had found it necessary to continue to turn as though nothing had happened.

Someone had been in the room while I slept. I had a quilt draped over me and my photograph had been placed back on my dresser. Momma's red shoes were placed neatly beside the bed where I could easily see they had not disappeared.

I arose feeling refreshed and more relaxed. I pulled a wash cloth from underneath the sink and warmed it with water and cleansed my face of the tears I had fallen asleep with. I licked my lips and decided to brush my teeth before I descended the stairs. I stood, looking at myself in the mirror and smiled. It was difficult, but there was work to be done and things to take care of. I would live to cry another day.

I walked into the kitchen to find my sisters gathered at the kitchen table. Julia sat on one end and Patience on the other. That did not surprise me. Gertie was holding Elisabeth's hands. Elisabeth looked discomforted.

I looked at Gertie and asked, "What's the matter with Elisabeth?"

"All that's going on has gotten her morning ritual disrupted," Gertie answered.

"She can't make her bowels move," Julia added with a grin and a wink at me.

"I don' understand it," Elisabeth moaned, "I move my innards ever mornin' right afta my coffee and today I ain't got nothin'. I is all locked up wit' the vapors."

"I don't understand why old people think they have to have a bowel movement every single day," Patience added to the conversation.

Elisabeth gave Patience the evil eye and asked, "Who it be you callin' old?"

Patience looked up at Gertie and Elisabeth, "Oh, well, no one really. I was just speaking in general. You know like a figure of speech."

Gertie bounced the conversation back to the subject at hand. "How many of you sisters remember Mamie lining us up to get a dose of that black draft?"

"What is black draft?"

"Oh, girl, hush yo' mouth," Elisabeth said laughing. "I 'member that shit. And I do mean shit, too. Goin' in and a comin' out. Make ya belly swell up somethin' ter'ble."

They all started to laugh, except for me. I was confused and again asked, "What is black draft?"

"I am just glad we had a bathroom inside and still had the outhouse. We needed both of them, but you know, we never seemed to ever get sick with Mamie's home remedies. And isn't everybody happy that an indoor bathroom was the first thing Mamie added to the house?" Gertie added.

Elisabeth raised her leg from her chair and farted.

"Y'all goin' have ta forgive me, but I gotta let this outta me," she explained.

"Oh, sister, that is just really bad," Gertie said to her.

"Well, I done tol' y'all I had the vapors."

Patience, holding her nose along with the rest of us, said, "That's not the vapors, that's just pure shit. Somebody get some spray."

The back door suddenly opened and Patrick came in and joined us in the kitchen. He started to speak, but the smell overcame him. He picked up each foot separately to make sure he hadn't stepped in anything. "Wow!" he said, "what is that smell?"

"It's Elisabeth. She's got the winds," Gertie said in her proper voice.

Patience took the can of air spray and sprayed it all around Elisabeth.

"That spray don't do no good. It just mixes with the gassy smell and makes it smell worser than it already do," Julia said.

"Well, it's better than suffocating with all of that flatulence she is spewing out," Patience said to Julia in a harsh tone.

"Sisters", Gertie said to avoid an argument, "Elisabeth and I have picked out the burial clothes we thought Mamie would want to be buried in. Her favorite yellow dress with the yellow and white scarf. Does anybody have any objections with that choice?"

No one did, but the statement silenced the room.

Gertie continued, "I thought we would also have her wear the small yellow hat with the veil that she loved so much."

"That was her favorite. I think she would like that, "Julia added somberly.

"We took the liberty to go ahead and run that down to the funeral home. We can change it, if anybody has any objections."

"No, Gertie, I think you handled it beautifully," I added.

"We stopped by the florist and ordered the family spray of flowers that will drape the casket. We chose wild yellow roses. Each of us will have a long stem red rose to put in with her at the grave side service. If there is anything special anyone would like to add to that, they are welcome to do so."

"We should include her Bible. The one she carried to church every Sunday," I said to Gertie.

"She will have that with her. She will have it in her hands."

I thought for a moment and mustered the courage to ask, "Is that how Momma was buried?"

My sisters looked at me with surprise when I asked that question wondering why I would be asking about Momma at this time.

Gertie touched my hand and said to me softly, "Momma died in this house. In the parlor. In Mamie's arms."

I gasped and caught my breath. "I never knew Momma died here."

Gertie continued, "We were all around her. Just like she wanted. You were just a baby. Elisabeth and I were still really young, but probably the only ones of us to really remember it. Julia might have some memories."

"I 'member it happenin'," Julia added, "but I really didn't understan' what was goin' on. Mamie always seem ta never want ta talk about it."

"Did Momma have cancer?" I asked.

"Momma was really sick. Mamie had her at the hospital many times, but they always told her that there was nothing they could do for her and sent her home. I remember she had terrible headaches and couldn't hardly keep down any food. She lost a lot of weight, and she suffered with a lot of pain. I think that is what bothered Mamie the most. Seeing her in pain and not being able to help her."

Gertie now had her arms around my shoulder when she explained this to me.

"Did Momma smoke?"

"I remember she did smoke, but it was not a lot. She wasn't constantly lighting up a cigarette. At night sometimes. When the day was over, she would have a cigarette on the front porch after she thought we were all in bed asleep."

"So, she did have cancer?"

The death certificate doesn't have a cause of death. It just says 'natural causes', but Mamie always thought it was cancer."

"Gertie, why didn't Mamie ever tell me about Momma?"

"Oh, she didn't talk about Momma to anybody much. She just kept herself busy on the farm with growing crops and put her mind on us. Maybe it hurt her too much to watch her daughter die and she wanted to protect us from the pain. Maybe she should have talked about her more. For herself and for us."

"Why didn't she sue the hospital for letting Momma die?"

"In those times? Being black? That would never have happened. And, the truth is that there probably really was nothing they could do back then even if Momma did have cancer. Besides, you know how Mamie was, it was never about money. The money would never have brought Momma back."

Julia finished her cup of coffee and we sat and reflected silently on the day and what lie ahead of us. The funeral home would call us when Mamie's body was ready for the family viewing and we would go. We dreaded the moment that we would have to raise our eyes and behold Mamie in a casket. We had seen her so alive in her yellow dress, and now we would have to look at her lifeless in it.

Elisabeth rose from her chair and headed to the bathroom. Behind her, she left a trail of gaseous fumes that made us all reach for something to cover our faces, but the scent had already hit us. Within seconds, we heard loud noises that embarrassed all of us. And, momentarily, we heard a flush and Elisabeth shout out in triumph, "Praise the Lord! Vic'try be mine!"

Patience shook her head and placed her forehead on the kitchen table. Julia arose silently and waved all of us, except for Patience, into the parlor. The rest of us quietly left our seats and moved away from the bathroom door which was right off of the dining area of the kitchen. We knew Patience would be angry that we left her there alone to endure the lingering odor. We adjourned to the parlor covering our mouths so our giggling wouldn't alert Patience that we left her.

We took a seat and discussed what we were going to do the rest of the day. Julia planned to go to the barn and complete some unfinished business there. Gertie offered to assist her, but Julia thought that I should help her instead. Gertie was to divert Patience and Elisabeth on something that would keep them out of the tobacco barn. She would get Elisabeth to drive her home for a while and would insist that Patience go along. Ava would stay at the house to entertain the early visitors coming to town to pay final respects to the family. We would all wait for the call from the funeral home for the first family viewing. We agreed they would probably call Julia and she would give us the details when she got them. That was it. We had a plan.

Patience and Elisabeth discovered where we had escaped to and came into the parlor.

Whatch y'all hidin' in here fo'?" Elisabeth asked with a chuckle while rubbing her stomach.

Patience looked annoyed at being deceived by our leaving. Ava sat and caught a glimpse of herself in the mirror to make sure her hair was perfectly in place.

"We plannin' out the day," Julia responded. "Gertie will 'splain it to ya."

Gertie explained, "We thought that while Julia takes care of some farm business, Elisabeth wouldn't mind driving me home for a bit to check on some things at my house. Patience, I would so love it if you would ride along. It has been so long since you have been there. It would mean a lot to me if you would go along with me."

"I'd like that, Gertie," Patience replied.

As we started to get started to our appointed tasks, Gertie stopped us with a reminder. "Don't forget everybody, the play is tomorrow night. Don't forget. That play was always very important to Mamie and Elisabeth's grandson, Nathaniel, will be playing a leading role this year."

"Oh, yeah, the p-p-play," Elisabeth said mocking Pastor Washington.

We parted company and hoped that everything would run smoothly. That, however, was not how our plans usually worked out.

Julia and I went down to the barn making sure all doors were secure behind us as we walked in. With all of the visitors we were expecting, we couldn't risk any unexpected guests in the barn. With us inside and the doors locked behind us, Julia walked over to the far left corner and I automatically went to the far right side. Like we had done what seemed like thousands of times before, we both reached down and lifted a hidden door that led us to our secret coveted crop. It is known by different names. Bud. Weed. Kush. Many different others. We only knew it as medicine.

As we lifted the large door, Julia and I both winced at the brightness of the room painted in a bright white flat paint.

"Damn, I never get usta how bright this room gets. Check the temp. Feels ta be a tad warm in here."

"Julia, it's ninety-three degrees. We have to lower it."

"Yeah, sho' do. Hit that side fan switch. That fan will get the air movin'.

I walked to the switch and flipped it up. We waited to feel moving air. We always wanted the temperature between eighty-five and ninety degrees. I watched the thermometer and after a few minutes told Julia the temp had gone down two degrees.

"I need ta get it a litta bit lower, but these plants are doin' fine."

"Do you need me to test the soil?"

"Nah, I checked the pH this mornin'. It's all good. Might wanna add more coconut coir and water to those plants on that end. Feels a litta drier than I like it. Next few months, we gotta be thinkin' 'bout repaintin' the walls. Light is good. This here gonna be the last of Mamie's crop."

"What was Mamie's first crop of weed?"

"Mamie started out practicin' on tomatoes."

"Really?"

"That's what she tol' me."

"Who gave Mamie the idea to start growing marijuana?"

"'Cordin' to her, she read 'bout it stoppin' pain and settlin' a upset stomach."

"She had to get the clones from somewhere. She started doing this a long time ago, Julia."

"Said she got some from a Chinese man somewhere in town. He taught her how ta grow it when he heard 'bout Momma bein' so sick."

"So our momma was why she started all of this?"

"Course it was. Why did ya think she's be doin' somethin' agin' the law? You knowed Mamie as good as anyone."

"She would only do it if it was the right thing to do. To help people."

"That's right. Now let's check the dried bud we got curin'."

I opened all of the airtight containers with Julia to release any moisture. We couldn't let any mold ruin the bud we had harvested earlier. We would freeze this a little later and make a butter with what we didn't freeze. Freezing it allowed us to have a year round supply. We froze butter, too. We never lacked for work and the demand for medical marijuana seemed to be racing supply. Demand was winning.

Elisabeth and Gertie sat in the front seat of the car. Patience sat in the back with Patrick, who she made tag along with them. Gertie had asked Patience to go along with them to their house to see the improvements they had made on it.

"Gertie, when Patrick and I drove in, I noticed that all the land around Mamie's place has been turned into farmland. Who bought all of this and cultivated it?

"Mamie bought it. Julia and the two summer farm hands cultivated it."

"You'd a knowed that had ya come home mo' often," Elisabeth said.

Patience ignored her and continued to talk to Gertie. "Patrick told me that small farms were not doing well economically. How is it that Mamie could afford all of this and the house, too?"

"Mamie was always wise with spending her money. When real estate prices dropped, she bought the land. And it's not like this is a large metro area or prime property, land around here doesn't cost all that much."

"Smart thinking," Patrick added to the conversation.

"Oh, just shut up. You don't even have a job," Patience said as she gave Patrick her up and down look.

"Patience," Patrick responded, "don't embarrass me in front of your sisters. That was uncalled for."

Gertie and Elisabeth glanced at each other and shook their heads in agreement.

"Well, you don't have a job. I'm just saying what is true."

"I was laid off, Patience. It was not as though I was fired for being a bad worker. I will find another job or I could get called back to the job I had."

Patrick turned his head and stared out of the window.

"Everybody has a streak of misfortune, Patrick. Don't let it worry you. We know you are a good man," Gertie said to reassure Patrick that he was accepted by the family.

"But, Patience, you jus' a bitch, girl. I is here to tell ya. Ne'va thought I'd cut one of my own, but I b'lieve ya could make me change ma min'," Elisabeth added.

Patience looked over at Patrick and said, "She won't cut me. She loves me."

Elisabeth slammed on the brakes. Patience and Patrick jerked forward barely catching themselves before they hit the back of the front seat. Elisabeth whipped herself around and looked Patience directly in the eyes.

"Let me tell ya somethin', sista. I will cut you. Ya betta start treatin' ya man right 'fore he finds hisself somebody who will."

Both Patrick and Patience had their world shaken by Elisabeth. Patience, because she never thought her own sister would turn on her. Patrick, because he felt the welcoming sense that he was safe from getting cut and found himself on the good side of Elisabeth. Always a good place to be.

"Come on now, sister, we can't be holding up traffic. Besides, we haven't seen Patience in years and we don't want to scare her into not coming back to see us, now do we?" Gertie reasoned.

Reluctantly, Elisabeth turned back around and resumed driving toward her and Gertie's house.

"I think you are going to like the house, Patience. Elisabeth and I have done a lot of work on it. We have installed air conditioning to both sides. One for upstairs and a separate unit for downstairs. Elisabeth said it would be better that way, right Elisabeth?"

"Uh huh," Elisabeth uttered.

"Just had the roof redone, too," Gertie said trying to subside any tension.

"I look forward to seeing your house. I am sure it is very nice," Patrick said smiling over at Patience.

They finally arrived and Elisabeth pulled into the driveway. The house was immaculately well cared for. The lawn was as manicured as the lawn at Mamie's house. The white vinyl siding was spotlessly clean. Both Elisabeth and Gertie smiled with pride as they ushered Patrick and Patience into their homes.

"This house really is awesome," Patience said with a little surprise in her voice.

"You thinkin' it was gonna be less?" Elisabeth asked.

"No, of course not. I was just wondering how much a house like this would sell for in D.C. area."

"A lot," Patrick responded.

"I'm really proud of both of you. You have a really beautiful house. We would refer to it as a duplex," Patience added.

They got the full tour of both sides of the old mill house. Patience had been correct when she told Patrick that they would have a door connecting both homes. Elisabeth said it was for security. We all knew it was for companionship. It worked for them. When Gertie came to the farm to help with the baking, Elisabeth watched Gertie's grandchildren. When the children went to sleep at night, Gertie would leave the connecting door open and go to Elisabeth's to watch television. They had both purchased a large flat screen together and decided to put it in Elisabeth's den. Elisabeth installed surround sound. They were happy.

As they were returning to the farm, Julia and I were finishing the chores we had been tending to in the barn. Julia was happy with the progress of the growing. I looked over the supply and figured that we had about three hundred plants in various stages in the sectioned parts of the barn. It would be a bumper crop.

"You 'bout ready to head up to the house?" Julia asked me.

"Yeah, I guess we better get cleaned up and ready. Folks will start dropping by. Not good to leave Ava alone for too long. She has probably done enough primping in front of the mirror."

"Ain't that the truth?"

We checked the temperature one more time and felt comfortable with it at eighty-eight degrees. We carefully pulled down the security door and made sure everything was locked down tightly. I had no doubt that Julia would return later to check on everything again before she went to bed. She always did.

Gertie and Elisabeth were in the kitchen when Julia and I had walked into the house from the barn. I noticed that some food had already started to arrive.

Gertie asked, "Julia have you heard from the funeral home?"

"Yeah, they told us to come down whenever we got ready. Now that you are back, I guess we could go down for the fam'ly viewin'. Jus' give us a chance to clean up with a whore's bath."

Patrick had just put a potato chip in his mouth and nearly choked when he heard those words.

We all laughed.

"Patience ain't never tol' you 'bout a whore's bath?"

"No, she's not used those words before."

"That's because I'm not a whore," Patience said emphatically.

"Oh, you shut up, hooker. You knowed you had as many whore's baths as any of us," Julia said directly to Patience.

"Well, I don't anymore. We have running water," Patience said back to Julia.

"Then why don't ya tell us all why you still stinkin'. Ya need to wash up that attitude you carry so close to ya."

Gertie explained to Patrick, "Mamie always called it that when we were young. It was when you just washed yourself without sitting in a tub of water."

"Oh, I see," Patrick said.

"The look on your face reminded me of my husband when he first heard Mamie refer to a bath like that. His eyes got as big as saucers."

"Miss Gertie, I have never heard much about your husband. Is he still living?"

"He sure is and I'm still married to him."

"You don't say?"

"We run into each other from time to time."

"I sho' wish I coulda run inta 'im," Elisabeth interjected.

"Yeah, but you want to be behind the wheel of your car when you do, sister," Gertie said laughing.

"Sho' do. Take my car straight on top of tha' fat bastard." Elisabeth took her fist and slammed it against her hand to demonstrate how she would squash Roosevelt flat.

We all laughed again. Listening to Elisabeth took me back to when Gertie and Elisabeth were young women and just married. My mind drifted back to that time.

Gertie

My sister, born Gertrude Irene Nesbitt, was not formally educated. At least, not with the kind of education that was awarded with a degree. She attended school until she reached the eighth grade. That was as far as she thought she needed to go. In the south, Mandatory attendance requirements were established in 1915. Regular attendance for black children was not exactly enforced, not really even tracked. If you were enrolled, then you attended, regardless of whether or not you were present.

Gertie, like the rest of us, was raised on the farm. She was proficient in planting, harvesting, cooking, and baking. She could milk the cow and clean horse stalls if she needed to, but those were not her favorite things to do. Her most favorite thing to do was read. She loved books and regardless of what chore she was doing, she had a book.

She loved romance novels the best. She never considered herself to be an attractive girl. In all honesty, she was not, by any means, one who could turn the heads of men. On physical appearance, most considered her mediocre with potential. But, in her books, she could transform herself into the leading protagonists and live vicariously through the fictional characters. She missed Momma and was probably the one of us who was closest to her. And when Momma died, a part of Gertie died, too. She withdrew into herself and Mamie worried that she had gone so far in that she might not ever return.

Her clothing was drab just like her world had become. She dressed in grays and mourning colors that made her blend into part of the scenery. Gertie was Momma's second child and that made her the first to receive Elisabeth's hand-me-downs. With the sadness in her face, she could make the brightest colors a dimming nimbus. Her soul was a wandering wasteland. Her eyes had dark circles that Mamie's cure-alls couldn't tackle. In today's world, a therapist would probably diagnosis Gertie as clinically depressed, but we had no such luxuries as therapists back then. Gertie seemed hopeless.

Then, Gertie met Roosevelt Hendrix. She had finally found the thing she needed to breathe life back into her. Gertie began to smile again. She was even laughing. Mamie was glad of that, but had little use for Roosevelt. She thought Gertie was a bright girl and could do better for herself and had prayed for it to be a passing fancy, but alas, when she was but sixteen years old, Gertie married Roosevelt.

Roosevelt had come from an ambitious family. They were hard workers and owned property. They owned a farm not extremely far from our family farm. We thought that would be a great thing to still have Gertie close. Elisabeth had already married and had two children and she lived in a home, also, not too far from Gertie. What was even better, Elisabeth could drive and had a car. They had constant contact and could visit often. However, like Mamie, Elisabeth was not that fond of Roosevelt either.

Had they both been men, Roosevelt and Elisabeth could have been the best of friends. They drank together, played poker together, and who didn't know that Elisabeth loved a good cigar? They smoked together. Elisabeth had heard too much about Roosevelt from her husband, Leroy, for her to like or trust him. And she had her personal experience of Roosevelt doing something he brushed off as accidental when he grabbed her ass. Although Leroy wasn't much better, Elisabeth had heard the talk about Roosevelt being a womanizer.

Even with all of the rumors, Elisabeth thought that marriage would be good for Roosevelt and he seemed to make Gertie so happy that she couldn't be the one to break her heart. It didn't stop her from threatening to break Roosevelt's head if he should ever hurt Gertie, but she still couldn't break Gertie's heart when she had seen her go dark for so long. They were sisters. While they could fight over chores and menial issues, they only wanted the best for each other. If Roosevelt made Gertie happy, Elisabeth would not stand in the way of that. Of course, it wouldn't stop her from keeping an eye on him.

Gertie and Roosevelt were married only two months and living with his parents when we all got the news that Roosevelt was moving Gertie to their own place. He told her it was time for them to be completely on their own and he intended to get her a house. He was a big planner, he was. He made large promises of new furniture and landscaped lawns. Gertie radiated light from his glowing affections. He was attentive to her and she was responsive, especially in the bedroom.

On moving day, Elisabeth showed up in her 1955 Mercury Montclair Coupe. I am sure that in its day, the car was high class. Today, we would call it a hooptie. You could tell that when the car had paint, it was a two-tone. Aqua and white. When Elisabeth drove it, it was rust. Not just in color, but true rust. Elisabeth was so proud of that car. It used more oil than it did gas and it only had one seat which was on the driver's side. She compensated passengers with folding lawn chairs that rocked and sometimes flew out of the missing rear window when she took a corner too sharply. But it made her happy to have wheels and it made Leroy happy to keep her happy. Not because he was a good provider, but it kept him distant from her anger. When Elisabeth got angry, Leroy had no peace. It wasn't as though Leroy had gone and purchased the car. He won it in a poker game and when he drove it home, Elisabeth and Leroy had a little poker game of their own. Elisabeth won.

She pulled the Mercury up to the Hendrix house. She was smiling, anticipating how lovely Gertie's new place would be. Roosevelt had kept the location of the house a secret. Not even Gertie knew where it was. Leroy pulled his father's truck in closely behind the Mercury. They would surprise Gertie and help her move her things to her new home. Leroy did not look particularly anxious to assist in the move. However, he was there and they both walked toward the Hendrix front porch.

Elisabeth's bottom jaw protruded forward as she peered at the front steps and leaned over to Leroy and asked, "I jus' wonder where dis fool is movin' my sista to. I am suspect 'bout this whole secret thin'."

She squinted her eyes and stared at the house. "Come on, let's go see where everybody's be at."

Leroy stayed a step behind as Elisabeth walked forward carrying her purse tightly to her body. She rang the doorbell and anxiously awaited for someone to answer. When no one did, she couldn't help but wonder why Roosevelt was taking her sister from this house to a place she was still unaware of. The thought, also, crossed her mind that Leroy knew exactly what Roosevelt was up to, but was afraid to tell her what it was. She knew those two to be as thick as thieves. Finally, Gertie showed up to answer the door.

"Hey Elisabeth. I'm the only one here right now. Roosevelt and his daddy have already taken all of our things down to my new house. I know it will be beautiful. He said it was brand new and had all new appliances. New furniture, too."

Elisabeth cut her eyes at Gertie and asked, "Are you sho' 'bout all this? You don't even know where he movin' ya to. Besides we brought the car and Leroy's daddy's truck to haul y'all's stuff."

"And we appreciate all that you've done, but Roosevelt said since everything would be new, we didn't have much to move. I already sent over the linens Mamie gave us for a wedding gift."

"So when is he 'sposed to be back ta pick you up?"

"He'll be back directly. He told me he wanted to have everything in place so he could carry me over the threshold. He can be so romantic."

Elisabeth rolled her eyes and stated, "You jus' keep yo' eyes open 'round that fool husban' of yourn. I don' mean to be judgin' yo' man, but how is he goin' ta afford a house and all these lux'ry things? I ain't seen him work a job since befo' y'all got married."

"He tol' me he worked fo' his daddy," Leroy chimed in.

"Oh, you jus' shut up, Leroy. No damn body asked you nothn'. Don't be takin' up fo' ya friend. And I betta not be findin' out that you in on all this secret business on jus' where this new house is 'sposin' to be. Whole thin' sounds like gravy to me."

Around about this time, a truck pulled up to the house. Roosevelt and his daddy got out and walked over to Elisabeth and Leroy. Mr. Hendrix shook Leroy's hand and they exchanged pleasantries. It was not customary for men to shake hands with a woman, but Elisabeth made Mr. Hendrix shake her hand, too.

Elisabeth looked around and proclaimed that since there was nothing to move except the newlyweds, everyone might as well go in one vehicle. Before anyone could say anything, she was in the driver's side and behind the wheel of her car looking out at Leroy, Roosevelt, and Gertie and said, "So what y'all waitin' on, Christmas?"

Roosevelt and Leroy looked at one another and waited for the other to take a step towards the car. Roosevelt felt a wave of panic and spoke, "Leroy, I don't want to get in that car with Elisabeth. I'll be feelin' like I'll be awake in my own coffin."

"Come on, Roosevelt. Me and Leroy will drop back by here and pick up Leroy's daddy's truck when we see this new house ya done went up and got." Elisabeth smiled as she spoke and gave a reassuring shake of her head to accompany the smile.

Leroy shrugged his shoulders and knew not to argue. He set three lawn chairs in the places where regular car seats used to be. The three of them got into the Mercury. The two men sat in the back with worried looks on their faces. A smiling Gertie sat in the front lawn chair. Elisabeth pulled on it to make sure it was secure. She really couldn't care less if the two men in the back either fell through the rusting floor board or went flying out the missing rear window.

Elisabeth gave the accelerator a kick and they were on their way. But to where?

Elisabeth cruised along the dirt road with dust flying up through the floor board and escaping through the rear window. Roosevelt's new clothes and dapper new haircut were getting sand blasted. No one could say that Elisabeth had done this on purpose, but the smile on her face could shame the bright morning sun. It said it all. Her smile faded as the car met the asphalt highway. She slammed on the brakes and caused Leroy and Roosevelt to come crashing forward. Their lawn chairs had collapsed and left them sitting on the rusting floor. Elisabeth turned and looked down on Roosevelt asking, "Well, sandman, do we turns lef' or da we goes right?"

Roosevelt sat huddled in the back with his hands over his face peering at Elisabeth between his sparsely widened fingers. He didn't want to tell her. He wanted to take Gertie to their new place alone to get her adjusted before he told anyone where they were going to live. After giving him a minute to get the dust out of his throat, Elisabeth grew impatient. "Well, whatcha say? We gonna be goin' left or right? We ain't got but one more choice an' that's to back up that dirt road again..."

A panicked Roosevelt managed to squeak out a response. "Left," he said, "just turn left."

That's all Elisabeth needed to hear. She turned the steering wheel to the left and they were off down the highway. She was skeptical that Roosevelt was so secretive about where he was taking her sister, but left was even closer to her house,. The closer she could get Gertie to her, the better she would feel. She still kept an eye on Leroy and Roosevelt in her rearview mirror. She suspected they were hatching a scheme and she gave them both the evil eye indicating they would meet with just rewards depending on their actions. They knew to be afraid.

It was just a few minutes before they passed the road to Mamie's place. Gertie and Elisabeth smiled and waved feverishly at the road even though there was no one there to wave back at them. Their past gave no beckoning calls for them to return. Elisabeth pressed the accelerator, eager to meet their future.

It did not take their future long to catch up with them. Elisabeth found herself in a familiar part of town. She peered at Roosevelt through the rearview mirror. Roosevelt reached from the back and rubbed Gertie's arm giving her reassurance of his affection.

"Well, well, well. Jus' look at where we are. Leroy! Did you know 'bout this? Did you know that no good, low bellied snake was movin' my sista to the projects?"

"No. No, darlin' I sho' did not," Leroy quickly responded to Elisabeth and looked over at Roosevelt with a shrug to let him know he was on his own. "I is just as surprised as you are Elisabeth. I can't believe he would do somethin' like this."

"Well, I'm a litta confused as to why ya so surprised. We live two doors down from 'em. No good bastards, both of ya. When I get outta 'dis car, they gonna be some ass whoopin' goin' on. All dat high talk 'bout new this and new dat.

Only thin' new goin' be goin' on 'round here is my new shoe up somebody's ass."

Leroy and Roosevelt couldn't figure out if Elisabeth was talking to one of them or both of them. They both looked at each other and raced to see who could jump through the back window first. Leroy had the advantage since he had more experience running from Elisabeth. Roosevelt gave it an earnest effort to escape though. Once they were out of the car, they both took to running not sure where they were running to. Elisabeth wanted to take off after both of them and fumbled with her car handle.

Gertie grabbed Elisabeth's arm to avoid a fight. She reasoned that she could not tolerate losing a sister. She assured Elisabeth that everything was going to be okay. She gently took Elisabeth's hand and gingerly placed it on her belly.

"I'm going to be a mama, Elisabeth. I'm going to have a baby. It doesn't matter where I live as long as I have you and my baby around. Everything is going to be just fine. You'll see."

Elisabeth hugged her sister and began to cry. Gertie took them as tears of joy. It would be years before she knew that Elisabeth was crying tears of sorrow because she knew that Gertie was now a part of the system and it would take nothing less than hitting a lottery, something at that time was illegal in the state of South Carolina, to get both of them out of where they both now lived.

The Mad Hatters

The white people squirmed in the pews, visibly uncomfortable. The family realized that it had most likely been the first time any of them had ever been inside an African Methodist Episcopal Church. We regulars often referred to it as the A.M.E. or Always Mettin' and Eatin'. For once, we were in our comfort zone while the white folk felt like outsiders looking in. If we had not been mourning the loss of Mamie, we would be laughing and talking incessantly until the church mothers hushed us with glacial stares. My sisters and I were at home here. We knew every pew, every timber, and every loop in the fading red carpet that covered the floor. We knew each and every person, both sitting in the pews and standing in the aisle. Even the white ones. They were here to show respect for Mamie and for that we were considerate and appreciative. Otherwise, me and my sisters would probably show some of the resentment we held in our memories of their past harsh judgments of us. Our blackness. Our desire to be who we were in a world they had so long, and some still, thought only they ruled. Mamie's memory was instilled in us and cut short Patience's desire to accidently on purpose trip Amy Rogers as she walked past her. Mamie's memory and Ava's hand forcibly holding down her tripping leg.

The family sat in front where we had often seen other families sit awkwardly as they received condolences, hugs, handshakes, and countless boxes of tissues for wiping away falling tears. I hated being on display for everyone to pity and swoon over. Elisabeth and Gertie felt important and were proud to take front row center. I didn't blame them. I felt that they, in their own right, deserved to sit and be recognized. They were the oldest among us girls and had had a much harder life when our mother, Patricia, had passed away. Julia was stolid and strong and, Ava, well, she thought the red carpet was put down just for her. She would expect them to roll it up and only put it back down the next time she graced it with her presence. She was prepared any day for the Queen of England to abdicate her throne so she could sit down. She often relied on her beauty to get her through another night of remembered torment. We could always tell she was troubled when we heard her brush going through her long coarse hair in the early morning hours. With her stellar beauty and light skin, we often thought that Ava should have been born white.

We did find some comfort in the weather. It was a warm April evening and the wind was blessing us with a cool breeze. The church was filling to over capacity and we could still hear the bustle of cars arriving with passengers to be dropped off to greet a standing room only performance. I turned to survey the crowd and wondered at the oddity of the white men, women, and children swaying from side to side and lifting themselves up and down. There was no music and the choir was not yet in place. Tonight was to be a play performance that Mamie had worked on with Pastor Washington. After all, it was Easter and Mamie always assisted with the play. The church planning committee and the pastoral committee both agreed that the play should be performed in honor of Mamie. It was the same damn play we had all seen at least ten times. But Mamie was persistent in having all the youth who attended the church take part in the yearly Easter play. This year was to be a special blessing for Elisabeth. Her youngest grandson, Nathaniel, was cast as the role of Jesus being crucified on the cross. Nathaniel was a special delight. Mischievous in some ways and pure devilish in others. However, it was his year to shine and make us all proud. Elisabeth sat with tissue in hand waiting on what she knew would be a stellar performance.

And the white people were still bobbing and weaving. My curiosity got the better of me and I laid my hand on Julia's leg and asked her if she noticed anything odd about the white folks. She turned around and allowed her eyes to cruise the church. To maintain her sophisticated nature, her movements were smooth and nonchalant. When she recomposed herself to her former position, she turned her head to me slightly and whispered, "It's the hats. They can't see the stage around or over the hats."

When Julia said that, I could hardly contain my laughter. I quickly clapped my hand to my mouth so no one would hear me, but what she had said made perfect sense. In black churches, women wore hats and not just your run of the mill, something to cover your head hats. I mean, elaborate, decorated, large hats. They wore them even to the point of it being a competitive event. The larger and odder, the better. They had feathers, flowers, and fur. But more than that, they had one for every outfit they owned for Sunday church services. Their hats were color coordinated to match their clothes. If they were married, their husbands dressed to accentuate their wives' hats. Their children were accessories to the hats. There was even a hat committee at the church and as peculiar as it might have appeared to anyone sitting in the audience who found it a redundant article of attire, to a black female, touching or heaven forbid, asking her to remove or adjust her hat, was like taking a gauntlet to her face.

My sisters and I were accustomed to it. It was second nature to be encumbered by a flopping wreath of feathers blocking our view of the pulpit on Sundays. We were trained early to compliment a lady's hat even if we would never have dared own it for ourselves. Of Mamie's granddaughters, only Julia wore a hat and that was an old fedora that our grandfather had left in the barn that she had found. It was her bargaining hat.

Patience appeared agitated and considered tonight's play an intrusion on her time. She looked down at her watch and peered at the curtain on the stage as though she could push time forward and force the festivities to begin. I really don't know why my mother would have named her Patience, or maybe I did. Her name was the only kind she would ever have. I remembered how Mamie would always tell her that patience was a virtue. She would only scoff, but

95

Julia gladly announced that Patience didn't have any virtue. Mamie would hold up her hands to ward off both of their tempers. She knew one harsh word would beget another until Julia had Patience on the floor crying for help. Even as youngsters, Julia and Patience were sworn enemies.

A voice from a side microphone stirred my thoughts back into the present day events. Pastor Washington was announcing that the play was about to begin and encouraged everyone who could find one to please take their seat. The choir took their place on the stand and allowed the pastor to welcome everyone to the presentation. The church mothers hurriedly fetched their hand held fans. A clear signal to inform the pastor that he was getting a little too long winded was when the church mothers started fanning their faces with fans with vigor. Something the church mothers were readily prepared to do. The pastor acknowledged the attendees presence that night and continued to speak.

"Welcome all t-t-tonight. We of the A.M.E. Ch-Ch-Church, sure do thank all of y-y-you for coming out t-t-tonight to view with us the c-c-c-c…"

"Commemoration!" someone from the audience yelled out.

"Commemoration," Pastor Washington continued.

"The commemoration of that h-h-horrible day that J-J-Jesus died for all our sins. Well, maybe not a h-h-horrible night, but a g-g-good night b-b-because the Lord J-J-Jesus died for all of us s-s-so that we could b-b-be absorbed in the bl-bl-bl-blood of the Lamb. Not that it was a g-g-good thing that Jesus died. Well, b-b-bad for Him, but g-g-good for us. Cause if He hadn't d-d-died, then w-we w-w-would all die, too, you see. We all know g-g-g-good John, Chapter Three and v-v-verse Sixteen wh-wh-where it s-s-says that God s-s-so loved the w-w-world that He g-g-gave His son, J-J-Jesus, so w-w-we could all be s-s-saved in the bl-bl-blood. We all know that only b-b-because of J-J-Jesus and his gr-gr-gr-great s-s-s-sacri-f-f-fices that w-w-we all able t-t-to j-j-join the Father and sit on the r-r-right s-s-side of the thr-thr-throne and...and...and we know th-th-that Jesus is w-w-watchin' us now and...and...and He knows th-th-that we b-b-be-l-l-long to him. B-B-But only if w-w-we gives ourselves t-t-to him w-w-will we be s-s-saved. Can I-I-I hear an 'Amen'?"

Most of the congregated people looked in awe and confusion. No one gave an 'Amen'. Elisabeth was beside herself and looked at Gertie with frustration. Patience looked disgusted. Julia and I were accustomed to Pastor Washington, but we both knew what the other was thinking. And that was that Pastor Washington had to be calmed down before he went into full salvation mode. Julia glanced at the church mothers who had their fans on ready and motioned for them to start fanning. On most occasions, it would only take three of the women to start their fans as the silent signal that it was time for Pastor Washington to either calm down or wrap it up. But these church women knew him well. All ten of the church mothers took to fanning as if their lives depended on it. If the pastor thought he had a captive audience, he would go on for hours like he was in a tent revival meeting and was leading the Israelites out of Egypt. And no one had time on this night to bolster his ego. Everyone had come to see a play, not a soul saving mission.

The fanning by the church mothers was successful. Especially since Sister Gist, a full-bodied bulldog faced woman gave him her raised eyebrow. And everybody knew not to get on the bad side of Sister Gist. When we were children, we all believed that Sister Gist had killed her husband and had buried him single handedly behind the church. Everybody became more suspicious when there was a fresh mound of dirt behind the church that Sister Gist declared holy ground. Every time a fresh grave was dug, we would all dare each other to go and look into the hole to see if Sister Gist had murdered someone else and threw them into the grave. We never found anyone. We did find a small animal bone once that Ralph Nordstrom swore was a finger, but we weren't ever convinced that a finger bone could ever be nine inches long.

When we were older, we discovered the so called, "Holy Ground", the very place where we thought a murderer buried her victims, was actually a replaced septic tank. Bulldog Gist was apparently innocent of breaking one of the Ten Commandments. We were all a little disappointed that the mystery was solved. We wanted to pass down the story to our own children if not to only deter their misbehaving nature as Mamie had done to us. We often were told that we would be taken to the Holy Ground if we did not mind our manners. We dared not argue or fight during church services for the fear of falling into the open hole in the ground. I suppose it is not really much different from today when we are taught that behaving badly will cause our eternal suffering in a fiery pit.

However, the septic system was not without true torments. Our church was located in a secluded area which meant there were no city or county sewage lines. So, during a Sunday service, breathing could become a chore after half of the church attendees held a service of their own at Smalley's bar and grill the previous night. The Saturday night pig picking was the absolute worst. The fish fries ran a close second. What might have appeared appetizing going in, certainly did not have the same appearance coming out. And the smell was worse. A flushing toilet was a signal to panic or pray. We did both. The fear we had for the septic tank could never have compared to what it feared every Sunday morning. Cleaning out the septic tank was almost always a topic for the church maintenance committee. The honey truck was a familiar sight at the A.M.E. Church.

Sister Gist, not ever one to miss a service, attended the Saturday night social and the Sunday morning service. One might say she was full of the spirit. The Lord provided some and vodka provided its share. We could never really tell when she would say loudly she was full of the spirit exactly which one she was referring to. But her breath couldn't lie.

The play was ready to proceed. The choir opened with singing a song of praise and then nestled back to enjoy the show. Elisabeth smiled and looked as though someone had poured a pitcher of sunshine over her entire body. Nathaniel would be a shining star tonight and she could hardly wait to see his performance. He finally appeared as he was carrying a stake he was to be crucified on. He wore a wreath of thorns and nothing else except a sheet cut to fit him loosely. He struggled with the large plank and almost dropped it twice, but regained control much to Elisabeth's applause. Gertie tried to settle her, but to no avail. She was a proud grandmother and prouder still that Nathaniel was tonight's star.

After the Roman soldiers had driven the last of the nails into Nathaniel's hands and feet, they stood up the wooden plank and inserted it into a pre-constructed orifice to keep the plank upright and steady. By the time the church was gaining spirit and many stood waving their hands back and forth reaching to the heavens. The choir began a vibrant rendition of "The Crossing Ova to Get Ova Yonder", a song the choir committee was proud to have written themselves. As they sang, several of the choir members begin to get into rhythm and started dancing to the vibrant beat of the music. The play's cast members followed their lead and eventually they had the entire audience rocking to the festive beat. Then the dancing really began and the stage itself began to rock. They danced and waved their entire bodies like flags in a wind storm. At first, Nathaniel's head movements went unnoticed. The swaying of his foot to the music was more obvious. Then the unusual happened. In all of the excitement, Nathaniel, who was supposed to now be a dead corpse, jumped down from being crucified and showed off his dancing skills. He was carrying on like a master of performance. Pastor Washington, who stood on the side of the stage becoming stunned at the performance, began to wave frantically in order to get Nathaniel's attention. Unable to do that, Pastor Washington jumped upon the stage showing some dancing ability of his own and scurried over to Nathaniel.

"Nathaniel! W-W-What you be doin'?" Pastor asked him in a frustrated tone. You s'posed to be dead. Get yo'self b-b-back up on the tree! You dead! You dead!"

When Nathaniel realized what he had done, he was unable to assume his previous elevated position so he stood by the plank and winked at the audience. Then, came a recognized voice from an audience member, "Lawd have mercy. Look, Ann, Jesus thinks he be on Soul Train."

Nathaniel's performance and Uncle Franklin's comments caused an uncontrollable outburst of laughter from the audience. And we all knew if Uncle Franklin had an audience he would be difficult to tame. Half of the church mothers even threw back their heads in laughter and the other half tried to hide their amusement and could only sit and shake to mute their desire to join the other mothers' hysteria.

 Uncle Franklin continued by shouting, "I bet Jesus didn't have moves like that."

As much as Gertie didn't appreciate the remarks of Uncle Franklin, she knew that keeping Elisabeth calm during all of the demeaning chatter was her number one priority.

"It's all right, sister. Mamie would be proud of Nathaniel. She loved his spirit and you know how Uncle Franklin can get," Gertie said to Elisabeth as she wrapped her arm around her shoulder. "He's just a senseless old fool."

Uncle Franklin, however, couldn't help himself. He was on fire and the laughter he was getting from the crowd added fuel to his flames. "I can hardly wait for the encore!"

Elisabeth had had enough. Her control, what little she had, left her. She jumped up from her seat and turned to confront Franklin and said, "Oh yeah, Franklin. I goin' ta give ya a encore."

Before anyone could manage to grab her, Elisabeth had kicked off her shoes and was standing in the pew where she was previously sitting. In one swooping jump, she leaped and superman punched Uncle Franklin squarely in the jaw. Everything went into slow motion mode. On her assent to stand on the pew, Elisabeth's wig flew backward from her head to expose several unkempt braids of hair. Uncle Franklin's face froze in fear. He could already feel the pain before it had even arrived. He yelled out, "Lawd have mercy. Ann, she's really gonna knock me out!"

Uncle Franklin's glasses lay cockeyed on his face. The parishioners sitting close to him including his wife, Ann, had scattered to safety. Franklin was out cold and had slid down in the pew. Elisabeth regained her composure and put her hands on her hips still arguing with the unconscious Franklin. "Ain't nobody gonna sit and bad talk my baby when he be in the house of the Lord. I wish ya would wake up cause I got some more fo' ya." Elisabeth began to swing her arm around as though she were pitching in a softball game. "I wish I had my razor!" Elisabeth said still talking to Franklin.

When Elisabeth said that, the entire audience hit the floor. The play had come to a dramatic end and the entire stage had been deserted. However, the floor show was the one that most attendees would forever remember. The dilemma only ended when Gertie finally stood up and found herself relieved to utter, "It's okay, everybody. I've got her purse."

Through the Looking Glass

The morning following the dramatic events of the previous night found us gathered together at the farm in Mamie's kitchen. The past evening faded as we looked around us at the bounty of food that smothered our kitchen counters. Even with all of that, Julia busied herself with cooking breakfast for the army who would be dropping by offering condolences. She knew they would expect to eat and she would not disappoint them. She had blueberry pancakes, eggs, grits, gravy, biscuits, bacon, sausage, baskets full of toast and would even take special requests if it were simple and easy. All the condiments were there: butter, ketchup, homemade syrup, molasses, honey, sugar, cream, and practically anything anyone could wish for was sitting on the counter next to the refrigerator. At a separate table were ten pitchers of iced tea and three large coffee carafes surrounded by foam cups. Large coolers of ice sat underneath the table to be easily accessible to visitors. Julia had left a corner table cleared for the food and desserts she knew would be arriving by guests and sympathizers.

Gertie and Elisabeth, the only two sisters dressed in black, sat at the kitchen table sipping coffee and pinching at a butter and molasses covered biscuit. A southern favorite. They had arrived early that morning from their own homes only a few miles down the road. Elisabeth got her youngest grandson ready for school and Gertie, who had been left as guardian for three of her grandchildren, had gotten them up, fed, and on the bus. Both women had long, sleepless nights and rubbed the back of their necks to massage their tired bodies. Julia glanced over at them and wondered if they were thinking the same thing she was. That getting older meant that they, too, were not as invincible as they once thought they were. Having someone close to you die makes you embrace the reality that life is shorter than you could ever have imagined as a child and that death was an inevitability. Days were not quite

103

as long as they used to be and even years seemed only to be passing moments. They appreciated what Mamie had done for them. Even when they heard the things they used to hate to hear her say coming from their own mouths.

Julia ran the kitchen as well as the entire farm which was now the family's primary source of income. Mamie had chosen her to take over and trained her to do just that. With Elisabeth and Gertie married with children and now grandchildren of their own, Ava, the victim of an abusive relationship, Patience, Ava's fraternal twin, out in the world to seek fame and fortune, Julia was the logical choice. Mamie had worried that she had prevented Julia from making her own choices. She often wondered if Julia would have sought out other alternatives for her life, but as she watched her grow, Julia was a natural at what she did. Mamie died knowing she had made the right choice.

The work was hard, but Julia took to it and had better bargaining skills than Mamie herself had. She had discipline and was a born negotiator. I was the youngest and eager to please and learn. Julia considered me to be her right hand assistant. Sometimes I felt she was grooming me to step into her shoes and at other times, I thought she only gave me specific chores to make me feel as though I had a purpose. I didn't mind that. I admired Julia.

I often wondered why Julia never married. Jonathon would be the natural choice for her. He seem to understand her and neither of them ever dated anyone else on a steady basis. She would only say that she was married to the business and no man was worth giving up her freedom for. She also said that it was time for the woman to flip the old saying, "Why buy the cow, when you can get the milk for free?" And I believe she did just that. She dated and had her pick of any man she wanted, but there was always a barter involved. When Julia needed new furniture, she dated a man in the wholesale furniture business. Our new roof was the courtesy of a roofer she dated in the next county. She even got Mamie new prescription glasses when she dated an optometrist. To Julia, she had something men wanted and they were not going to get it unless she got something in return. It was only when the truck needed new tires that we thought things would change for her. She met Jonathon and the tires didn't come until months later, and we were not entirely sure she didn't have to buy those.

However, we never went without. Anything. The farm was doing incredibly well. The magic in the barn was making the farm a fairly decent profit. Folks came from all over to buy produce, fruits, canned jellies and jams, but the things that sold the most were Julia's baked goods. They seemed to fly right out of the kitchen as soon as they came out of the oven, especially the brownies. To Julia, it was all about the bargaining. When we saw Julia grab her fedora and adjust it on her head, she was ready to deal. On that, she was a champion. While no one was turned away due to their inability to pay, donations for the special baked goods were always appreciated. And, the special baked goods were not there for general public consumption, those only went to the people with special notes from doctors written in a code only few could decipher.

As breakfast was reaching its conclusion, more guests were beginning to arrive and I was to be the first to welcome them. They brought cakes, cookies, casseroles, and more food than any four families could feast on for weeks. Fried chicken in both boxes and barrels were stacked five high and people were still bringing more. Bertha and Bulldog Gist brought a fresh garden salad and banana pudding. Marlene Thomas and her mother brought napkins, paper plates, extra cups, and rolls upon rolls of paper towels. And still, they came.

Ernie Murdoch pulled his fish fryer out to the back lawn and prepared to set up the afternoon food fest. Outside, there would be an entirely separate southern smorgasbord of food. Fish with hot sauce and tartar sauce galore. Burgers and hot dogs for the kids and smoked sausages, hash, barbecue all served on buns. It would be a spectacular event. An outsider would consider this to be more of a family reunion than a wake. Both men and women would carry their pint bottles of brown liquor in either their jacket pockets or closely beside them in their purses. Little brown bags would be continuously passed among the continuously gathering crowd. And, of course, there was ample supply of the homemade distilled liquor available to those who preferred it.

All of the cousins and still living relatives were here. I could only imagine the airlines and train schedules being altered to accommodate the onslaught of people coming to Mamie's home going. I met people claiming to be my relatives that I didn't even know existed until that very day. And, then, there were the people who we were all too familiar with who began to arrive. One voice could be heard above all others and when we heard it, all of our eyes focused on Elisabeth who was still sitting with Gertie munching on her biscuit.

"Lawd, have mercy. Ann, just looky here at all these fine people," Uncle Franklin came through the door wearing a pair of what appeared to be a pair of women's sunglasses. "How y'all folks doin' today?"

Elisabeth, still being watched by the people in the kitchen, turned her head as to ignore Uncle Franklin's entrance. However, he was a hard man to ignore. Especially in those dark, feminine sunglasses.

None of us sisters really understood why we called Franklin our uncle. We were not even sure if he was related to us outside of our church family. Mamie always called him that and we followed suit.

Except for Elisabeth, we acknowledged him with a nod of our heads. Of course, we knew why he was wearing the dark shades. We could only imagine the size of his eye that Elisabeth had nearly knocked out just the previous evening. What we were all curious about was how Uncle Franklin was going to present his swollen face and the story he was going to tell as to how it happened. We also knew that we wouldn't have to wait that long to hear it. His yearning for attention couldn't be bridled.

He casually walked to the table holding all of the coffee and fixed himself and his wife a cup. He knew exactly how she liked it. Three artificial sweeteners and two rounded teaspoons of creamer. He just drank his black. He liked to actually taste the coffee. He carried one cup in each hand and found his wife, Ann, sitting at the table with Gertie and Elisabeth. He slowly walked over to the table to join them. You could tell he really didn't want to approach them. The three sitting women felt his awkwardness. Elisabeth broke the silence.

"Well, Franklin, why don' ya take off yo' wife's sunglasses and sit fo' a spell? You want us ta dim the lights since ya actin' like ya is light sens'tive?"

Gertie joined in with, "I think Uncle Franklin might be sporting something he don't want anybody to see."

"Don't you ladies start up no nonsense 'bout my vision. I had a unfortunate accident las' ev'ning when I got up and went to the bathroom. Ann can tell you."

He looked over at his wife as though he wanted her to help him create a scenario that would give him cover from any embarrassment.

107

"Tell these people, Ann, 'bout me trippin' las' night over the rug leadin' inta the bathroom. Go ahead. Tell 'em."

Ann sat with her head slightly downward and took a sip of her coffee.

Elisabeth had a look of disgust on her face and said to the people surrounding the table, "Well, now I have jus' about heard it all. A growed man askin' his wife, a saved Christian woman, to lie fo' 'im 'cause he is too embarrassed to let peoples know that he got his ass knocked out by a woman. Ain't no shame in the man."

Gertie looked at Elisabeth shaking her head in agreement.

"Well, you ole cheese eatin' sow pig! Ain't no woman ever knocked me out!" Franklin argued with Elisabeth.

Cocking her head with a slight shake, Elisabeth said, "Then I guess you betta take off them sunglasses befo' ya trip over yo' lyin' mouth."

This was the moment we had all been waiting for and the tension was rising. We all leaned in to get a glimpse of Uncle Franklin's face when he took off the shades. Ann held her head low trying not to laugh. We figured that she had already seen the damage Elisabeth had done to Franklin's face.

Franklin looked like a defeated warrior in battle who had to surrender his sword. He was going to have to take off his sunglasses in front of Elisabeth and account for his surrender, but damn if he wanted to do that. He knew he would be ridiculed by his entire family and at Mamie's wake, where family from every nook, cranny, and crevice would be there to witness it. People he hadn't seen in years would be privy to the knowledge that Elisabeth had knocked him out at the church. But he relented. He knew it would have to be done. He stood shaking because he was so mad at both Elisabeth herself and the fact she hit him. He jerked the darkened glasses from his face and stared at Elisabeth through one eye and asked, "Is this what you been waitin' to see?"

Everyone standing around waiting to see Uncle Franklin's eye through a hand over their mouths in disbelief. It was bad. Really bad.

"Holy shit!" proclaimed Elisabeth, I don' think I ever seen a eye that look that bad befo'. I probably should have hit a litta lower so I coulda broke that jaw. Mighta been able to keep that big mouth of yourn shut. Go ahead and put them shades back on. That face might scare the chil'ren."

"His face is scaring me," Gertie added. Looks even worse than what you did to Leroy that time. You remember that, Elisabeth? The time you walked in and he was with the neighbor in your bed?"

Elisabeth thought for a moment and responded, "Oh yeah. I believe Franklin do look worser than Leroy's did. That no good basta'd deserved it though. He dead now, but he still deserved it. I'm jus' sorry I wasn't what killed him. Mamie was right. Leroy was a no good devil."

We all took a careful look at Uncle Franklin's face. Gertie and Elisabeth were right. It looked worse than Leroy's face did after Elisabeth beat him over the head with a shovel. She beat the neighbor he was with, too. But she wouldn't hit her in the face. She took the shovel and beat her ass until it bled. She told her she was getting the ass whooping her daddy never gave her. That woman didn't sit down for a week or two. But Elisabeth never told the woman's husband that she had caught his wife with Leroy. Elisabeth thought a good ass whipping was punishment enough.

One of the distant cousins asked Elisabeth how Leroy died. She was more than happy to tell him.

"His drunk ass got hit by a car. He was walkin' down the road and was hit by some white woman. I was mighty mad 'bout it."

The cousin asked Elisabeth, "You mean you was mad 'cause he got hit by a car?"

"Hell no! I's was mad 'cause I couldn'ta been the one to a run 'im ova. White woman had insurance tho', so I got some money outta that. And don' think I didn'ta keep the bas'tad's life insurance paid up. Still wish I coulda been the one to kill 'im though. Couldn'ta collected if I'd a did it. Policy was writ that way. But I sho' wanted to."

With her last statement, Elisabeth had her finger pointed at the cousin who asked her how Leroy died. Gertie had to remind her that it might not be proper to talk about killing her husband at Mamie's home going. Elisabeth looked at Gertie and acknowledged with a shake of her head to the affirmative. They both continued to eat.

The hours passed and more and more people dropped by to see us. Some came with deepest, sincere sympathies, some came in tow of their parents or family, and some came just to eat. The liveliest of the crew came to sit beneath the old maple tree in the left hand corner of our backyard to reminisce and drink. Sipping whiskey made its rounds as both men and women swapped stories about their lives and how they had been enriched by the departed loved one they were preparing to lay to rest. And Mamie was loved.

Judge Holcombe and his young wife stepped into the kitchen and dropped off a chocolate cake. All of the black women looked on and nodded appreciatively while they knew that cake was bought at the local grocery store. That kind of gesture might be acceptable to white northern folk, but no self-respecting southern black woman worth her grits would take something to a wake that was not handmade or home cooked. You might just as well stop and buy a bag of ice to keep the drinks cold. But to save the judge any embarrassment, I took the store packaged cake with a gratuitous smile and placed it on the table reserved for guest brought foods after I threw away the box and placed it on a plastic cake plate with a cover. Then, I led the judge and his wife to comfortable seating in a more quiet part of the house. His feebleness became more apparent to me as I held his arm to steady him in a chair. I knew there was no wonder why he was a steady customer of Mamie's for years. He thanked me and asked me if Julia had made any of her delightful brownies.

"Why, yes," I responded, "I am sure she did. Let me get some for you."

111

The judge's wife stared off into the distance and I wondered if she even had a clue. While the entire town wondered why he would ever marry such a young idiot, my family knew well and understood completely. His wife had died and he needed a caretaker. Not for pleasure, but for company and friendship. She was a lovely young widow with three children and had passed Mamie's test for a suitable mate for her dear friend. I left them there as I went to retrieve his special request from Julia. As I walked into the kitchen, I answered the incessantly ringing phone.

"Gertie! It's the school. They need to speak to you about Roland," I yelled to Gertie as though I were screaming into the wind. I heard her manage to get to the phone then heard her gasp and very loudly say, "He said WHAT?"

Only hearing one side of the conversation through Gertie's comments was difficult to make sense of. Most of it was Gertie saying, "Uh huh" or 'I see." Elisabeth came to stand beside her to get the full story as soon as Gertie hung up the phone.

"What's the matta, sista? What be goin' on down at the school house now? Always some kinda shit goin' on."

"Elisabeth, I am really not sure. Something about some cussing and something about his neck."

"Neck? Roland too young ta be neckin'."

"It's not that kind of neck. They said it was some kind of game where the kids slap you on the neck. I'm not sure, but they want me to go and pick him up."

"Well, you'll need a ride. Come on. I take ya down there ta go and fetch 'im."

"Thank you, Elisabeth. I need to get to the bottom of this."

Elisabeth grabbed her keys and firmly stated, "Oh, yeah, ya can count on us gettin' ta the bottom of it. You wantin' me ta take my razor?"

As they left, Elisabeth snuggled her purse squarely beneath her arm. On their way out, they both looked at Uncle Franklin and chuckled. Elisabeth turned to Julia and asked if she needed to bring anything back from the grocery store.

Julia looked around the kitchen and said, "Are you kiddin' me? You might wanna drop in and ask 'em if they need anythin'. And, by the way, don't you two be startin' no trouble at the school now, ya hear?"

"Who, us? What could we poss'bly do. Hurt you'd think such," Elisabeth said to Julia. "Tho' ain't 'bout ta make no promises."

Julia waved her hand in the air until she got my attention. When she did, she pointed at Elisabeth and Gertie. Without saying anything aloud, she mouthed her words to me, "Go with them."

I nodded to show her I understood what she meant and pushed my way through the filled kitchen to get behind my eldest sisters.

"So, do you two mind if I tag along? I need to get a break and could use some fresh air."

Elisabeth gave Julia a disgusting smirk and replied, "No, litta 'un, we don' mind if you hang with us."

Memory Lane

Elisabeth, Gertie, and I mangled our way through the crowd gathered in the kitchen to make an exit to the back door and managed to get to Elisabeth's car. Although both Elisabeth and I could drive, there was never a discussion as to who would. Elisabeth always drove. Gertie was always her co-pilot and whoever rode along with them knew they had to take the back seat. I didn't mind. The back seat was spacious and having no one near me was a relief. I was never one for crowds of people, especially those I wasn't familiar with.

The chattering between the two in the front seat began almost immediately after Elisabeth started the car. It usually began with Elisabeth telling Gertie she needed to learn how to drive. Gertie would have none of it and argued the point of why she would never get her driver's license. She made good points. She would have to buy a car, pay car insurance, learn how to drive, and she was always with Elisabeth who would never let her drive anyway. Driving was not appealing to Gertie like it was to Elisabeth. Elisabeth liked the control driving the car gave her.

As we passed the various places in town, my two eldest sisters would point out how things had changed so much. It had been a long time since they were both young and married. Elisabeth pointed out 'welfare row' as she insisted on calling it and brought up the first day Gertie and Leroy had moved there. "Do you remember that dirty bas'tad tellin' us how he had foun' a new house for you to live in that had all new 'pliances and furniture?"

"Sure, I remember it. How can I forget it? It was true to a point. It was new. To us, anyway. The couch was one that his daddy had kept in the barn and took several cleanings to get the smell out of it."

"You know, Gertie, I woulda killed him that day if you woulda let me."

"I know you would have sister, but it wasn't worth the trouble. I was young and in love or I thought I was. That was a long time ago and water under the bridge."

"Look over there, Elisabeth. Do you remember our children sitting on the steps to that basement watching us get our food surplus supplies? They only let three or four of us in at a time. Place was crowded. Remember the cheese and peanut butter we used to get? Our kids would have starved without that food and what we got from the farm from Mamie."

"Sho' do. 'Member it well. Our chil'ren sitting on those steps with their noses to the windows singin'." When Elisabeth mentioned that, they both broke out in song. "Bringing home the cheese. Bringing home the cheese. We will all rejoice when ma brings home the cheese."

Both women busted out laughing and so did I. I could visualize my nieces and nephews doing just what Elisabeth and Gertie described.

"As soon as we got back home, we must have made twenty grilled cheese sandwiches. And the powdered milk, do you remember that?"

Elisabeth let out a laugh. "Yeah, and mixin' it with watta and real milk from the farm to make it last longer. And the corn flakes. No sugah or nothin' on 'em. Just plain ole corn flakes. Couldn't afford much sugah so had to measure out jus' a half a teaspoon per bowl per chil'. Times were tough, but we made it through."

"You still 'member them fifty pound bags of flour?"

"I'll never forget them. It was rough carrying those up from the basement, but we made fresh biscuits and homemade breads, and rolls. I did most of the baking and we had that old freezer. Made up enough to freeze for both of our families. But always saved enough flour, sugar, and eggs to make a cake or two once a month."

"Yo' pound cakes were the best, Gertie. You still makin' 'em? I don't recall having one in a while now."

"Do most of the baking at the farm now with Julia. We experiment with different things. Fun to try new recipes."

"What new kinda experimentin' y'all up to at the farm?" Elisabeth asked curiously.

"Just different things. Adding a little more butter to this and that. Like you and I used to do when our children were young. We're seeing what we can do with wild parsley on a few things now."

"Wil' parsley, you say? I don' 'member us eva to be usin' nonna that. Parsley be bitter. Don't like tha' much," Elisabeth said as she turned up her lip and scrunched her nose.

I loved hearing the stories that Elisabeth and Gertie told. As much as they say how bad the earlier times were, you could tell they remembered a lot of it fondly. Unless it was about Leroy or Roosevelt. Sometimes, though, I wondered if even those memories were as bad as they made them sound. When she thought no one was watching her, Elisabeth softly rubbed the finger where her wedding band once rested and gazed distantly to the wind. Gertie still wore her band. She was still married. Never did divorce Roosevelt. As long as they didn't have to live together, they could be civil. It was all the times they were living in the same house that were unforgettable. It could certainly never be considered a civil union.

The one time that most significantly stands out in my mind was when Elisabeth and Gertie were going to set Roosevelt on fire. To keep them talking I asked them about it.

"Do you two remember when you had your minds determined to set fire to Roosevelt?"

Gertie turned a little and gave me a slight smile as though she knew I was going to bring that up.

"Yes, little one, I certainly do remember that. It was Elisabeth's idea though."

"Now wait, jus' a minute there," Elisabeth blurted defiantly, "I told you to set a fire underneath his ass. I didn't figure you to really strike a match to 'im."

Gertie chuckled, "I was so mad at Roosevelt. He and Leroy would go off gambling and come home with nothing to show for it. He was so drunk, he couldn't even tell me where he had been. So, when he fell across the bed, I called Elisabeth and she came to our apartment. The kids had gone to school for the day. That's when Elisabeth told me to light a fire under him. So…I did. I tore up some old newspaper and made me some kindling. Tucked it around Roosevelt and struck the match, and I set his ass on fire."

"What happened then, Gertie?"

"Bastard woke up. Then, I was mad 'cause he woke up. How he managed to do that, I will never know. The only new piece of furniture in my house were those brand new mattresses and he sat up and it looked like he had a dead man's chalk mark drawn around his body."

Elisabeth chimed in with excitement, "The evil bastard just wouldn't die. And, I was mad, too, sista. I wanted to put Leroy beside 'im and make it a bon fire."

"Yeah," Gertie added, "That would have been a real weinie roast."

"But, do you ever miss him, Elisabeth?" I asked solemnly from the back seat.

She stared straight ahead and thought for a moment.

119

"Well, if I had to be completely honest, I 'spose I do or, maybe, I miss what it coulda been. All womans want to be loved. I think me and Gertie fell in love wit' bein' in love and never was in love wit' who we married. But he dead and gone now to be wit' the devil, so I 'spose it really ain't matterin' anymo'."

Gertie reached over and touched Elisabeth's arm gently. "That was very well said, sister."

I rarely saw the softer side of Elisabeth and what she said almost brought tears to my eyes. I reached to the front of the car and placed my hand on her shoulder.

"What is the matta' wit' you two? Don' be touchin' me like you sympathizin'. The bastard is dead and burin' wit' his daddy, the devil 'imself."

Gertie and I both started laughing and took our hands from Elisabeth and put them back by our sides. I am not sure if Gertie was thinking about the same thing I was, but I imagine it was. That being Leroy's funeral. It was another one of our family's unforgettable moments.

I remember Leroy's funeral. He and Elisabeth had separated a long while earlier, but they never divorced. Leroy moved up to Spartanburg and was living with another woman. Rumor was that he had two more children by this woman, but Elisabeth would never accept or deny it. And, obviously, Leroy had not informed the woman he had not divorced Elisabeth. When we showed up to the funeral, Leroy was laid out in the most elaborate casket we had ever seen. We overheard his new woman say it was mahogany with gold inlay handles. He was dressed fine, too. New suit that had to run the woman, at least, five hundred dollars. You could tell she was broken up about his death and had spent several thousand for the funeral. The crying stopped when Elisabeth walked in and announced that she was Leroy's wife.

I thought Leroy's new woman would explode. She had the funeral director strip him of his brand new suit. By the time it was over, Leroy lay in a pine box, wrapped in a sheet, and buried in potter's field.

About a month later, Elisabeth showed up in a new Cadillac. Bright red. Leroy's favorite color. Mamie fussed at her for spending money on such a wasteful, worldly possession. Elisabeth countered the argument by telling Mamie that it was her tribute to Leroy. "He always wanted one."

"A headstone is a tribute, Elisabeth," Mamie said.

"Well, after I drive it to death, I'll park it at the head of his grave. I'll even engrave his name on it," Elisabeth said in a serious tone and left Mamie only shaking her head at her oldest granddaughter.

Gertie and I, still sitting in the car as Elisabeth drove towards the elementary school, laughed audibly. But we let the subject drop as not to get Elisabeth started before we went into the school. I was, after all, the one sent by Julia to be the peacekeeper. And we were close to the elementary school now.

"Well, here we is. Sista, I will let you and the little 'un out by the do' and I'll go fin' a parkin' space. I be in d'rectly."

"Thank you, Sister, I just don't know what I'd do without you."

"God willin', I hopes ya neva have to fin' out."

"See you inside, dear. Oh, and Elisabeth, you might want to leave your purse in the car. It tends to make folks a little nervous when they see you carrying it," Gertie cautioned.

"I don' know I feels too comfortable wit' leavin' my purse in the car. They got some hoodlums in this place, and I ain't talkin' about the chil'ren."

I attempted to help Gertie by saying, "Well, how about you leave that straight blade razor under the seat. I don't think anyone will see it and that way, you will have your purse in case you need to show your I.D."

"I.D.? I.D.! You kiddin' me. Ain't a sumofabitch in 'ere that don't be knowing who I is. Maybe I should take my razor and leave my purse in the car."

Gertie and I both knew that arguing with Elisabeth was useless. We just smiled at her and told her we would meet her in the office. She agreed and told us she would be in shortly.

As soon as Gertie entered the door, she was lavished with love from the school. Teachers had found aides to mind their classes to come to see Gertie.

"On behalf of all of us, Gertie, we just wanted to let you know how much we miss you around here. The cafeteria is just not the same without you. We miss your cooking and all of the wonderful desserts you made. But, we especially miss your ever present smile."

"Oh, I miss all of you, too. And, I so miss all of the children. Each and every one of them."

"Gertie," one voice said from the crowd, "Do you think you could make us some of your fresh biscuits?"

"Yes, I surely will. I'll drop them off one morning."

Another teacher spoke up, "Gertie, we are so sorry to hear about Mamie. You and she are so much alike."

"Thank all of you so much. You all don't know what that means to me and my family," Gertie said with tears welling in her eyes. "Now you all better get back to class before the principal comes out here and fires all of you!"

Gertie took a moment to get a tissue from her purse and wiped her eyes. She missed running the school cafeteria. She spent so many hours in this building. Making sure everyone was well fed and well nourished. Her food was fresh.

She didn't open cans containing all the preservatives in them. The school district contracted with Mamie's farm for fresh produce and vegetables. It benefited Mamie's farm financially and benefited the children physically. Mamie and Gertie knew that all of the children would get two good meals per day. Those who came in late were allowed to go to Gertie's cafeteria and get an egg biscuit or a bowl of cereal with fruit. Gertie always said, "No child can benefit from school without at least a little something on their stomach."

These days, Gertie busied herself with working the farm to still keep the contract with the school district and helping Julia with the baking. Even though she missed working at the school and seeing all of her friends there, things were good now.

We proceeded to the desk to check in and registered on the sign-in sheet. We signed our names. Martha Nordstrom was the volunteer working the front reception desk. As Gertie signed, she said to Martha, "My sister will be here shortly to join us."

Martha looked at her cautiously and squinted her eyes and asked, "Which sister will be joining you?"

"My sister, Elisabeth," Gertie replied with a smile.

Martha immediately picked up the phone and dialed the office while giving Gertie and me a nervous smile. When the call was answered, Martha partially covered the mouth piece of the phone and said in an audible whisper, "Gertie is here with two of her sisters to pick up Roland."

We were unable to hear the voice on the other end of the phone, but from Martha's reaction, we were certain that the office had been alerted that Elisabeth was going to be entering the building.

Martha hung up the phone and graciously told us to go in and have a seat in the outer office and Principal Jackson would be with us shortly. Lagging slightly behind Gertie, I chuckled to myself to hear Martha pick up the phone once again and call security and put them on notice that there may be some turmoil in the office. It was obvious that Principal Jackson and Elisabeth had met before.

A few minutes later, Elisabeth came through the front door. "Well, damn! I musta walked a mile through the parkin' lot." She looked around and began walking toward the reception desk.

"Hello, Elisabeth," Martha said. "Your sisters are waiting for you right inside the office door. Right through there."

"I need to sign somethin'?" Elisabeth asked Martha as she set her purse on the receptionist's counter preparing to give her an I.D.

"Oh, no. No. You just go right on in. Gertie told us you were coming and I went ahead and put your name down on the register." Martha was nervous upon seeing the purse that she surmised was holding Elisabeth's straight blade razor.

"Well, thank ya, Martha. 'Preciate that. I'll just go on in here with my sistas."

Martha smiled and shook her head to acknowledge her agreement.

Elisabeth walked into the front office and came over to where Gertie and I were sitting to wait on the principal. She squeezed in between us and we could see she was sweating from her walk from the car.

"Gertie, you gotta a cloth so I can wipe my face?" Elisabeth asked. "Walking through that parkin' lot is like walkin' through hell. I am sweatin' like a slave. I hope my deodorant holds up. Ever since the doctor told me I was goin' through menopause, I can't seem to stop sweatin'. Exactly, jus' how long is menopause 'spose to last anyway? I am seventy year old and still sweatin' like a slave pickin' cotton. I need to 'just that thermostat. And, damn it, men don't do no 'pausing, why they got to go and call it, 'men-o-pausin'? And the monthly cycle. Womans always gettin' the short end of the stick. Men gets a whole month with no interruptions. One of our weeks is stole away from us. Kinda shit's that?"

"Elisabeth, you're not seventy years old," Gertie told her.

"My bones tell me diff'rent," Elisabeth responded. "How old I be, Gertie, I fo'get."

"You'll be fifty-eight on your birthday."

126

"Well, I be dipped in shit, don' know why I thinkin' seventy."

I nudged Elisabeth with my elbow and said,"Shh! Everyone can hear you, Elisabeth!"

"Well, I don' care if they hear me. They knows it's true."

Fortunately for all of us, the women in the office had a sense of humor and all snickered while continuing to work. Elisabeth had cooled down and sat back seemingly relaxed. Principal Jackson finally came out of his office and walked toward us. The school resource officer was with him. He greeted us politely and offered his condolences concerning the death of our grandmother. We thanked him politely in return.

Gertie got down to business quickly and said, "Principal Jackson, I understand that you have had some problems with my grandson, Roland. Do you think we could discuss that?"

"Most certainly, Gertie. Why don't all of you come in my office? I have the guidance counselor and two of Roland's teachers in there, also. I would like them to weigh in on the situation that we have here with Roland."

"I would like to have their input also, if you think it will help us get to the bottom of the problem."

"Come right this way ladies and have a seat."

127

Gertie, Elisabeth, and I went into the principal's office almost as though we were the ones who were about to be reprimanded. We all sat together on the leather sofa against the wall.

Principal Jackson began the conversation. "Gertie, I am afraid to have to tell you this now. Especially since I am aware of the loss of Mamie that must have all of you very saddened. However, Roland and his behavior over the past few days must be addressed before it gets completely out of hand. I think you know the teachers here and the guidance counselor."

"Yes, I do and it is very nice of all of you to be here," Gertie replied.

"Jus' what is it that the boy has gone and did? And what is the neckin' game Gertie mention to us?" Elisabeth added.

Principal Jackson said, "I am going to let the guidance counselor address that first and, then, we can discuss it."

He nodded toward Ms. Mabry with consent to speak to Gertie and her sisters.

"Hello ladies. It has been brought to my attention that Roland has been being verbally abusive to his fellow classmates. We were a little surprised that this is happening with Roland because he has always been a model student."

Elisabeth spoke up and asked, "Exactly what is it ya mean by verbally 'busive?"

"Well," Ms. Mabry continued, "Roland has been using a lot of, well, curse words."

"Whoa! Whaaat? Roland? I don' believe I ever heard that boy sayin' anythin' outta the way." Elisabeth looked genuinely shocked with what she had heard.

Gertie added, "What curse words has he been saying? Could he have picked something up at school? Mr. Jackson, you know me and I would not allow a child in my home to speak inappropriately with curse words. What has the child said?"

Ms. Mabry, feeling embarrassed to say the words aloud, leaned over to whisper to Gertie with Elisabeth listening in to hear the words, "He called another little boy a 'son of a bitching bastard'".

"Oh, my goodness," was all a shocked Gertie could say.

"Well, now," Elisabeth said as she held her hand to her face. "I jus' don' be knowin' where the lil' bastard woulda be gettin' that kind of talkin'. Umm Mmm Mmm."

The people in the office looked at Elisabeth and then, at each other.

"You know," Elisabeth continued, "I think, maybe, Gertie and me should have us a word wit' Roland. We can prob'ly get to the bottom of all this. Bring that youngin' down here and let me and Gertie step out in the hall wit' 'im."

Gertie went out into the hallway and waited for Roland to be sent for. Elisabeth followed her out and I noticed they left the office door partially cracked. Principal Jackson looked at me still sitting in his office. "Don't you wish to join your sisters in the hallway?"

"Oh, no. I don't think that will be necessary," I responded.

In only a few minutes, through the partially opened door, myself and the entire office staff could hear the talking to that Roland was getting from his grandmother and his Aunt Elisabeth.

"Roland! What is this I hear about you saying curse words in school? You know we don't do that!"

"That's right, Roland. Ya little pecker head you!" Elisabeth was pacing back and forth as she spoke to Roland. "I have tol' you and tol' you that if they needs to be somebody cursed out, then you shoulda come to me and I'll be the one ta cuss out the lil' summabiches. Now, boy, don't you go makin' yo' auntie go throwin' down on ya. And, damn, boy what is tha' on yo' neck?"

130

"That's just from a game we play at school, Aunt Elisabeth. When somebody says something stupid, the kids yell out, "Neck!" and they commence to slap you upside your neck."

"Well, from the looks of yo' neck, you been sayin' some really stupid things. Yo' neck looks like a nes' of waspers has stung into it. And what yo' go playin' some stupid game like tha' fo' anyway? Damn, boy, don' tell me them other boys' necks don' look as bad as yourn. 'Cause if yo' tell me somebody been whoopin' up on ya, then they is a lot more necks down here at this schoolhouse goin' to get swole up!"

Roland began to start moving to place himself behind Gertie before he answered, "No Aunt Elisabeth, it's not like that. It's just a game we play."

Gertie looked at Elisabeth and stated, "Sister, why don't you go back in the office and tell the principal that we are just going to take Roland home with us for the rest of the day and he can return to school tomorrow."

"Yeah, all right. I tell 'im. But I ain't gonna forget that neck game. I'd like to slap evabody 'round here tha' says somethin' stupid upside they head," Elisabeth said as she retreated to the office to do what Gertie asked of her.

She entered without noticing that the door had been cracked and everyone in the office had heard their conversation. Although, I don't think she particularly cared. She matter-of-factly came in, told me we were taking Roland home for that day and looked over at Principal Jackson and said, "He be back in the mo'ning." Without much more ado, we were out the door in the unbearable heat heading toward Mamie's house. Roland had fallen asleep in the back seat lying against me. I put my arm around him and he nestled even closer where I could see his slightly swollen neck. A cool cloth would make him all better I reasoned to myself. Then, I giggled silently and repeated softly, "Neck."

Snow White

After arriving back at the farm, we were amazed to see the myriads of people who had arrived in the short time we were gone. There had to be at least fifty more cars parked on the road than there were since we had left. Elisabeth was a little put out that someone had taken her usual parking space.

"Elisabeth, just find another place to park this time. I am sure all of these visitors didn't realize they were taking your spot," Gertie said trying to reason with Elisabeth.

"Sista, ma name is on the damn tree that has the 'Park Here and Die' sign nailed ta it. They can't read that they's blind and otta not be behind the wheel. I find 'em. They goin' move they car."

Elisabeth laid on the horn and blew it until everybody came over to her. Gertie and I escaped into the house with Roland to avoid the confrontation.

While she had everyone's attention, Elisabeth said, "Who here parked their piece a shit car in my place? Ain't none a y'all got no home learnin'? I's goin' go inta the house and relieve my bladda and when I get back out here, my space betta be freed up."

We had no idea who owned the car, but when Elisabeth went outside her space was free and she moved her Caddie into her normal spot. I told Julia what had happened at the school. What could she do, but shake her head?

Gertie put Roland in an upstairs bedroom to sleep and came down to help with the serving of food. Working in a cafeteria was useful in a time like this. Most of the people were now outside gathered around Ernie and the cooking fish. They couldn't seem to get enough of it. Elisabeth found herself a comfortable chair under a cool tree beside of Ann and stopped some of the men passing by with their brown bags and had herself a sip of whiskey. We knew that would either put her to sleep or get her into another fight.

I looked around the house and asked Julia, "Where's Patience and Ava?"

Julia replied, "Ain't seen 'em it a while. Find a mirror and you'll find Ava. Ain't no tellin' 'bout the other one."

Julia rinsed her hands and dried them on the hanging kitchen towel. She looked at me curiously and said, "Let's go find 'em."

We searched the lower level of the house and they were not there. That left upstairs, outside, or one of the barns. Neither of them were barn people, so we decided to ascend the stairs. We could hear voices when we reached the landing.

"You will have to ask Julia about what Mamie wanted to happen to the farm, Patience. She never discussed those things with me," Ava was saying to Patience.

Julia pushed open the door to Ava's room and peered at Patience and said, "Yeah, you would have ta ask me 'bout the farm."

"I was her granddaughter, too, Julia," Patience said both disgusted and embarrassed at getting caught interrogating Ava in private.

"That's the difference in us, Patience. I still am her granddaughter," Julia said emphatically.

Patience glared at Julia and said, "Well, I guess we will just have to wait and see. Come on with me, Ava. I want you to help me shop for a dress."

Ava reluctantly uncoiled from her fetal position that she reverted to when she felt conflict in the air. She obediently followed Patience down the stairs.

"So, where do you buy your clothes, Ava?"

"I don't go out a lot. I like staying close to home. I feel more comfortable here."

"Well, I'm with you. Let's go shopping. I'll get you a new handbag or something. Where is a good place to go?"

"Lots of the women in town like Amy's shop on Main Street."

"Perfect. Let's go there."

Patience led Ava out of the house and into her car. She saw Patrick on the way out and told him she was taking Ava shopping. He didn't like it, but he knew he couldn't stop her.

When they were in the car, Patience grilled Ava on how she had ended up back at the farm. She could tell Ava was not going to say much, and answered as simply as possible.

"Mamie told me what your husband did to you, Ava."

"Then, you know."

"Why did you allow him to beat you? You don't have to take that from a man."

"Couldn't stop him."

"Don't tell me that. There's things you could do. Why didn't you report him to his commanding officer?"

"Not that easy."

"It was as easy as making a phone call, Ava. That's all it would have taken."

"Not that easy."

"Women like you just kill me. You let men run over you and don't lift a finger to help yourselves. Maybe you liked it."

Ava reached for her purse and took out a bottle of pills. She threw one down her throat.

"You can't solve anything with drugs, Ava."

"You can solve a lot of things with drugs, Patience."

They didn't talk again until Patience parked on Main Street in front of Amy's store. The sign said, "Designs by Amy". Patience doubted that.

The store had a lot of traffic. It was small, but large enough to have a storage room in the back to have different sizes of the clothes on display. Amy was there and had a girl who looked a lot like her assisting her.

"Patience Nesbitt! As I live and breathe. Girl, I haven't seen you in ages. How you been?"

Amy Rogers had the brightest smile that Patience had ever seen. She removed her sunglasses, looked at Amy, and decided to slip them back on. Amy caught on to what she did.

"I know, right? I just had my teeth bleached. I just love how it makes my teeth feel. I mean, you can't have a fashion store and go around looking shabby, now can you? What brings you girls in today?"

"I came to look for a dress. Black. Maybe navy blue?"

"Oh, well, of course. You're going to want to look for something for Mamie's funeral. Didn't bring anything with you from D.C.? Mamie told me you were an attorney now. She would come in just to tell us how proud of you she was. She was the sweetest thing. Everybody in town just loved your grand mama."

"Yeah, and my last name is Snow now. I'm Patience Snow."

"Oh, yes, Mamie did mention you got married. Good for you. Last time you and I talked you had hair out to here. We really never did think you'd ever get married. You say your name is Snow now? I guess that's a good name. You always did wish you were white. I recall you having a big chip on your shoulders about being colored. Not that it ever bothered me any. I never saw what all the hoopla was about myself. It's not like we have colored bathrooms anymore and you can go and do pretty much anything you want to. What size you looking for, hon? About a sixteen?"

"I wear a size nine," Patience said with a hint of anger in her voice.

"Really? A nine? Wouldn't have ever guessed that one. Sales clothes are against the wall right over there. Let me know if you find anything. I'll be just right behind the counter. Oh, and I just wanted to let you know that I loved that play your church put on. I was just hysterical over it. And, my goodness, my hat sales are booming. All the white ladies are just mad over the colored hats."

"The colored hats?" Patience asked inquisitively.

"Oh, yes! Those big red, blue, green, yellow hats. Just looked like a rainbow at the play with all those lovely ladies wearing all those hats. I'm here to tell you that business has been outrageous cause of those hats. Animal prints are in these days. Been getting a lot of requests for hats. Yessiree."

"Amy," Patience asked, "why do you call them colored hats?"

"Well, because they're colored silly. Oh, I know what you're referring to. You thought I meant the colored folks were wearing them. No, hon. But you

139

know, now that you brought it up, I do think that always was the problem between me and you. You always felt lesser than. But, darlin', I'm here to tell you the gospel truth. I've never owned slaves and you've never picked cotton. Everything against that wall is fifty-percent off. Well, hello there, Ava."

Patience was speechless and Ava stood looking at the shoes and handbags while she twirled her hair in her fingers and glanced at herself in the mirror. Patience grabbed Ava's arm and literally pulled her out of Amy's store and pushed her into the car.

"I just cannot believe that woman. What a bitch! I don't know how she stays in business and why would a black woman ever shop there? They should boycott her and her damn hats!" Patience fussed and jabbered to herself until she parked in front of another store.

"Ava!" Patience screamed and looked at her twin in disgust. Don't you have anything to say about what just happened?"

Ava looked at her and calmly said, "Drugs solve a lot of things."

Patience rolled her eyes and ordered Ava to get out of the car and go into the department store. Ava obeyed.

The store was spacious and lovely. It had the one thing that was mandatory for Patience, an absence of Amy Rogers. Ava found a full length mirror and looked at her beautiful shape and face. Patience was off to find her dress. She was successful. She found a stunning navy blue sleeveless dress with an

140

accompanying jacket. She felt black would have been too traditional and she also took into consideration that she could wear her new purchase to work. With the new shoes and purse she bought, she felt she could make an impression without standing too visibly out. When she went to the counter to pay, the clerk asked her if she would be interested in purchasing a matching hat. She gave her a simple response, "Hell, no."

Ava was trying on a pair of long white gloves. Patience stood back and looked at her admiring her beauty. She could show up at the funeral in a housecoat and stand out more than any person present. She had a natural presence about her that was majestic.

"Ava, have you found a handbag that you like? I promised to buy one for you," Patience asked.

"No. I already have all of these. But, thank you."

"You mean you already have every single purse in this store?"

"Yes, and the matching shoes."

"You told me you never went out much. How did you get all of those things?"

"Julia."

"Julia! Our sister, Julia? She has bought all of this, every single handbag in this store for you. I've never seen the woman out of her bibbed overalls. This is not a cheap store, Ava. How does Julia afford to buy you designer clothes?"

"I don't know."

"Would you tell me if you did?"

"I don't know."

"Come on. Let's go. We need to get back to the farm."

The crowd had thinned out a little when Patience and Ava pulled into Mamie's yard. The fish were still frying and the men were still sipping on their bottles. Patience noticed Elisabeth among them. She got her bags from the car and looked around for Patrick.

They arrived in the kitchen and found Patrick in an apron helping Julia and Gertie clean up what the many guests left behind. I was keeping a log of who had brought what in order to send thank you cards. The list seemed endless.

Patience sat her bags in the floor and told Patrick he needed to take them up to their room.

"I'm a little busy here. Do you think you could take them up?" Patrick asked as he emptied another trash can and replaced the bag.

"Patrick, I'm tired and I have just finished a stressful encounter. Have any of you ever shopped at that witchy Amy Roger's shop on Main Street?"

Julia responded, "No, don't get in there too much. Around here, we work."

"Well, it is just a horrible place. She won't have to worry about getting any of my business. No self-respecting black person should ever go inside those doors. However, Julia, she did mention that Mamie went there from time to time and from the sounds of it, she went there to brag a little bit about me and all of my accomplishments," Patience said smugly.

"Well, now that I recall," Julia responded, "Mamie did go in that shop on occasion. Ever now and again when Mamie got to missin' you, she would go in there and talk to Amy."

"And, just how did that allow Mamie to deal with missing me?"

"She came into contact with your white mirror image," Julia replied as she dried the large kettle that she had finished washing.

"Oh, you are just jealous, Julia. You never did anything to give Mamie reason to brag about you. She wanted her granddaughters to be more than just some crop growing, kitchen help country bumpkins."

"Patience!" Patrick voiced in disbelief.

"Patience, you simple minded fool. Take your lazy black ass and get yo'self and these bags outta my kitchen or I will put you and them in the trash. Tell me I won't," Julia said with angered eyes staring at Patience.

Patience was reluctant to move until Julia took a step towards her.

"I will sit the bags on the steps and when Patrick goes upstairs to my room, he will take them up. That is what true gentlemen do."

"Let's me and you get somethin' straight, Patience. I didn't want you here. I don't want ya here now. If it weren't for yo' husband bein' a decent man, you would not be here at all. And I would be a litta careful 'bout callin' that room you usin' yourn."

"Mamie would not leave me out of anything. You and I both know that. It's just something that you are going to have to accept, Julia."

Julia threw the kitchen towel over her shoulder and turned her back to Patience and only said, "We'll see."

Patience sat down at the table and said, "Patrick, I need a glass of tea. Would you mind getting it for me?"

Julia arched her back as though Patience's request had sent chills down her spine. She pulled the towel from her shoulder and whipped herself around to look at Patience and said, "Why don't ya let me get that for ya? I don't want ya ta strain ya'self by pickin' up the tea pitcher."

"Why, thank you, Julia. I would so appreciate that, and could you put it in a real glass, not one of those plastic cups that the guests have been using?"

"Of course," Julia replied as she opened the cabinet and retrieved a large glass and filled it with ice.

Julia smiled as she poured the tea over the ice and listened to the crackle of the ice melt as the tea hit it. She placed a wrung out dish cloth underneath the glass to catch any spillage and walked over to Patience where she sat at the kitchen table.

"Here ya go. Tea was just made so you might want me ta add mo' ice ta it."

"It will be just fine, I'm sure. Just sit it on the table," Patience requested and started flipping through a magazine.

Julia stood looking down at Patience still holding the glass of iced tea.

"Oh, Patience?" Julia said with a lift to her voice.

"Yes..."

As Patience looked up from her magazine, she was blinded with a deluge of iced tea being poured over her head. The ice cubes and lemon slices had slid down her blouse and she started to scream out.

"Julia, you bitch! You lousy heifer bitch! Just look at what you've done to my clothes. It took me hours to do my hair!"

All of us in the kitchen started laughing uncontrollably. Especially Patrick. We were shocked at what Julia did, but the look on Patience's face was priceless.

"Don't get mad at me," Julia chuckled, "I'm just the kitchen help."

"Oh! This is outrageous!" Patience yelled and stomped out of the kitchen and headed to the stairway to her room.

Julia called out behind her, "And don't fo'get to take yo' damn bags up with ya!"

With Patience gone, we held our stomachs and rolled with laughter. It would be an incident we would all remember. Patrick knew he would pay for it, but he let out a laugh that came from his belly and we could all tell it was heartfelt. Me, Gertie, and Patrick reached for dish towels to wipe up the mess

Julia had made with the tea. Afterward, Patrick sullenly went up to check on Patience. They argued, and Patrick retreated outside. We felt so badly for him, but understood that he needed some time to himself to cool down.

Five Dollar Fridays

Patrick was furious after arguing with Patience. She never fought fair. Yes, he was between jobs. Yes, he was having a tough time with being unemployed, but she had no right to bury his nose in the debt they were incurring because of the lay-off. She, who for the majority of their marriage was the frugal one, had begun lavishing herself with expensive clothing and all of the material things she had never before really even had an interest. He thought she might be having an affair, but it was just a thought that didn't linger in his mind very long. And that was because he couldn't imagine anyone who would want her. However, the bitch she was turning into remained on his mind constantly. Coming back to her home town only enhanced her bitchy nature as she still harbored so much resentment for the town and the people in it. Too many memories. He felt the rain begin to fall and pulled his collar around his neck and shoved his hands into his pockets.

The rain was welcomed. The road leading to Mamie's house was still mainly dirt with splotches of leftover asphalt from county paving projects. Mamie had wanted the road paved, but it was a poor county and most side roads were left with a covering of tar and gravel. She did, however, with the bribes of freshly baked pies and cakes, make arrangements to have any scraps of asphalt remaining from county road paving projects put on the road to her house. It was an easy bargain and the mayor could always win a few votes with no expense to himself. The rain helped to hold down the dust and made breathing a little easier.

Patrick had no idea where he was going. Walking felt good and the loneliness felt better. No one liked being around death and he was no different. He reckoned over being back at the house to comfort the family in their grieving time, but the thought of putting distance between himself and Patience made him decide to pick up his pace until he met the highway. The rain started to fall with more intensity and other than cars turning in to go to Mamie's farm, there was little traffic. He decided to go right and head toward town. It was not very long before a blue truck stopped and asked him if he would like to get out of the rain. Patrick didn't recognize the vehicle or the driver and was a little hesitant to approach the truck.

He weighed his options. He could get into the truck with a white man that he did not know who might kill him or he could kindly refuse and return to be with Patience. The cab of the truck felt warming to his chilled, wet body. He began to rub his arms to create friction in hopes that would warm him faster.

"Thanks for the ride. I appreciate the shelter from the rain. By the way, my name is Patrick. And you would be?"

"Oh, it depends on who you ask."

"I beg your pardon," Patrick asked with a little confusion.

"Well, when I was born, my parents weren't getting along too well, so my daddy named me Harold and my mom named me James, but most people just call me Buck."

"I see," Patrick said still confused. "How did you get the name Buck from Harold and James?"

"Beats the hell out of me. I think my grandmother said when I was just a baby that I bucked like a mule and since no one could agree on my name, Buck it was and is."

"So, your birth certificate has the name, Buck, on it?"

"Oh, no. My mother won that fight and my real name is James, but regardless, the name that stuck is Buck."

"Okay, then, Buck it is. Glad to meet you Buck."

"Glad to meet you, too." Buck gave him the look over and asked, "I don't recognize you, so you must be new in town."

"Oh, no, I'm just visiting. A death in the family, you know."

Buck looked over at Patrick sympathetically and asked, "You in town for Mamie's funeral?"

"Yeah, as a matter of fact, I am. Did you know Mamie?"

"Everybody knew Mamie. She was a great woman and most people in town still don't care for black people. No offense or nothin'. But everybody in town loved Mamie. She had a charm about her. Made everybody feel comfortable and welcomed. Sure goin' to miss her. I work at the hospital. Was there when she died. Whole place went quiet and sad. Her death had a big effect on most everyone who knew her. She was a good woman."

Buck shook his head as he spoke and Patrick could feel that he genuinely meant what he was saying about Mamie.

"Patrick, if you don't mind me asking, how did you know Mamie? You a cousin or somethin'?"

"No, I'm not a blood relative. I am married to her granddaughter, Patience."

"Oh. Her."

"Yeah, her. I married her." Patrick was the one who sounded sympathetic now.

Buck realized his sadness and quickly added, "Oh, she is the one who moved to Washington, D.C. and is working in the Capitol. A great girl."

They glanced at one another. They both knew what the other was thinking and Patrick finally said it.

"No, she's not!"

"Well, now, let's not be too hard on her. She might be grieving and might not be acting like herself."

"Buck, I appreciate you trying to make the situation lighter than it is, but Patience is Patience. The same bitch she always has been and probably now a little worse. She complains more. Spends more. Goes out more. Gets on my last nerve more. I could go on and on. Look, we just met and I don't mean to be laying all of my problems on you."

"You know, Patrick, if you knew what she was like before you married her, then why did you go ahead and marry her anyway?"

"My mother."

"Your momma? Your momma made you marry Patience? Your momma hate you or something?"

"No, she hated Patience."

"I don't understand. If your momma hated her, then why would she have anything to do with you marrying her?"

Patrick wiped his head and began rubbing his temples. He looked over at Buck and asked, "Is there anywhere around here where you can get a beer?"

"You are talking my kind of language. I know the perfect place, and it might cheer you up, too."

"Whoa, now. Let's not go to any honky-tonks, and I need to express 'honky'. No offense, but you have already mentioned that folks around here don't like blacks." Patrick put his hands up to emphasize his sincerity.

"Not to worry. You're with the Buck. You'll be safe. It's just a few miles out of town."

Patrick was not entirely convinced, but had gone this far so he figured he would continue on. They drove for a few miles and reached a sign that read, "Turner's Drive-In". Buck pulled up to the ticket booth and gave the man there a five dollar bill.

"Oh, wait, I have some cash. Let me pay for this, Buck."

"Don't worry about it. I got it. Besides, it's Five Dollar Friday."

"Buck, today is Wednesday."

Patrick said the last statement slowly as to emphasize his confusion.

"It don't matter. Ole man Turner is a hundred years old. All you have to do is hand him a five dollar bill and say, 'Five Dollar Friday', and he'll let you in. Hell, he'll let a loaded bus in here for five bucks as long as you follow that rule. Now, you sit tight and I'll go get the first round of beers at the concession stand. Be right back."

Patrick sat in the truck waiting and looked around the drive-in. He was realizing that this was Americana. The southern part of it. He had never been to an actual drive-in movie before. And they sold beer at the concession stand. He was born and raised in Arlington, Virginia and had never been this far south. When he and Patience had married, both sides of the family had traveled to Washington for the ceremony. Not a day he really wanted to re-visit at the moment. But just because he hadn't been here didn't mean that he was unaware of history. He knew well of racism and knew also, that it was not contained to the south. It was much larger than that.

Buck returned with two large cups of beer and two bags of boiled peanuts. He called over to Patrick to unlock his door as he had accidently locked it getting out.

"Sorry about that. I don't usually lock my door unless I'm parking for the night."

"No problem, I do that myself. I live in D.C. You lock your doors out of necessity. Larger cities have larger crime rates. What are those soggy things in those paper bags?"

Buck laughed and said, "Boiled peanuts. Don't tell me Patience has never told you about eating boiled peanuts. Try some. Might take a little getting used to, but they are good with beer. I think Mamie used to make them and sell them on the farm. Not sure if they still do."

Patrick opened the bag carefully and pulled out a soggy peanut. He held it up to examine it and was a little mystified as to why you would even put a peanut in water.

"I am going to try one, but I am going to have to say that they do not look very appetizing."

He unwrapped the soaked skin and popped a mushy peanut in his mouth. "Well, it's different and it's really kind of good." Patrick was pleasantly surprised.

"Okay then, here is your beer. Now let's find us a parking spot to watch the movie. Looks like it is pretty busy tonight. Wednesday nights usually are. People come here after church lets out after Wednesday night Bible Study. Hey, can you reach over and hook that old sound system to the truck? You might have to hit it to adjust the volume. Those things are as old as dirt. The old man never has done any major improvements to the place."

Patrick reached out the window and talked as he did what he had been instructed. "What is the name of tonight's show?"

"I'm not sure, but they only play four different ones, so we will know in just a minute. I've seen 'em all so many times, I couldn't begin to tell ya. So, tell me about your momma and Patience and all that."

"Oh yeah." Patrick had to take a large swallow of beer. "Well, Patience and I met in D.C. My mother lived not far away in Arlington, Virginia. After Patience and I had gone out about five or six times, my mother wanted to meet her. I knew it probably was a bad idea, but I figured that if things were to get serious between Patience and myself, then they would have to meet sooner or later. I discussed it with Patience and we agreed to have dinner with my mother. And if they were going to meet, then Patience should get the entire overview so we made plans to have dinner at my mother's apartment. Now, that was just a big mistake."

"So what happened?" Buck asked curiously.

"When we walked in, my mother had dead chickens hanging in the kitchen and live chickens walking around in the apartment." Patrick began to rub his head again.

"Well, damn," Buck said to hearing about the dead chickens. "You need some more beer?"

"Buck, I could use a keg of beer. Here, let me get this round."

Patrick handed Buck a twenty dollar bill. Buck happily took it and headed to the concession stand. A few minutes later, he returned with ten large cups spilling over the top with beer.

"They don't sell kegs, so I got as much as I could carry in cups. But be careful, this beer ain't fancy, but it can pack a punch and give you a hangover you'll never forget."

Patrick reached for a cup before Buck could set it down.

"It's all good. I appreciate your hospitality, Buck."

"Well, you're in the south. The heart of hospitality. Drink up."

"Yeah, well, I sure as hell didn't get a southern belle bathed in hospitality with Patience."

"Patience always did carry a bit of a chip on her shoulders. Just so you know, it's not just you. I remember her in high school. She was always a really smart girl. She was ambitious and was shootin' for the stars. Have nothin' against her for that. She was just always so damn mean. Always seemed to think somebody was out to take somethin' from her. Especially, Amy Rogers. They had an unspoken hatred for one another. You know, like when you walk into a room and feel tension, but nobody is even sayin' anything?"

Patrick raised his eyebrow at the mention of Patience as a younger girl.

158

"Oh yeah, what was that all about. Patience doesn't talk much about her youth and growing up. Although the name you mentioned, Amy Rogers, that sure does stand out. Patience had some kind of run in with her today and from what little I understand, it didn't go so well."

"I'm surprised you haven't heard it more. Amy is an okay girl. I always thought Patience and Amy had a lot in common, but were always in competition with one another. Amy is a white girl. I always thought Patience was angry because she was black. It was like if Amy won an award for somethin', Patience would always say she got it because she was white and if Patience won an award, Amy always said they had to give it to the little colored girl. Things like that that most people grow out of feelin'. Maybe Patience never has."

"No, maybe not. I just don't know. Maybe, Amy hasn't either," Patrick said quietly almost under his breath.

"Well, now, I know you know that Ava and Patience are twins. Fraternal. Ava is just drop dead gorgeous. And has light skin. Patience was not as pretty and is definitely not as light. Now, don't' get me wrong, Patience is a nice looking woman, but she could never compare to Ava. It was as though Ava got the beauty and Patience got the brains. I will never forget when Mamie, Julia, and Elisabeth went down to Atlanta to get Ava and brought her home. Ava's husband beat her up pretty bad. They brought her to the hospital here. I saw her in the x-ray department. That man almost killed Ava. Broke her jaw and messed up one of her eyes pretty bad. Doctor said she would always have a scar above her eye. I guess she wears make-up to cover it. She was terrified to look at herself in a mirror.

"Wow, Buck, I never knew that. Patience never told me about it."

"Patience was in D.C. when that happened, but I think y'all were married at the time. Maybe she didn't know. Mamie wanted it kept quiet. But you're family so I thought you might already know."

"No, she never told me. Even though, they are twins, they never seem to have any special bond between them. But, Buck, you seem to know them better than I do."

"Patience didn't like it that Ava had light skin."

"There was a time when black folks wanted to have lighter skin. They thought it would get them more advantages and if you look at history, I suppose it did. You know, the lighter skin black folks got to work in the big house and the darkies had to work in the fields and in the barns. Today, though, they are prouder of their heritage. They want to be dark. Hell, even white people flock to the beaches to get tanned. I always thought that was funny. Hating black people and then go tan yourself to become more like them."

Buck shook his head to the affirmative and looked at Patrick and said, "You have a point there."

Patrick smiled and said, "I have a point and I believe I will have another beer."

160

"Hey," Buck said, "I think the movie is about to start."

Patrick was feeling the buzz of the beer and was, by this time, completely warm. He looked over at Buck with matter-of-fact eyes and said, "Brother, you sure as hell were not kidding about this beer. I feel like it has little fists that are coming out of the cup and punching my ass. However, I have to piss like a race horse. They have restrooms here, right?"

"Oh, yeah, just behind the concession stand. Men's room is on the right."

"Uh, just one more thing. I couldn't help but notice that I am the only man of color here. I'm not going to get attacked or anything, am I?"

"Not unless you start a fight."

Buck laughed out loud and smiled at Patrick.

"You will be fine. People have already asked me who you were when I went and got the beer. I explained that you were a relative of Mamie's. So, it's all good. You're safe."

Feeling reassured, Patrick hopped down from the truck and was off to the restroom. He looked around at the drive-in and nodded politely to the passers-by. They nodded back respectfully. Patrick headed to the restrooms and when he arrived at them, he found them to be somewhat unusual. He was accustomed to individual stalls and urinals along a back wall. Here, he

161

found a long trough of running water for men to urinate in. As strange as he found that to be, his bladder was busting and was glad to stand beside two white men and relieve himself. He let out a sigh of relief. The buzz from the beer kept him from being nervous. He shook himself, zipped his pants, washed his hands, and then headed to the concession stand for more beer. He bought four more cups. Two for him and two for Buck. He reasoned that would be his limit, but after stumbling back to the truck, he realized that his limit had been reached several cups of beer ago.

He handed the beer to Buck and pulled himself up into his seat. When he sat back, he realized the movie had already begun. After looking, he had to do a double take at the screen. Patrick rubbed his eyes and then stared, unable to blink. Without removing his eyes from the screen, Patrick asked, "Buck, are those two doing what I think they're doing or is it just the alcohol affecting my vision?"

"If your vision is showing two people having sex, then your eyes are fine and it's not the alcohol."

"Are you insinuating that this is a porno flick and I am sitting in a porno drive-in?"

"Yeah, I thought you could use some cheering up and this is about the best place around to do that."

"No shit. I'll be damned. And I really will be damned if Patience finds out that I came to a porno movie when I should be at home with her grieving." Patrick continued to talk while looking straight ahead in disbelief. "You have to give it to southern hospitality. There is nothing like it."

Patrick's head turned with the movements of the bodies in the movie until his head was almost upside down.

"Whoa there, Patrick, you are going to twist off your head."

"Holy Mother of God, how does she move her body like that and get into that position?"

"It's just a movie, Patrick."

"Then, I would give my right leg to be a movie star. That heifer is hot! Man, my pants are getting tight."

"You sound like my uncle when we come to Turner's. He said he could screw a rock pile with a snake in it."

"Hell, Buck, I'd screw the snake if you hold its head."

Buck laughed as he watched Patrick get into the movie. He had a buzz going on himself, but as he had explained to Patrick, he had seen all of the movies several times. Sometimes, it was more fun to watch the first timers. He sat back and let the movie take Patrick away from his problems. He reminded himself that he would have to ask Patrick about his mother and the chickens.

"Patrick, I know you probably won't notice I'm gone, but I gotta hit the head myself."

"Go ahead. Go ahead. I'll be right here."

Buck got out of the truck and headed to the restroom. Not long after that, he returned with a fresh bag of boiled peanuts to find Patrick still glued   to the screen with saucers for eyes."

"Hey, you want some of these?" Buck asked as he held out the bag to Patrick.

"No, no thanks."

"It's about time for the intermission," Buck said as he munched on the peanuts.

Several minutes passed and the screen came to a close and Buck confirmed that intermission had started. It was obvious that the movie had paused as many car doors opened and the men got out to adjust their pants and the ladies fixed their hair. The concession stand had three lines about ten people deep getting French fries and hot dogs. Some of the women yelled out their orders from the cars for milkshakes or cherry limeades. You could hear them shout, "No onions," or "Make sure mine's a slaw dawg, sweetie."

Buck looked over at Patrick and asked him if he would like to get out and stretch his legs.

"No, I'm good. And I think I'll just lay off the beer for tonight. By the way, what kind of beer is this anyway?"

"Gee, Patrick, I don't think it has a name."

"What do you mean? It's got to have a name. That is some really good beer. Wouldn't mind looking it up when I get back home."

"Well, I don't think you're going to find it up there. Probably only going to get that around here. It's home brew."

Patrick's eyes got large again and he asked, "You mean, this is illegal alcohol? I have actually been sitting here for over two hours drinking illegal alcohol?"

"I guess it is, if that's what you want to call it."

"Buck, you can go to jail for this."

"I kinda doubt that, but if you want to make sure, you can ask the sheriff. He's sitting about three cars down."

Patrick, getting a little paranoid, sunk down in his seat and managed to utter, "Buck, this is some serious shit here. I can't get arrested. Patience would kill me if I got arrested."

"Calm down, nobody's gonna get arrested. Hell, the sheriff's drinking it too. You just need to sit still and let that buzz start wearing off. I'm going to take a look around and see who all is here tonight."

Buck opened his door and stood up on the side board of the truck. He peered out at the crowd and this time he was the one to do a double take thinking his eyes were deceiving him. Excitedly, he reached in and honked the horn several times and began waving frantically. Then, he shouted, "Mom! Dad! What are y'all doin' down here?"

The only thing heard from Buck's parent's car was a frustrated, "Ah, dammit!" and the screeching of tires as they peeled out of the drive-in.

"That is really unbelievable. How many kids can say they went to a porno drive-in movie and met up with their parents? It's funny as shit though," Patrick said as he began to laugh.

When Buck saw Patrick laughing, he couldn't help but laugh himself.

"My dad will probably give me what for tomorrow."

"I imagine he will, Buck," Patrick said, still laughing.

"Well if it's okay with you, I think I better head home myself. I have to work in the morning."

"Sure. Sure. I should be headed back to the house, too. And, you know, I would rather face your father than face Patience right now. Life can be such a bitch sometimes and life with Patience is a bitch all the time. Hey, thanks for a memorable evening. I don't think I'll ever forget it."

"You are so very welcome. Maybe we can do it again sometime."

Patrick smiled and said, "I sure hope so."

The ride to Mamie's house was quiet. Patrick had a lot on his mind. When they arrived, Patience was standing at the door with her arms folded to her chest.

"Uh oh," Buck said softly, "looks like you got trouble."

"Yeah, the bitch is up."

Buck waited for Patrick to shut the truck door and turned off his lights. He backed out of the driveway and coasted past the house. When he felt he was out of Patience's sight, he turned his lights back on and made his way home. The last thing he thought about before he drifted into sleep was that Patrick forgot to tell him about the chickens.

Hell Hath No Fury

"Just where in the hell have you been?" Patience asked Patrick as he stumbled through the rear door of the house and attempted to enter Mamie's kitchen.

"Well, let's see. I took a walk, met a friend, watched a movie, and got away from you. Other than that, not much," Patrick replied and added a belch that smelled like the home brew he had been drinking and was still feeling the effects of. As he walked forward and away, he still felt the effect of the beer he had consumed, but Patience always had a sobering power over him.

"You wait just a damn minute. You just leave. Take a walk, my ass. You don't just walk away from me when we are arguing. I got news for you. When I talk, you are going to listen and you are going to like what I am saying regardless of what it is. I don't know who you think you are, but you just don't walk off from me and not even tell a soul where you be goin'. Ain't you got nuttin' to say?"

"Yeah, Patience, I do. First thing is that you lose your pompous shitty attitude and revert back to your old southern twang shitty attitude when you are angry. Have you ever noticed that? Second thing, you can ruin a perfectly wonderful buzz, and third thing, why have you never told me about boiled peanuts?"

Patience's head appeared to turn three hundred and sixty degrees. Of course, that could have been the way Patrick saw it after all of the beer he had been drinking. But as much as we, those of us still gathering to pay respects for Mamie's passing, scorned the interference of the fight between Patience and Patrick, we found it brought a welcomed break in our grief. We turned our attention to them, but tried to appear not to notice.

"Boiled peanuts!" Patience screamed at Patrick. "What in the hell does boiled peanuts have to do with this?"

"I ate some tonight at the movies, you know, the drive-in on the outskirts of town. They looked really nasty at first, but they were rather tasty once you got past their appearance. I really enjoyed them. Yeah, I have to say they were really good. This whole new southern dining experience might get me into trying grits or something. You know what I mean?"

Julia, who was standing in the kitchen, cleared her throat. Not exactly to remind Patience that other people were in the room, but to let her know that not a soul present wasn't aware where Patrick had been. This was a small town and by the next day, everyone would know everyone's business.

Patience managed to control her external appearance and whispered loudly through gritted teeth that they would take this upstairs. He obeyed, not because he was afraid to confront Patience, but because he was actually looking forward to it with his beer buzz to lean on. Fortunate for us was that their bedroom was just above the parlor, and if we were to retreat there, we could hear the entire thing. Patrick wasn't the only one to have entertainment that evening. People scrambled for a seat and I followed the crowd with a carafe of coffee and a pitcher of tea. On the coffee table in front of the couch were already placed several plates of desserts and finger foods accompanied with napkins, plates, and eating utensils. I am sure I am not the

170

only one who thought that popcorn might have been more appropriate. We huddled closely and readied ourselves for the show.

I knew that keeping Elizabeth quiet could be a chore as she would want to comment on each exchange between Patience and Patrick. She had a rating scale for sarcasm. It averaged from a one to a ten. Elisabeth, according to only her, had ever received a full ten perfect score for a clever comeback response in an argument. She had had the most practice and relished her honed skill in arguing. To try to muffle her, I placed a large slab of chocolate coconut cake on a plate. I knew she would have difficulty resisting it as it was her favorite, and I also knew, that the frosting was so thick, it would get in-between her dentures and make talking a grueling task. To be fair, I set a cup of hot coffee and a fresh glass of iced tea coastered on the side table beside her. I then scurried to plant myself in a corner chair to hear the match.

"You damn near fell down the stairs. I know you been drinkin'."

"You damn skippy I been drinking. I mean, I've been or I have been. Damn! Patience! I am losing proper grammar being around you."

"You need to hope that's the only thing you gonna be losin'."

With her mouth full of cake, Elizabeth held up three fingers to indicate her rating of Patience's sarcastic response.

"Now you betta start talkin' and tellin' where exactly ya been and how ya got there."

171

"I made a new friend. His name is Buck, or James, or Harold. I can call him Buck though. He remembered your mean ass from high school."

"Yeah, I know who that cracker is. So, where did you and your new friend go off to?"

"Some place called, 'Turner's'."

The listening crowd below all had their mouths gapped open and peered at one another.

"You tellin' me that your black ass has done and gone off to a porno movie drive-in? We here for only a couple of days or so, and you already found one of the scummiest places in town?"

Uncle Franklin looked around and commented, "Oh, Turner's not be that bad. Girl don't know what she's talkin' 'bout."

That comment got a slap to his sore cheek from his wife. He flinched.

"Come on, Patience, that place is not as bad as some of the places around D.C."

"Well, my family can't see you walkin' in drunk from a porno movie when we are in D.C."

"Nobody has ever seen me walk in drunk from a porno movie. I have never seen one before. But, at least, at the movie, I got to watch somebody getting some action. It's not like I am getting anything out of you!"

Elisabeth nearly fell into a convulsion over Patrick's comment. It was difficult for her, but she held up both hands and gave him an eight for his response. The rest of us sat with our eyes bulging in disbelief.

"What exactly does that mean?"

"Exactly what it sounded like! You are a cold, mean bitch, Patience!"

Everyone below acknowledged what Patrick said with a positive nodding of their head to imply full agreement with him. Especially, Julia who seemed to have a mixture of both elation and sadness in her face.

"Well, maybe I would be a little warmer if I didn't have to support your sorry ass and have to work all the time!"

That statement drew a hush on the crowd congregated below.

"You know, Patience, I don't even know why we stay together. All you ever do is complain about how miserable your life is. Well, let me tell you something. You're not exactly Suzie Sunshine yourself. I was laid-off, Patience. Laid-off. I didn't quit my job. It's not like I'm living large on your dime. I look for work every day. Don't worry, I will find work. I am a CPA. Believe it or not, Patience, you are not the only one who has a degree. So, just let it go. And, besides that, you are the one always spending money. Money we don't have and on things that you don't need!"

"I'll spend my money on what I want! If I earn it, I should get to spend it!"

Julia looked around and commented, "That greedy bitch. Got a better man than any of us got and she treats him like dirt."

We had to agree with her. It was true. Even Uncle Franklin's wife, Ann, shook her head in agreement much to Uncle Franklin's disgust.

The yelling from up above us continued.

"What are you doing? Watching my spending now?"

"Of course, I do. We have to eat. And if you spend all of the money on clothes and jewelry, well, you can't put that in a pan and cook it!"

"Patrick, right now with the way you have made me look bad, I don't care if your ass starves to death!"

"That's what it's always about with you, Patience! You are so damn worried about what other people think about you that you forget to feel good about yourself. I don't even know if you can! I was thinking you might be having an affair, but I can't think of anybody who would want you!"

"Oh, I get it. You think I have another man! After you, why on God's green Earth would I go and look for another one? You don't exactly set any high standards for men! But just so you know, I do have another man."

Everybody in the downstairs who was listening to the argument sat straight up with widened eyes in astonishment with what Patience had just said. Patrick had no comeback to it. He stood with his eyes focused on her not exactly surprised.

"Don't stare at me like that, Patrick! Ask me what his name is! Go ahead and ask me, damn it! I know you want to know!"

"Okay, Patience, what is his name?" Patrick asked in the most sober voice ever spoken by a drunken man.

"He has a lot of names. But I can call him Bill. There is electric Bill, water Bill, car Bill, credit card Bill, insurance Bill, grocery Bill. I can go on and on if you'd like, Patrick. And one damn thing is for sure. I can always count on him to be with me. He shows up even if I don't need him. Sticks to me like glue. Follows me around and keeps me company. A man who is always on my mind. I give that man some attention and the very next month, he's right back for more. I go to bed thinking of him every night and wake up with him on my mind every morning. I'd like for you to meet him one day."

"Oh, I know that bastard. I've been sleeping with him, too. Sometimes, he gets so close to me that I think I'm turning queer."

Elisabeth was sitting on the edge of the sofa when she said, "Well, damn, seems like evabody be fuckin' Bill. He have sho' fucked me enough, I can tell ya that much. 'Specially, them early years."

Franklin's wife, the quiet, ever silent and obedient mousy person, commenced to say, "I know he's sho' fucked us and it ain't like no pleasurable, private moments. Sometimes it jus' feels like the bastard wants a be raping ya fo' ever last cent ya got."

At that very moment. Time. Just. Stopped. Everyone's head turned with their mouth gaping open to face Ann. We had never heard that language from her before. The woman who hardly ever spoke a word even made Elisabeth speechless. We sat so motionless, we were unaware we had stopped breathing. Suddenly, we gasped and it was Uncle Franklin who broke the silence.

"Well, Lawd have mercy! Ann, where you get that kinda filthy trash talk?"

"I am so sorry evabody," Ann said and put her hand to her mouth as if she would rot in hell for what had just spouted out of it.

"Oh, shut up, Franklin. Po' woman never gets a chance a speak 'er own min'. Always got that trap of yourn flappin'," Elisabeth said with a stern look.

"Don't tell me to shut up, you ole mouthy heathen."

Elisabeth gave Franklin her evil eye as she sat her plate and fork on the table and responded, "I'm gonna whoop your ass."

When those words came from Elisabeth's mouth, we all retreated to a safe corner. We almost had a tussle between ourselves trying to be the one most secured to the inside leaving others bare to a possible punch.

Gertie spoke softly to Elisabeth from a safe distance, "Now sister, we need not be acting like this. It's not a proper way to be behaving. We have to show each other respect and love."

"Don't a be tryin' a stop me, sista. He been askin' for a ass whoopin' and I be the one to make sho' he gets it."

They were both standing. Both refusing to step down and allow the other to claim victory. Gertie eased down to the floor and crawled to pull the coffee table from their path realizing that if the table was to be knocked over, the food would be the new carpet. Elisabeth still stood strong with the evil eye covering Franklin and Franklin stood, barely able to see from the eye

Elisabeth had already blackened. Everyone huddled in the corners took small breaths so as not to be noticed and catch the glance from either one of them.

Elisabeth pushed up one sleeve and then the other. With two quick moves she was out of her shoes. Franklin threw off his glasses, much to everyone's disgust, revealing a nasty, swollen eye. Elisabeth didn't flinch. She was a tall, thin woman and had a clear advantage over Franklin's short, stocky stature. It was on!

Franklin took the first swing aiming at Elisabeth's jaw. He was hoping for redemption and bragging rights over the first beating she had given him, but failed to calculate how his swollen eye would alter his judgment. Elisabeth dodged the swing and was winding her arm around like a seasoned softball pitcher ready to go in for the strike. It was a swing and a hit. Her aim was spot on and landed on poor Uncle Franklin's healthy eye. He couldn't rebound from the hit and fell backward onto the sofa now totally blind and in excruciating pain. It was the smack heard 'round the world.

"Lawd, have mercy! Ann! Ann! That crazy woman has blinded me! Help me!" cried Uncle Franklin.

Elisabeth stood holding her right hand to her chest as though it were injured waiting to see if Franklin would move toward her. There was doubt in everyone's mind that he would. The one thing that no one doubted was that Franklin would awaken with two black eyes so swollen that he would need a guide dog in order to function. Breathing would be about the only thing he would be able to do on his own.

Next it was Elizabeth's turn to call out. "Sista, I believe that ole fool done forced me to break my hand. It be throbbing somethin' terr'ble."

Gertie rushed to her aid. We all looked at both of them in disbelief. The teenage boys who witnessed the fight reenacted it to one another showing how Elisabeth came down across Uncle Franklin's face. They were quickly hushed and reprimanded by the adults in the room.

I looked at Elisabeth's hand and knew she would need a doctor. Gertie, visibly upset and as nervous as I had ever seen her, put her arm around Elisabeth and started moving her to the back door. Then, in an almost unbelievable move, Gertie swooped up Elisabeth's car keys from the kitchen table.

"Gertie," I said softly, "where are you going with Elisabeth's keys?"

"To the car to take Elisabeth to the hospital."

"But, Gertie, you…"

"Don't you think she needs a doctor? I think she has broken her hand. Can't you hear her crying out in pain?"

"I most certainly do, Gertie. I think she is going to have to go the emergency room, but Gertie…"

"What! Just help me get her to the car so I can get some help for her. Why do you keep holding me up? I need to get her to a doctor!"

"I understand, but Gertie…"

"Look! You can help me get her in the car or you can get out of my way," Gertie said in a high toned, panicked voice.

"Gertie," I said in a reasoning softer tone, "You can't take Elisabeth to the emergency room."

"Well, I don't know why in heaven's name I can't!"

"Because. Gertie, you can't drive."

"Oh, yeah, you have a point there. Here, take her other arm and we will get her to the back seat of the car and I will sit with her. You can drive while I try to comfort her."

I had already managed to wrap Elisabeth's hand in ice while trying to reason with Gertie. Elisabeth struggled with immense pain being pulled by Gertie to the back seat of the red Caddy. I don't know who was in more shock; Elisabeth, Gertie, or Uncle Franklin, who still remained on the sofa moaning, holding now two wounded eyes. Gertie and I couldn't think of him at that particular moment. Gertie and I knew that our sister was injured. Regardless of how we might have bickered over mundane things in the past or how we knew we were going to give Elisabeth grief over this most recent incident with Uncle Franklin, we had a more immediate concern. We had a sister who was injured and in severe pain. She was one of us and sisters always took care of their own.

The drive to the hospital was uneventful, but the x-ray findings of Elisabeth's hand were startling. Three broken bones in her right hand. Fortunately, she would not need surgery, but the way the doctor had to wrap her hand was just so Elisabeth. Her middle finger was sticking straight up. With pain killers and Julia's special baked goods, if needed, she would be just fine.

With Elisabeth stabilized, we would have only imagined that the night's happenings, although with incident, would subside and we would live to fight another day. We probably over shot that assumption. Shortly after we had arrived, Uncle Franklin was brought into the ER by ambulance and accompanying him was the sheriff.

The paramedics had placed bandages over Uncle Franklin's entire head leaving only small crevices for him to see through. However redundant the crevices were, Uncle Franklin had insisted that they be there. Gertie and I couldn't help but laugh as he looked like he had just been dug out of an Egyptian tomb. Elisabeth almost peed on the hospital gurney when she saw him. Her euphoria was exaggerated by the pain killers and she continuously pushed her emergency button to call the nurse to tell her King Tut had entered the hospital.

The county hospital was not a large medical trauma unit so Elisabeth and Uncle Franklin ended up being placed in side-by-side ER cubicles. If we had not been related to them, we might have been able to step back and watch the vaudeville act, but we had our hands full. Not being able to see, did nothing to close Uncle Franklin's mouth. The back and forth between him and Elisabeth was hopeless usually beginning with Elisabeth holding up her injured hand with her middle finger sticking up at Uncle Franklin. He was beside himself with anger and the angrier he got, the happier it made Elisabeth. He could not fully see that Elisabeth was not intending to fly her middle finger at him. Well, actually, we couldn't be sure of that. The truth was she probably did know what she was doing and continued to do it even after Uncle Franklin reached for her blindly with outreached arms. We were helplessly and hopelessly in the middle of a horror movie that just didn't seem to have an end.

The sheriff stood at the nurse's station and we could see he was talking to the doctor. All we needed at the time was for Elisabeth to have charges brought against her. We waited patiently for him to come and speak with us. It wasn't long before he did.

"Evening ladies," he said to us while removing his hat.

"Hello, Sheriff. How you doing this evening?" replied Gertie for all of us.

"Well, I was doing pretty good Gertie, afore I got this call, that is. Seems like there is some sorta family dispute here 'tween Franklin and Elisabeth."

"Sheriff, you know how Elisabeth and Franklin get when they are around each other," I interjected.

"Oh, yeah, I heard about how Elisabeth knocked him out over at the church. Course there wasn't any charges filed on that and with Mamie passing, I figured it was just anxiety and all."

Gertie responded, "That's what we thought, too. Just pretty much passed it off as nervous tension."

"Well, tonight Franklin over here wants to press charges against Elisabeth for assault. What do you all think about that?"

Gertie and I looked at one another with grief stricken faces.

I replied, "I don't know why Uncle Franklin would want to do that. Maybe because he feels a little embarrassed that a woman got the better of him or something like that."

"Yeah. Yeah, I can see how that could weaken a man's character by having that happen, but y'all have to understand that it is part of my job to get to the bottom of this. Since he swore out the complaint, I have to investigate it."

"Of course, you do, sheriff. We all want you to do your job. We wouldn't want any special treatment or anything like that. Oh, no, sir," Gertie stated adamantly.

"Well, the doctor said Franklin's eye is looking pretty bad and since her hand is broken, I can only see that she hit him. His hands are clean."

"Sheriff," I said, "Uncle Franklin took a swing at Elisabeth and she returned one in due course."

"Just tell the man, I whooped his ass! Franklin just cry babyin' 'cause I beat his ass good!" Elisabeth said after being quiet for a while.

"Don't mind her, Sheriff, the pain medication is making her talk out of her head."

"Tell me this, ladies, were there any witnesses to the fight other than the two of you?"

I cupped my hand over Elisabeth's mouth and replied, "The entire room was full of people who will tell you exactly the same thing we did, Sheriff."

"Well, if that all checks out, then, I think this will just be written up as self-defense."

"Oh, thank you, Sheriff. We surely do think it was. So, can we take Elisabeth home now? Is she free to go?" asked Gertie.

"Just as soon as the doctor releases her. I can't see why not. Oh, and do you think you can give this to Julia. I almost forgot to give it to ya. It would be a donation for the baked goods I picked up for my momma. Please, let Julia know momma's appetite has picked up real good since she's been eatin' the blackberry pie."

"Why, now, thank you Sheriff, Julia will be so glad to hear that."

We thought the sheriff had intentions of staying and talking longer, but his radio went off and he was receiving a call. All we could hear was him say in response to the dispatcher was a disgruntled, "Damn moonshiners. That's the third report we got on 'em this week."

Gertie and I both took in a deep breath and released it at the same time. The nurse came over and gave us several pages of documents to sign and several more pages of instructions on how to deal with Elisabeth's broken hand. We thanked her. I decided to go to the hospital pharmacy to fill the pain medications for Elisabeth. Gertie helped the nurse get her dressed.

When I got back from the pharmacy, Elisabeth was already in a wheelchair with a hospital porter ready to take her to the car. As we passed by the cubicle Uncle Franklin was in, he was still lying in bed, but now quiet. That was short-lived by Elisabeth raising her injured hand in the air extending her middle finger directly at him. This was all that was needed to get Uncle Franklin started again. We told the porter to hasten the pace, and we exited the Emergency Room doors quickly.

Once settled in the car, I started the engine and headed home. I followed Gertie's instructions to take them to her home. It would be more convenient for her to care for Elisabeth there since they lived side-by-side in a two family mill house. I offered to stay and assist Gertie with Elisabeth's care that night.

Actually, it was by that time, early morning and we were all fairly exhausted. Gertie said she could handle it.

I helped get Elisabeth settled in and then, got myself back into the car and started for home to find a bed for myself. I remember thinking to myself that I had one hell of a family. Neither war nor peace had anything on us. That night would go down in family history as the two-story war. Patience and Patrick upstairs and Elisabeth and Franklin down below.

Morning Glory

I turned the knob on the back door. I thought of Mamie when I did that. She had always taught us to turn the knob before entering the house to make sure the door was actually locked. If you knew the door should be locked and it opened without the key, then someone could be in the house. She had always tried to look out for our safety. The door opened without the key and I found myself to be surprised. I cracked it slightly and held my ear in the opening to see if I noticed any familiar voices. I didn't have to look inside. The smell of coffee was making its way through the crack. I knew it would have to be Julia waiting for me to get home.

I entered quietly and removed my jacket and placed it on the coat rack in the mud room. Then, I stepped into the kitchen and noticed the smell of wild honeysuckle. It was coming from a small candle still lit and glowing on the kitchen table. Julia was there, too, with her head bent down into her hands. I walked closer to see if she was asleep. Before I could lean over, she raised her head and acknowledged my presence.

"How is Elisabeth?" she asked me with a worried tiredness that I had never seen in Julia.

"Other than a broken hand, she is herself. Gertie is taking care of her. How is Patience?"

"Haven't heard a word out of them since you left with Elisabeth and Gertie last night. Probably thought the ambulance sirens coming ta get Uncle Franklin was the police comin' out here ta get them. I guess they either worked it out or they killed each other tryin'. To tell ya the truth, I'm too tired to go up and look."

"You look exhausted, Julia."

"I am a litta tired, but time is only friendly to children."

I knew what she meant. When you're young time creeps by. Days seem like years. As you get older, years seem like days. Children shouldn't have a worry in the world. Most don't. The aging process brings on responsibility, worry, and wrinkles.

"Have you spoken with Ann? We saw her and Uncle Franklin at the hospital last night. Came in a little after we arrived with Elisabeth. He had the sheriff with him. You talking about a three ring circus. Just wait until you see how the doctor had to wrap Elisabeth's hand."

"What was the sheriff doin' there?"

"Seems like Uncle Franklin wanted to press charges against Elisabeth."

"Well, no, he didn't."

"Yep, he sure did. They will probably come around asking the ones in the parlor, who saw the fight, who threw the first punch."

"Oh, well then, I ain't too worried about that. Uncle Franklin did regardless of whether he did or not. I tell ya. I just don't know what we are going to do wit' those two. If they weren't related, I would think they shoulda gotten married. Fight as though they were."

"Julia, can I fill up your coffee cup? I see you about empty. Oh, and before I forget, here is a donation from the sheriff and he told me to tell you that his momma is getting her appetite back."

"Oh, good to hear that. She was looking mighty frail when I seen her last."

Julia did not tell me if she wanted coffee so I picked up her cup and fixed her a full one. Just the way she always liked it. Three sugars and two heaping teaspoons of creamer. I just left the spoon in her cup. Julia liked to stir when she had things on her mind.

When I turned to set the cup in front of her, she had already opened the sheriff's envelope containing the donation. I waited for her to say if it was satisfactory. We ran part of the farm on a donation basis only. The fruits and vegetables were sold a little below market value. We did fairly well.

"Well, I think I might have to send the sheriff a thank you card."

She began to count the one hundred dollar bills aloud and was on five when we heard a creak on the stairway. Our eyes met, and she had to quickly stuff the money back into the envelope and stick it inside her shirt.

Patrick and Patience stumbled into the kitchen. Patrick looked rested and Patience still looked angry. Patience always looked angry.

"What are you two doing up so early?" I asked.

"What are you two doing up so late?" Patience responded.

"Look, about last night, I really want to apologize for all of that. I disrespected your house, and I did not have the right to do that. I just want you to know that I don't behave that way very often. I am really not a drinker and when I do, I don't seem to be able to handle it very well."

Julia looked understandingly at Patrick. "If I lived with Patience, I would probably be an alcoholic. Made a fresh pot of coffee just a bit ago. Have some. Patience, get this fine man of yourn a cuppa coffee."

"That fine man of mine knows how to get his own cup of coffee. He can get me a cup, too. He knows how I like it."

Julia rolled her eyes and said, "Yeah, I bet he does. After what we all heard last night, sounds like you don't know what he likes though."

"What do you mean about what you heard last night?"

"Just what I said. We were in the parlor and heard the big argument y'all was havin'."

"Just who is we?" Patience asked with insistence.

"About twenty of us. Why? You embarrassed?"

"Julia, you told me Mamie had reinforced the floors and insulated them so the rooms had more privacy."

"Yeah, well, about that...I lied."

"Patrick," I interjected, "Please, sit here, and I will get you both some coffee. I think Patience likes it black, how about you?"

"With a little sugar, if you don't mind, but I can get that. Really, I should be serving you."

"You're a guest in this house and you are family. Now, you sit down in that chair and hush yourself."

My southern hospitality opened itself up and swooped Patrick up. I could tell he liked being cared for and not being the one taking care of someone all the time. In due time, I think we could straighten him out enough to where he wouldn't have to endure Patience's abuse as much. Unfortunately, Patience recognized the southern prowess and intervened to quickly change the atmosphere.

"Isn't today the day we meet with Judge Holcombe to review Mamie's will?" Patience asked.

Julia began to stir her coffee and our eyes met. I shrugged my shoulders. Julia continued to stir her coffee and finally lifted her eyes from her cup and asked, "Got the will on ya mind, do ya?"

"I've thought about it somewhat."

Julie commenced to stirring her coffee a little more intensely now and without looking at Patience, she questioned, "Are you hopin' that you gonna be in it?"

"Julia, I am an attorney. I think it would only be proper to have someone with legal experience to represent the family, don't you agree?"

"I've never agreed with you, Patience, why would today be any different?" Now it was Julia displaying insistence.

"If you don't want me there, it's fine. I will just get a copy from the courthouse. It will be on file there."

Julia, getting angry, responded, "Yeah, I imagine it would be. They open at nine. The rental agency called. Your credit card is maxed out, and they need you to return your vehicle or give them a different card to charge."

Patience closed her eyes in obvious embarrassment. Smoke seem to be pouring from her ears, and she looked as though she wanted to explode.

"Patrick! You should have taken care of that!"

Julia replied cutting Patrick short, "He couldn't. Don't ya remember? He ain't got no job. And you too busy buying clothes and jewelry."

Furious now, Patience peered at Julia and stated, "Well, at least, I don't sell myself to get the things I need!"

Calmly Julia replied, "You ain't gonna get a car with what you got. Not even a rented one."

As she continued to stir her coffee now slightly slower, Julia looked over at Patrick.

"I put the rental on my credit card for two weeks. After that, you can tell your wife, she can take her rented ass back to her wonderful life in Washington. Patrick, you are welcome to stay, if you'd like, but that bitch gotta go."

"Okay, now. Here's a cup of coffee for Patrick with two sugars and one straight black for Patience. How about some pastry with that coffee?" I asked.

There was a dead silence in the room. Folks who didn't know these two sisters of mine would blame their animosity on the stress and anxiety of Mamie's death. But I knew differently. None of us really ever got along with Patience. We simply tolerated her. If we missed Mamie, it would be her absence of ending confrontations. Coffee and pastry could never replace that.

"Nothing for me, but thank you. It's a little early for me," Patrick said trying to cut the tension.

"I have to get to the market for bakin' goods," Julia remarked with an effort to be thankful for the offer.

"Baking goods! You have got to be kidding me," Patience exclaimed and waved her arms around the kitchen bringing to Julia's attention all of the food already there.

"Patience, I know you may not understand this, but I still have a business to run. The farm doesn't tend itself. I ain't able to put in a slip and leave my job for a month. The pigs and chickens would keel over and die. All of us here may not have a college degree, but we ain't stupid neither. And before you go off about bakin' goods, you might want to know how many baked goods and how much work it took to bake them to put you through law school."

Julia knew that her sentence structure may have been a little off, but the reality check she wrote to Patience made even Patrick feel ashamed. He hung his head and raised his eyes to look at Patience. He was glad Julia could tell her off and put her in her place. He admired Julia for it. So did I.

"Little 'un, I'm gonna be goin'. I should be back in about two hours. Truck gets to the store soon and I'll be there to meet it. Morris will hold out my shipment. You get some sleep, at least 'til I get back. Make sure Ava is doing good this mornin'."

"I'll see to it, Julia. You be careful out there. Love you, sister."

Julia took a swallow of coffee and rose from the table and looked around the kitchen as though she were looking through us. She was looking for her hat. She always said that she didn't think she could think without it. I spotted it on the table beneath the phone. It was lying on top of a Bible with its dark brown felt almost blending into the color of the painted walls of the kitchen. Chocolate. Mamie had picked out that color. Just as with Patience, we tolerated it. It wasn't that we didn't like the color. It was more the name of it. We baked so many chocolate cakes, pies, brownies, and cookies down in the barn's kitchen, we wanted a more relaxing tone in the house kitchen. Maybe a serene blue or a soft green.

Julia and I spotted her hat at the same time. Before I could retrieve it, she had already grabbed it and put it on. She picked up the truck keys and headed for the door.

Before she left, she turned to me and said, "Don't forget to put out that candle before you to go up to bed."

I nodded that I would.

"Just a minute," Patience slapped her hand to the table and said in a stern, loud voice, "I'm going with you. I want to take a look at how this business of yours is working."

Julia looked at her suspiciously and replied, "Is that right? Are you sure you wanna go wit' me?"

"If I am in the will, then, I need to understand how things operate around here."

I held my breath in fear that Julia might go off on Patience again. But she didn't. She kind of smiled and told Patience to get the lead out because she had people waiting on her.

Patience swallowed down the last of her coffee and hurried to the door.

"Let's go, Julia, I'm ready."

Julia looked her up and down and smiled.

"Well, okay then, if you say so."

Patrick sat in his seat and rubbed his finger up and down on the side of his coffee mug. You could tell he had questions about our family but was too polite to ask. Of course, that didn't mean that I couldn't ask him the things we had always wondered about.

"Patrick, you can tell me that it's none of my business, but why did you ever marry Patience?"

He looked up at me and responded, "To be completely honest with you, I don't know. My momma told me life would be hard with Patience. But when you're young, sowing your oats, wanting to prove that you're a man, you tend not to listen to the things your momma tells you. I guess I thought I could make her love me. Maybe because I thought I could change her and make her a better person. Maybe because I thought I loved her. I don't know."

"Do you love her now?"

"I don't know if I love her or I have become complacent over the years. She goes to work and, well, I, well, I'm sure you were in the parlor, too, and already know all about that."

197

"You will find another job, Patrick. You are a good man and with our history, good men are more rare that good jobs. We just can't figure out how Patience got the good man being as mean as she is."

He blushed and thanked me. He was genuine.

"Can I ask you a question now?" Patrick asked politely.

"Sure, ask away."

"Do you and your family love her?"

"Ooh! Now that seems like a loaded question. If you want to know if it would be okay to leave her here and you run off without her, then the answer is no. But, seriously, of course, we do. We don't have a problem loving Patience, we have a problem liking her."

"You know, I think you have answered it perfectly," Patrick said. "I do love Patience, I just don't we like her very much."

We both laughed and it felt good. It felt so good that we continued to laugh until the small honeysuckle candle was no more. The wick had ended and it went out without our even noticing it. If it hadn't been for the stench that came after a candle burns down to nothing and becomes more smoke than pleasant aroma, we could have laughed with the sunrise. But as all good things usually did, it came to an end with a thump. From up above us, something had hit the floor.

"Oh, no!" I gasped. "Ava!"

It seemed like in the blink of an eye, Patrick and I were hovering over Ava. His face had horror in it as he watched her shake with her eyes wide open.

"What's the matter with her?"

"She must have had a bad dream. She has severe panic attacks. She got herself involved with one mean man and it didn't work out well for her."

Patrick looked at Ava helplessly. He wanted to comfort her, but didn't know how.

"It's okay Patrick. I can handle this. Go downstairs and call Julia's cell and remind her that we have a meeting this morning. Go on now. Call Julia."

He stepped backwards from Ava's room and turned to go down the stairs to the kitchen. Ava and I were alone in her room. I bundled her in a quilt that Mamie had made for her and rocked her back and forth until the shaking stopped. I sang to her the lullaby that Mamie had sung to us when we were children.

"It was just a dream, Ava. Everything is okay now. Remember what Mamie told you? When you have this quilt around you, there is nothing bad that can ever happen to you."

I continued to rock and finally, Ava spoke to me.

"He was here. Adrian was here with me in this room. He tried to kill me."

"No, Ava, it's just you and me in here. Adrian can't bother you. He is far away and there's no way he would take the chance to come around Elisabeth. Remember? She cut him. He's afraid of her and he knows she protects you. And you have me, Gertie, and Julia. You are safe. Take some deep breaths and just let those bad dreams go."

She finally calmed down and I helped her get back into her bed. I would have to talk to Julia about taking Ava back to the doctor. As of late, the dreams had been recurring much too often. I did get her back to sleep and was hopeful that she would not recall any of this in the morning when she would be fully awake. I left her room and left the door cracked in the event she called me. I went back down to make sure Patrick phoned Julia.

"I phoned Julia and Patience. They are on their way back. I mentioned Ava, too, and what happened. I hope that was okay."

"Yeah, that's fine."

"If you don't mind me asking you, what happened to Ava?"

"Patience didn't tell you?"

"Patience doesn't really tell me anything to do with her family."

"Well, I don't have to tell you that Ava is beautiful. It's okay. You can go ahead and say that you've noticed that. Anyone would be blind not to notice it. She married a military man. His name is Adrian. Ava was very happy at first and we corresponded often through phone calls and letters. Then, all of a sudden, the communication dwindled down to nothing and Ava became very distant. Mamie worried herself sick, so we decided to go to Georgia to visit with her. Well, actually, I stayed here with the farm. Mamie, Elisabeth, and Julia went to check on Ava. We all thought it would make us sleep better if we could see her with our own eyes. You know?"

"I can understand that," Patrick replied.

"Ava and Adrian lived in base housing. Mamie and my sisters tried to get on base. They had a difficult time getting in, but were allowed to when Mamie explained to the base commander that she was worried that her granddaughter might be extremely ill. Finally, they were escorted to the small house where Ava lived. When they walked in, Julia said it looked like a war zone. No mirrors in the house were left unbroken. Adrian had obviously gotten really upset and had broken everything in the place. He stabbed Ava in the belly with a chard of glass. Come to find out, Ava was pregnant. Adrian decided he didn't want any added responsibility and Ava refused to get an abortion. So, he did surgery on her himself."

"How far along was she?"

"The doctor guessed she was around two months along in the pregnancy. And her face. He smashed her face in with his fist. Broke her jaw and she has lost some of her vision in her right eye."

"What did the military do to him?"

"The military or Elisabeth?"

"Both."

"Ava was taken by ambulance to the hospital and Mamie went with her. Elisabeth and Julia stayed at the house to pack up Ava's things. They swept up the glass after the military police did their investigation and took pictures. Then they waited on Adrian. Mamie tried to discourage them and told them they would just make matters worse, but Elisabeth was ready to kill him. And if she had a gun, he would be dead now. I guess it was late afternoon and he tried to enter the house through the back door. Julia stood behind it and when he opened it, she slammed it in his face. I guess he thought it was Ava and he came in and was looking Elisabeth in the eyes. She had her razor and she left her mark on him. He wasn't going to be such a pretty boy anymore. She broke his jaw, too."

"Where were the MP's?"

"Oh, they were looking for him, but I guess he managed to get around them somehow."

"And Mamie brought her back her to the farm?"

"After a few days in the hospital there, she did. She is not the same person she once was, but her 'regalness' comes out a little more often every day."

"What about the mirrors? She always looks in mirrors."

"She couldn't for almost two years. She had several reconstructive surgeries and with a little make-up, she still looks just like Ava on the outside. The inside will take a little longer, but we keep working with her. The therapist told us that she has to look in the mirror to make sure she is still alive. Many think she does it to admire herself. We tease her sometimes about primping too much, but she knows what we mean. If Ava opened up to you, you would probably find out that she thinks she's a very ugly person. She still sees the ugly person Adrian made her out to be."

"Where is Adrian?"

"Adrian and Ava are divorced and Adrian is in prison. I'm not sure what sentence he got, but I don't think he will ever come near this family again. He's afraid of Elisabeth."

"Yeah, so am I."

We both laughed.

"I am so sorry that happened to her. To the whole family. It must have been devastating."

"We are family, Patrick. Things happen, sometimes they are not good things, but we see each other through."

"You are a wonderful family, too."

"I think I hear Julia pulling up now. Whew, this is going to be another long day. I guess I better get out there and help Julia unload the truck."

"No, let me. I'm the one who got sleep last night and it's the least I can do," Patrick said thoughtfully.

"You have no idea how much I appreciate that, but I will have to ask Julia first."

Julia and Patience could be heard arguing outside. That was not unusual. That was the normal. Patrick and I walked outside and saw them standing face to face, both with their hands on their hips.

"Julia, you could have told me I still had my pajamas on!"

"You told me you was ready to go. You got want you wanted. Now, you can get your ass ready to help unload the truck. You wantin' to know how the farm operates, well, this is it. Now bend yo' big ass over and let me load some of this on ya back."

"You ain't loadin' my back with anything. You'll break it."

"We can only wish, but that would keep ya here longer and ain't none of us want that!"

"Julia, I can help you with unloading all of that," Patrick said.

"Uh, Julia, I think I should be the one to help," I said with my eyes growing large.

Patience started walking toward the house and looked back and said, "Yeah, all of you can do it. I'm going up for a bath and a fresh change of clothes. Help them, Patrick."

"Don't forget to douche. I could smell ya in the truck."

As Patience walked away, she turned and shot Julia her middle finger.

"Patrick, pull down that tailgate and hop up on it. We will take this load down to the barn kitchen. Get in the cab litta 'un," Julia said.

I obeyed and so did Patrick. When I shut the door to the truck, I asked, "Julia are you sure you want to let Patrick this close to the tobacco barn?"

"You know, I been thinkin' 'bout it. We ain't ever goin' know how he feels 'bout what we do, 'til we ask 'im."

She had a point, but what a risk we were taking. I worried that he would tell Patience. Then, again, maybe he wouldn't. I would let Julia make that decision.

We were at the kitchen built behind the tobacco barn within seconds. It was spacious and allowed four of us to move around freely when we were making our baked goods to distribute from the farm. It's where we also stored our wild parsley which was our code name for the marijuana we put into some of the baked goods. To be completely honest, the kitchen was an illegal marijuana distribution center. You would never know it to look at it. It was spotless. The stainless steel appliances were well maintained and you could see your reflection in the oven doors. We also had an attached walk-in freezer for storage. It was not a commercial size locker, but it was plenty big for us to manage what we needed to do. We even got an "A" rating from the Department of Health and Environmental Control. We loved seeing that big blue "A" on the door as we entered the front kitchen door.

"Wow," Patrick said, "you have a restaurant kitchen. This is the first time I have been in here. This is awesome. You ladies really have it going on. Has Patience seen this?"

"Nah, I doubt it," Julia replied.

"So where do you store the flour?" Patrick asked ready to help by carrying a large bag of flour on his shoulder.

"Patrick, before ya start doing that, I need to talk to ya for a minute," Julia said with a little reservation.

"Sure, Julia, what's up?"

"I need to know how ya feel 'bout somethin'."

"Well, okay."

"How do ya feel 'bout medical marijuana?"

"I'm sorry. I thought you said medical marijuana. Can you repeat the question?"

"That is what I asked ya, Patrick. How do ya feel 'bout medical marijuana?"

"Why in the world would you ask me about something like that?"

"I was just wonderin'."

"Oh, so you really want me to answer?"

"I sho' do."

"Well, I can't say that I would be against something that could help someone medically."

"So, ya would be for it."

Patrick looked at Julia and myself suspiciously and asked, "Is this a joke or something? I still don't know why you would ask me something like that just out of the blue."

"'Cause we grow it."

Patrick laughed. "Yep, I knew the question was some kind of joke."

"Come with us, Patrick. Bring that sack of flour with ya," Julia instructed.

We went through the kitchen and through the swinging doors to the locked connecting double doors to the tobacco barn. Julia pulled her keys out of her pocket and looked for the one with a green plastic top cover on the key. She opened the first door and then, fumbled with her key holder to find the key with the red plastic top cover. When she flung the second door open, Julia exposed the segmented portion of the tobacco barn. There, before the three was our next crop of wild parsley. We heard the flour sack hit the floor. It had fallen over his back and fell crashing and burst open to cover the floor as white as the blinding white walls. We looked at Patrick's face.

It looked white, too. At first, we thought it was from some of the flour that now seemed to be everywhere, but there was no flour on his face. There was no color in it either.

"Patrick," I said as I waved my hand before his face, "are you okay?"

"You...you...you...you weren't kidding."

"Nope."

"Julia," Patrick said calmly, "This is marijuana!"

"Well, you asked us where we stored the flour."

Patrick fell backwards onto the package of flour that had fallen from his shoulder. When he landed he created a cloud of dusty flour and now his face was truly white. Not from shock this time, but from all the flour searching for a place to settle. Julia and I got dusted, too, and we laughed at each other not knowing that we both looked silly.

Patrick wasn't laughing. He was just stunned. I put my hand on his shoulder.

"Patrick," I told him, "it's okay."

"No, it's really not okay. It's really, really not okay."

"But you said that you agreed that weed could be used for medical purposes," I reasoned.

"Yeah, in theory, it sounds like a wonderful and rightful thing to do. But when you can see it and you know it's illegal, and it's right there in front of you, you begin to have second thoughts."

"Patrick," Julia said, "I told ya because I thought I could trust ya. Right here is where the rubba meets the road. You have ta let me know we can all trust ya."

"How long have you five ladies been doing this? This is not something that you just thought you'd try out. This place is well designed. It's...It's...It's illegal. That's what it is, and I am sitting here with it. I don't know."

"First of all, only four of us have anything to do with growing it," I told Patrick. "Elisabeth doesn't have a clue."

"And Patience? Does Patience know about this?" Patrick asked.

"Oh, hell no. That bitch would love nothin' betta than to try ta get me arrested," Julia responded.

"Well, I don't know if you two ladies have noticed, but she wouldn't mind them hauling me in with you."

Patrick looked around taking it all in and after a few moments, he continued to talk.

"Look, here's the deal I will make with you two. I won't mention anything to Patience about all of this, but let's just pretend I never saw any of this. I have about a million things running around in my brain right now. Sweet little Gertie grows marijuana. Hey, why doesn't Elisabeth know?"

"You seriously have to ask that?" Julia answered. "Elisabeth gets tipsy and lets that mouth of hern run a litta too much."

"So how much of this stuff do you ladies smoke?"

"Smoke? None of us have ever smoked it," I replied.

"We jus' cook it," Julia added.

"How much do you cook?"

"That always depends on what the doctor needs fo' his patients," Julia responded.

"Doctors! You are working with doctors?" Patrick asked in disbelief.

"Look, Patrick. This might have been too much to just spring on you all at one time. Let's all of us just step back and take some breaths. Take some time to think it over," I said to him.

"I've got to clear my head. I will help you carry the rest of the bags in and then, I think you ladies have a meeting coming up soon. Just don't bring me back in this barn. I don't think my health can take it."

Patrick helped us unload the truck, but only carried things to the front kitchen. Julia and I used the hand trucks to get the things stored in the barn to its designated area. I know Julia was feeling the same way I was. It sure was nice having a strong man around to help out. When we had finished bringing in all of the goods Julia had purchased that morning, we shut the tailgate to the truck and drove it back up to the house.

Ava was on the stoop at the side of the house, cutting fresh flowers to keep in the house. She thought they made the house look so much prettier and smelling good. We couldn't disagree.

Patrick looked around and didn't see the car he and Patience had rented for the trip. He looked at Ava and asked if she knew where the car was.

"I don't know."

"Did Patience drive away in the car?" Patrick asked Ava.

"She did."

"Did she say where she was going, Ava?" I asked.

"Didn't say."

"I betcha I know," Julia said.

"Where would she have gone, Julia?" Patrick asked.

"To try ta get her hands on Mamie's will."

"That bitch," Patrick said more loudly than he thought.

Julia added, "You learnin'".

"You have a plan, Julia, as how all of us are going to get to the judge's office for the meeting for the will reading?" I asked.

"Well, we still got Elisabeth's car from where ya drove 'er home from the ER las' night. Litta 'un, go wash yo'self up and scoot over there to carry 'em to the judge's office. Patrick, ya think ya could take the truck and you and Ava get to the judge's office? Ava can tell ya where it is."

"Sure, Julia, but how are you going to get there?" Patrick asked.

"You don' have any nary mind 'bout me. I'll be there. Tell Judge Holcombe I be on my way."

214

"Oh, my goodness," Patrick said and stopped in his tracks.

"What is it, Patrick?" I asked him.

Patrick looked at Julia and myself and said, "I'm going to have to take a whore's bath."

We all laughed and rushed to ready ourselves for the meeting. I had still not been asleep since the previous night. I was running on adrenaline and I was going faster and faster.

The Reading of the Will

Patience checked her watch and stood on Main Street in front of Judge Holcombe's office tapping her foot waiting on Alvin Carpenter to arrive. Julia had spoken with Alvin the previous day to arrange a meeting with Judge Holcombe. The judge could not meet with her so she spoke with Alvin, his law clerk. He agreed to meet with her privately before Mamie's will was read.

If there was anything Patience hated, it was tardiness. She was always early regardless of where she was going. Her opinion always was that if you get somewhere earlier than expected, you could manage to get the upper hand. It was now ten a.m. and Alvin was late.

She checked her watch again and turned the doorknob of the judge's office. To no avail. It was locked. She noticed some movement walking toward her. But when she saw how the person was dressed, she realized it couldn't be Alvin. This character was dressed like they were going to be in a theatrical ensemble. In the heat of the spring, they had on a full dress suit. Complete with a double breasted vest with a single breasted jacket. He was wearing cuffed pants and of all things, he was wearing a top hat. Patience wanted to laugh, but was too angry about Alvin being late to accommodate humor.

This odd person was carrying an umbrella that he was using as one would a walking cane. He looked as though he had just stepped out of a speakeasy. Patience turned her back and continued to wait.

Suddenly, she felt a tap on her shoulders. Convinced it had to be Alvin, she turned around with a smile. A smile that soon turned to scorn as she saw in front of her the same man she wanted to laugh at only moments ago.

"Can I help you?" Patience asked the stranger.

"It would appear that since you are standing at my employer's door, that I would be the one who might help you," said the stranger.

"Are you Alvin?"

"That would be I."

Patience gave him the up and down look almost not believing what she was looking at. This foolish looking man was wearing spatter dashes. It was as if he stepped out of time and entered into present day from the 1920s.

"Hello, Alvin. I'm Patience Snow. We spoke yesterday on the phone."

Patience put out her hand to Alvin which he looked at, but refused.

"Yes, I recall that we did, Ms. Snow. Let me unlock the office door that we might have some privacy."

"Yeah, that would be nice."

Alvin unlocked the door. Patience remembered the office well. There was a stairway that led upstairs. Judge Holcombe's office used to be located up there. She had played on the staircase many times as a child while waiting on Mamie to visit with Judge Holcombe. It was in that office that she talked to the judge about becoming a lawyer. He was very encouraging for her to pursue that career. He had written a letter of recommendation for her to attend law school. She had no doubt that a letter from a man of his stature and recognition helped her more than anyone realized about her being accepted into an Ivy League school.

Today, however, they did not ascend the stairs. Instead they passed the stairway and entered a narrow hallway that opened into a larger more modern law office. It looked to be an addition to the older building that had existed on the main street for probably close to a century. Patience was impressed with the lavish styling and mahogany furnishings.

"This office is very impressive," Patience remarked.

"Yes, it is nothing like the office the judge used to occupy upstairs."

"No, it certainly isn't."

"When I began to work with him, I convinced the old scrooge to spend some of his money on refurbishing the office into something a bit more befitting a man who works in the area of enforcing justice."

"Yes, well, you and he did a fine job at upgrading the old building. And, since you remembered that we spoke yesterday, you might recall what we spoke about."

"I most certainly do," Alvin responded.

"So, will you let me have a glance at the will?" Patience asked.

"Well, I'm afraid that I won't be able to do that."

"And, just why not?" Patience asked.

"Ms. Snow, I realize that you and I do not know each other for if we did, you would know that I do not venture into any type of activity that I do not see any reward for myself in."

"I beg your pardon, Alvin."

"Well, to be more succinct. What is in it for me?"

"What exactly do you want to be in it for you?" Patience asked while she handed Alvin her business card.

Alvin accepted her card and glanced at it briefly.

"I already know who you are, Ms. Snow, and where you work. I have heard the judge and your grandmother speak of you often. I'm not intimidated by your business card or the people you work for. You came in here and asked me to do something that I don't think my employer would approve of my doing. Why don't you just scoot up to the courthouse and see how your little business card works on them?"

"I checked with them and oddly, the will was not on file there."

"Well, that is certainly odd."

"Alvin, I bet you could probably check your computer and see if there is a copy scanned to a file."

"Yes, I most certainly could. But then that would bring us back to my original question. What is in it for me?"

"And I would ask you again what it is you want."

"Perhaps a job with the U.S. Department of Justice?"

"Alvin, do I look like a Human Resource Department? I don't hire people. The very least I could do would be to pull up your resume and see it gets into the right hands."

"But I have no guarantee that you would keep your word."

"My family and the judge will be here in under an hour. My word is all I have to give you."

"Hmm. Write down your name, work number, work address, and your supervisor's name and numbers."

"Do you have a pen?"

"Most definitely, I do."

Patience wrote down the information he demanded. While she wrote, Alvin began searching for files in his computer.

Patience handed Alvin the paper and Alvin reviewed it using a pair of Lorgnettes. He seemed satisfied and continued to search the files.

"Eureka!" cried Alvin after only a moment.

"You found it?"

"Of course, I did. But I don't think you are going to be satisfied with what it says."

"What do you mean, Alvin?"

"Well, it appears you will not get the farm and you aren't getting any of your grandmother's life insurance monies."

"You have got to be kidding. Were there ever any codicils to the will?"

"Does appear that there were several, but they don't change anything about any inheritance for you. Oh, wait. There was one about a year ago, that does leave you in the life insurance, but you won't get the farm. Sorry."

"What are you sorry for? I don't want the damn ole farm. The house is nice now, but I want liquidity. I am looking for the cash benefits. Can you print that latest codicil? It would override the will."

"No, there is one after that that leaves you out entirely."

"Look, Alvin. The judge is getting pretty old and he may not remember a new one was added. When he asks you to print the documents for today's reading, simply print the one I'm in."

"That is really going to cost you. I could lose my license for doing something like that."

"You can always say it was a mistake. Mistakes happen all the time."

"Ms. Snow, aren't you just a fine little trickster. Sounds as though you might have done things like this before. Learn that in the DOJ, did you? Sounds like I could get along just fine in that place."

"Yes, I think you could. So, we are clear on what the judge receives this morning."

"As soon as I confirm the numbers and addresses as accurate, I think we do. Oh, and Patience, don't forget that I won't forgive those who cross me."

"Neither do I," Patience responded and turned to leave.

"Just a moment, please, Ms. Snow."

Patience turned back around to look Alvin in the eyes.

"I was just curious as to why you wouldn't want the farm."

"I'm no farm girl, Alvin. I want more from life than digging potatoes and filling bushel baskets with fruit."

"So, that's how you think the farm has become so successful."

"It's the only thing I have seen going on there. The house is nicer, the farm is still the farm with all the labor included."

"I see. So, the other sisters haven't let you in on the secret of what they are producing on the farm?"

"I already told you that I saw nothing different as far as the crops go compared to when I was young."

"So, you haven't been inside the barn?"

"The barn? Me? No, and I have no intentions of going in the barn. Julia can milk the damn cows."

"Well," Alvin said, "don't say I never told you. But if I were you, I would rather have part of the farm and forego the life insurance money. Besides, you don't even know what the policy is worth."

"Mamie always told us she would have enough to give us so we would be self-sufficient."

"So, you really don't know, do you?"

"Know what, Alvin?"

"The rumors are all over town about what goes on over there."

"Rumors? Don't you know not to put stock into rumors?"

"Certainly, but how else do you explain the vast changes in the farm?"

Patience couldn't deny that she had wondered how the farm had become so prosperous. She recalled Ava telling her about owning all of the shoes and she became more interested in what Alvin had to say.

"Okay, Alvin. What are these rumors that you have heard about the farm?"

"Julia has a still in the old barn. She's making illegal whiskey and selling it over two or three states. Your grandmother started doing it about forty years ago. It appears that sister Julia is keeping up the tradition."

"Alvin, that is about one of the most absurd things I have ever heard. Do you not really think that if my grandmother and sister were producing and distributing illegal liquor that I wouldn't know about it? I grew up on that farm."

"Well, missy, do you think old Grams would put up an advertisement all over town? It's not like she would go around saying, "Arrest me, arrest me. My sorry ass is breaking the law!"

"And you have proof that this was happening?"

"I had to drive the old coot over to the farm the other day with his bride who is about one-fourth his age, which is an entire other story, but you should have seen the people going into that barn. Going in walking perfectly fine and coming out not even able to walk upright."

"Alvin, how do you know they didn't carry the liquor in with them? I am aware that some drinking was going on. Nothing out of the ordinary."

"Well, you might just want to mosey on down to that barn and take a look for yourself. Would be quite a feather in your cap to come home and be able to find something illegal to report back to the DOJ. I'm sure you lock elbows with someone from the ATF who would be interested in getting involved in some illegal activity. Transporting that venom over public highways is a big no-no, if you know what I mean."

Alvin glared at Patience as though every piece of gossip in town went through him and he would have to determine if it were worthy to be spread around or smoldered out like a burning campfire. Still, Patience knew that in order to get what she wanted, she needed to humor Alvin.

"I will check it out. Today, after the reading of the will. I won't have time to do it before."

"You will include me in the report, correct? I mean, I am the one who informed you of it."

"Of course. I would never leave you out of something as large as busting up a moonshine conspiracy."

Patience wanted to laugh, but held off to not let on that she thought Alvin was a cheap town gossip. She bid him adieu and left the office.

Gertie and Elisabeth sat at their home and waited for me to arrive to pick them up to attend the reading of Mamie's will. Elisabeth was in good spirits and had a comfortable night considering she was suffering from a broken hand after punching out Uncle Franklin. Gertie was the one who was a bit restless.

"I have never been to a will reading," she told Elisabeth.

"Me neither, sista, but it's jus' a meetin' with Judge Holcombe.

"Yes, but it seems so formal. So definite. It will be like Mamie is talking to us when we know she's passed on. It will feel like hearing Hamlet's father."

"Who's that?" Elisabeth asked.

"You know, Shakespeare."

"Nah, I never read that shit. Always give me the creeps."

"I feel like that now. I feel something isn't right, but I just can't put my finger on it."

"Well, I tell ya somethin' that'll calm ya down. Somethin' I been thinkin' 'bout gettin' fo' a long time now. Come on ova here and sit down and relax. I tell ya 'bout what I goin' ta do."

"What is it, Elisabeth? What do you have in mind?"

"Well, ya know I don't jus' go off and do nothin' and not give it consider'ble thought."

"Oh, no, not you. You never do anything spontaneous like knock people out."

"That's right. I think on it first."

Gertie looked at Elisabeth and gave a slight shake of her head.

"Why, jus' the other day, I was sittin' on the front porch and seen that litta Haskel boy tryin' to get inta the Maynard's winda. Had to throw a rock at the boy ta get 'im to get away from there. I tell ya Gertie, things be getting' worser and worser in the neighbahood. Ain't like it use ta be."

"Elisabeth, did you hit the young man with the rock?"

"Course I did. But I didn't kill 'im. He got up afta a few minutes."

"What are you leading up to Elisabeth?"

"That what I's gettin' to. And, I goin' to tell ya what I goin' ta do. I is goin' to buy a gun."

"No, Elisabeth. You cannot buy a gun. I have children in my house. What kind of example would that set for them? No, I just can't have that."

"Now, Gertie, tell me whatcha goin' do iffin' some no good rascal tries ta break inta our house?"

"I'll call the police."

"By the time it takes 'em ta get here, I woulda already shot their sorry asses."

"But, then, you would still have to call the police and explain to them why you shot someone."

"Cause they be breakin' inta ma house."

"What if the intruder tells them something different? Like they heard a cry for help and was trying to see if they could assist one of us?"

"Oh, sista, they won't be doin' much talkin' afta I shoot they ass."

"Elisabeth, you have never even handled a gun before. You don't know anything about them."

"Sho' do. Shot at Leroy a few times. He had hisself a gun."

"If it was his gun, how did you get it?"

"I whooped his ass and took it from 'im."

"And, then, you shot him?"

"Nah, I didn't hit 'im or nothin'. He shit hisself though."

"Elisabeth, I know that your intentions to own a gun are good, but I just don't think it is a good idea. You could hurt the children or yourself. So, let's just put that idea to rest. Besides, Julia keeps granddaddy's gun in the old barn. Maybe you could go out to the farm and shoot when Julia's with you. You are not to go and do it by yourself. Do you understand me? Do you. Elisabeth?"

"I be doin' me some thinkin' on it. I want one, though."

Gertie breathed a sigh of relief. She would never want Elisabeth to have a gun, but she was grateful Elisabeth told her that she had been thinking about getting one. That alerted her to watch her a little closer.

"Hey, look Elisabeth, I believe that I see your car pulling up. I guess we better get ourselves to the judge's office."

"I got my purse."

"Well, I'm going to step in and get my sweater."

"Why, it ain't cold, Gertie?"

"I know, but I feel a chill in the air. Something is just not quite right."

Julia explained to Ava that she was to ride in the truck with Patrick to the judge's office. She looked anxious at hearing that. Her large round eyes grew larger.

"It's okay, Ava. I trust Patrick. I wouldn't let ya be with someone none of us trusted. You goin' ta need ta show him how ta get to the judge's office. Elisabeth'll be there."

Ava shook her head and agreed. Julia saw that Ava and Patrick got into the truck and watched them drive off. She went inside and called Jonathon to take her to the will reading. She knew she could have gone with Ava and Patrick, but she also knew that it would be a good exercise for Ava to begin to trust men, again. Patrick was kind and Julia truly did trust him.

"Ava," Patrick said softly, "your sister told me part of what happened to you in Georgia. I want you to know that I could never do anything to hurt you. I want you to understand that. I'm sorry that all of that happened to you. No man should treat a woman that way. I do know what it's like to lose a child. I don't know if Patience ever told anyone in her family, but she had two miscarriages. I really wanted children, but Patience wasn't able to carry a child to term."

Ava bit her bottom lip, but did not look at herself in the mirror. She looked down and touched her stomach. For a moment the pain of her past came back. Patrick reached over and touched her hand. She touched his back and began to smile. She felt comforted by him. She felt she could trust him, but still pulled her hand away from him. Patrick pulled his hand away, too, but he would have left it there had his touch been better received by Ava. He thought Ava was the most beautiful woman he had ever seen in his life. She probably was.

Jonathon arrived at the farm about ten minutes after Julia had called. He knocked on the door and Julia opened it with a smile.

"You know ya lucky ya caught me before I left town," Jonathon said with a grin.

"Oh, yeah, where you be headin' outta town to?" Julia responded smiling back at him.

"Well," Jonathon said while pushing his ball cap back on his head, "you just never know. I might be out to find some sweet litta Georgia peach."

"Then I guess ya betta high tail it outta here to go and fetch her, but I'm here ta tell ya that Georgia peaches ain't got nothin' as sweet as what I got growin' right here."

Jonathon grabbed her and held her to him tightly. The embrace was genuine and Julia returned it.

"I know that's right."

"Come on, we ain't got time for this right now. We goin' be late for the readin' of the will."

"Couldn't we just do it over the phone?"

Julia pulled away and said, "I wish we could, but I gotta be there. Judge insisted."

"Marry me, Julia," Jonathon said in a sincere voice.

"We goin' be late, Jonathon."

"One day you going to say you will marry me, Julia. You can't keep pushing me away. I know you feel it, too."

"Maybe, if ya play ya cards right, I might not say no."

Jonathon kissed her lightly with a smile of self-confidence and said, "Let's go or you gonna be late."

The parking spaces along Main Street were full. Fortunately, there was additional parking in the rear of the building. Me, Gertie, and Elisabeth were the first sisters to arrive. Patience came strolling up the sidewalk and was the only one of us who was parked in front of the judge's office. When I asked her where she had disappeared to earlier that morning, she would only respond with telling me she had errands to run. I quickly dismissed her and turned my attention to getting Elisabeth and Gertie in the judge's office without incident.

Next to arrive was Patrick and Ava. Patience glared as they walked in together. Patrick took a seat next to Patience. The coldness between them remained like an icy barrier. Much to his surprise, Ava sat down beside of him. He smiled and nodded. Patience's spine tensed and she cleared her throat. She gave Ava a raised eyebrow look. Ava remained seated beside of Patrick.

Pastor Washington, Uncle Franklin, and Ann came into the office next and it was already getting crowded. Alvin brought in extra chairs and led Uncle Franklin to a seat like a guide dog. Gertie made Elisabeth promise to keep quiet and to avoid any urges to even look his way. His head was still completely bandaged and he still looked like a mummy. Ann followed behind Alvin and thanked him for bringing in the chairs.

236

Alvin started to leave, then turned around and said, "I think we are now only waiting on Julia and Judge Holcombe. I received a call from the judge and he is on his way. Can I get anyone anything to drink?"

Patience answered, "I think we are all good, but thank you."

"Jus' a minute there Fred Astaire," Elisabeth said mocking Alvin's clothing, "I would like a cuppa coffee, if you and Patience don't mind. Not evabody in here is just wantin' to get the money and run off."

"Certainly, I will get that for you," Alvin replied to Elisabeth's request and gave Patience a blank stare.

"What exactly does that mean, Elisabeth?" Patience asked as though she had been insulted.

"Just means if the shoe fits, ya should put it on. Just tellin' it like I see it. Most of us in here can see."

"And just what's that mean, ya old bat?" Uncle Franklin asked while he pulled up the bandages covering his eyes.

"Gertie," Elisabeth said, "please, tell Franklin I'm not talkin' to 'im like I promised to ya I wouldn't."

"Be a blessin' iffin she lost her mouth. Looks like whoever put her dentures in, forgot the teeth and put in a set a piano keys. Jus' look at her," Uncle Franklin said taking full advantage of knowing Elisabeth promised she wouldn't say anything to him.

Before Elisabeth could respond, the office door opened and Alvin brought in a silver tray. On it, he had a coffee carafe and several china cups with individual serving of sugar and creamer.

He looked at those gathered and asked, "I presume this will suffice your requests?"

Elisabeth looked confused and asked Gertie, "Does that mean he brung in some coffee?"

"Yes, sister," Gertie replied. "I am going to fix you some. You just stay seated and relax your hand."

"If you could jus' get her to relax her lips, we'd all be grateful to ya, Gertie," Uncle Franklin said still adding fire to the flames.

"Uncle Franklin," Gertie said addressing him like a school marm, "Elisabeth has acted quite like the lady ever since she walked in here toward you. It would be appreciated by all of us if you could treat her and the rest of us with the same type of respect."

Elisabeth smiled at Gertie as she reached for her coffee with the hand she was still able to use.

"Thank ya, sista," Elisabeth said victoriously.

The door opened again and Alvin made another entrance. He captured everyone's attention. He had changed from his double breasted vest to a bright red single breasted one. This time he appeared in spectacles that looked as though he stole them from an old movie set. They were very round, brassy in color, and appeared to wrap completely around his ear. His stature was of a military soldier standing at attention. We all bit our tongues to keep from laughing, except of course, for Elisabeth.

"Gertie, look what that boy got on now."

"Shh! Be respectful, Elisabeth," Gertie reminded her although Gertie as well as the rest of us wanted to laugh.

"Ladies and Gentlemen," Alvin announced, "I present to you the Honorable Judge Maquire Holcombe."

"Oh, cut that out, Alvin," Judge Holcombe said. These people know who I am, and I have known most of them all of their lives. Forgive my grandson everybody, he spent some time in England and now he thinks he's an English gentlemen or something."

"I feel the people of Cookham should respect the bench you preside over," Alvin said unapologetically.

"I feel that each and every person in this room does respect me."

"We certainly do, Judge Holcombe," Gertie confirmed.

"Well, now, who are we missing here today?" Judge Holcombe asked and begin to survey the room.

"Miss Julia is missing, judge," Alvin said. I will telephone her and find out what's keeping her."

"We can give her a few minutes, Alvin. We are in no rush."

Judge Holcombe took his seat behind his desk and opened the file that was before him. He cleared his throat and begin to cough. Gertie looked at him with concern. He took out his handkerchief and covered his mouth. Those of us who knew the judge well, noticed the red spot on the cloth and knew it was blood. Gertie went up and poured him a glass of water. It was the same water pitcher that graced his bench when he was the presiding judge when I was just a small girl.

Gertie leaned over and asked him if he needed something for the cough. He told her he had something in his drawer, but thanked her for her thoughtfulness.

Judge Holcombe retrieved his keys from his pocket and took a small key and unlocked a small drawer where he kept his medicine. He apologized to the ones in his office.

"Sorry folks, but I haven't had the chance to eat anything today. I hope you'll pardon me while I just grab myself a bite of this delicious brownie. I don't mean to be rude and not offer any to all of you, but this is my last one of a special batch. Extra peanut butter. My favorite."

"Please judge, go ahead and have a bite. Nourish yourself. We can't start without Julia anyway," Gertie stated.

Gertie and I knew the marijuana in the brownie would take around thirty minutes to begin to work so we chatted to pass the time. We silently hoped that Julia would be fashionably late. Many sat in silence wondering how Mamie split her estate and who would get what. Patience simply wondered if Alvin had done as she had requested. Trusting him was a long shot and she knew it. She kept looking for some kind of signal from him to acknowledge that everything was going as planned. However, Alvin held a stoic look and gave nothing away. She was feeling restless.

Fifteen minutes had passed and the judge appeared to have a little more color in his face and I imagined that the possible nausea he had earlier experienced was passing. He began to even smile and make small talk with people in the crowded office. Alvin sat outside the office still waiting on Julia.

After looking at her watch on every minute that passed, Patience asked, "Doesn't everyone think we should get started? I'm sure the judge has other matters he needs to tend to today. No sense in us taking up all of his time and forcing him to rearrange his schedule."

"Not to worry, Patience. I cleared my entire day for this. Mamie was a very dear friend of mine. I owe her this."

Just as the judge spoke, there was a loud crash from the back parking lot. All of us rushed to find a window. The sound was becoming fairly familiar. The sound that comes from a foot going through a windshield. Julia's foot, in fact.

"Oh my," said Alvin peeping through the blinds behind his desk.

"That's just disgusting," Patience said glancing out of the window only momentarily to see the commotion.

"I think it's spontaneously romantic," Patrick said aloud without thinking.

The judge, who remained in his chair, did not appear to be upset or startled by the disturbance. The brownie was taking effect on him and left him relaxed.

"Well, I guess we can be getting started soon," Judge Holcombe said serenely.

"Judge, I apologize for my sister's behavior. Having intimate relations in a parking lot is inexcusable," Patience said in a hopeful attempt to get in the judge's good graces.

"Come now, Patience, you mean to tell me you and your husband have no sense of adventure?" Judge Holcombe asked.

"No, your Honor, she does not," Patrick answered emphatically.

Hearing Patrick bothered Patience, but not as much as the passive attitude of the judge. She noticed the change in his demeanor within the last twenty minutes. He was smiling and almost giddy. Unusual for a judge, but she took her seat and remained hopeful Alvin would come through for her.

The front office door opened and we could hear Julia and Jonathon speaking to Alvin apologizing for being late. Alvin raised his eyebrow at Julia and she looked back as though she understood his judgmental glare.

Alvin said without looking up again, "Miss Julia, you truly are late and you might want to straighten up your blouse before embarrassing yourself in front of the judge, your family, and your pastor."

Julia looked down to notice that she had skipped a button while fixing her blouse. She adjusted it and said to Alvin, "Thank ya, Alvin. Did ya get a good view from the window? I see that ya might wanna make an adjustment yo'self."

"I don't know what you mean."

Julia pointed at the front of Alvin's trousers and wiggled her finger in the air without explaining what she was referring to.

Alvin grabbed the front of his pants and looked a little embarrassed.

"I can assure you that I have no interest in what you do in your vehicle, Miss Julia," Alvin responded.

"I'm sho' ya don't, I figured your arousal came from watchin' Jonathon."

Alvin slammed his hand to his desk. "Those rumors are entire falsehoods!"

"Calm yo'self, Alvin. You wanna tell the judge I made it?"

"I shall announce that you have finally arrived."

"Thank ya, Alvin."

Alvin opened the door to the judge's office and was less formal this time and simply stated, "Julia's here."

"Wonderful!" Judge Holcombe said jovially.

Jonathon and Julia walked into the room and sat beside of me. The room was getting a little warm with so many people in the room, but we were all glad that the meeting could finally get started. Of course, Patience raised her hand to the judge.

"Excuse me, Judge Holcombe, I don't think it is appropriate for Jonathon to be present. He was not requested to be present by his honor and he is not in a marital status to anyone here."

Jonathon stood up and walked towards the door.

"I take your point, Patience, but seeing that I don't consider him to be a threat to this meeting and he walked in with Julia, your sister, then I don't see a problem with his being here. The will can be reviewed and inspected at the courthouse. Does anyone else have any objections to Jonathon being present at this reading?"

Everyone looked around and shook their head to the negative. We all respected Jonathon and could really not understand why Patience would object to his being here unless it was to punish Julia for being late and the scene she made in the parking lot.

"That's what I thought. Go ahead and take your seat, Jonathon."

Everybody pushed a little closer together and made room for him to take a seat beside of Julia. Patience was the only one to not slide back to accommodate him being there. She sat as though the room was much more spacious than it was. Her confidence was high that she would walk away with money and that is what she came home to get.

Judge Holcombe opened the file on his desk and pulled out the forms enclosed. He clasped his hands together on his desk and begin to address those of us present.

"Mamie Nesbitt was probably one of the best friends I have ever had. My heart is heavy to have to be here with you today, but I made a promise to her that I would be present when the will was read. It may not have gone over well in Cookham, but I probably would have asked Mamie to marry me if I thought she would have said yes, but I knew she wouldn't have. But I want her family and those close to her to know that I truly did love her. Well, let's get down to the brass tacks."

He picked up the first page and begin to read:

"I, Guinevere Jane Rhinehardt Estes Nesbitt, the testator of this estate…"

"Wait right there a minute, judge," Elisabeth said while she waved her broken hand in the air, we here fo' Mamie's will readin', not nary any otha 'un."

"This is Mamie's Will, Elisabeth," Judge Holcombe told her.

"Who is those names you callin' out?"

"Which one, Elisabeth?"

"That Gwen somethin' or nother."

"That was Mamie's name, Guinevere."

"What was the next one?" Elisabeth asked.

"Jane?"

"Ain't nobody ever tol' me her real name. Always knowed her as Mamie."

Judge Holcombe responded, "I know, Elisabeth, everyone called her Mamie. But this was her legal name."

"Well, did you call her a Rhinehardt?" Elisabeth asked.

"I did."

"When was Mamie a Rhinehardt?"

"That was her maiden name."

"Well, I be dipped in shit. We got relations wit' that crazy fam'ly? I hate them summabitches. Gertie, you know who they be. Stay on my last nerve. Can we takes that one offin' Mamie's name, judge?"

"That would be illegal, Elisabeth," Patience said sounding frustrated as she didn't appreciate the interruptions. "Maybe we should just let the judge read the entire will and then we can comment on what it contains."

Elisabeth shot daggers at Patience and it made Patience flinch and slump down in her seat.

"Oh, hell, pardon me Pastor Washington, we are all friends here. Let's do away with all of the lawyer talk of the will and skip to the bones of the matter," Judge Holcombe stated.

"Here it is in a nutshell," Judge Holcombe explained. "Julia and the two sisters already living there get the farm and all and any proceeds redeemed from what the farm produces. The life insurance is divided between Elisabeth and Patience with ten percent going to the church. Uncle Franklin gets one dollar."

"What is all of this worth, Judge Holcombe?" Patience asked.

"The farm would have to be measured on today's fair market value. Mamie didn't have any debt minus the costs of the funeral and I believe that will be taken care of through a burial policy Mamie had. The farm would also include any and all profits from farm production. The bakery and all of that still remains to those living there."

"No, judge, the value of the life insurance policy. What is that worth?" Patience asked impatiently.

"Yeah, that. Unusual of Mamie. The value of the policy is seven hundred and fifty thousand dollars."

"And it only goes to me and Elisabeth?" Patience asked in a pretentious questioning tone.

"Yes, it appears so. Unless the will is contested. Seventy-five thousand goes to the church and the remainder is to be split between you and your sister, Elisabeth. And if my math is correct..."

"Elisabeth and I each get three hundred, thirty-seven thousand, five hundred dollars," Patience said and smiled as she finished the judge's sentence."

"Well, yes, I believe that is correct," Judge Holcombe confirmed.

"You mean ta tell me ya pulled me outta ma sick bed for a dolla?" Uncle Franklin cried out.

I desperately wanted to talk to Julia about the will. I turned to her and she looked at me. We both knew something was wrong, but Julia smiled at me so I knew not to make a large deal out of the reading. We thanked the judge and began to gather our things to leave. We would come back later to sign some paperwork.

"One last thing to the family. Mamie did not want a long drawn out mourning period. She wanted the burial to be within a week of her death. I realize that is a little unusual for your people, but it was in her wishes."

"Of course, judge, and we will honor them," Gertie replied.

Patience had already left the room and was in the outer office speaking to Alvin.

"You did well, Alvin. I will keep up my end of the bargain. I can't make any guarantees, but I can certainly try."

"Oh, I know you will, Ms. Snow."

"What makes you so confident, Alvin?"

He reached inside his vest to an inner pocket and pulled out a small cassette tape and held it up for her to see.

"What's that?" Patience asked.

"Insurance," replied Alvin.

Patience angrily turned and left the office and headed to her car. She drove back to the farm alone. Her anger was toward herself for letting a snippy law clerk outsmart her. Her incoming inheritance would help her anger, but she knew Alvin would be a thorn in her side; a wound that had the potential to never heal.

Uncle Franklin and Ann left with Uncle Franklin still angry about only being left a single dollar in the will. I was to drive Gertie and Elisabeth back to the farm. Ava would ride with Patrick. Something I thought neither one of them minded. Pastor Washington was headed to the farm, too, to help with the next rash of incoming guests and relatives coming in and dropping by to pay their final respects to the family. Ava would watch over things until we all arrived with Patrick's help. Ernie would be there with the fish cooking on the grill. Julia would arrive with Jonathon, but she had some unfinished business with Judge Holcombe first.

Wills and Stills

Patience took some deep breaths and exited the rented SUV she and Patrick rented for the trip. Her mind was telling her to go inside and up to her bedroom and sleep in the comfort of knowing she could now easily get herself out of all the debt she had been incurring. Her heart, however, clung onto a twinge of guilt for taking something from her sisters that she knew was not hers to have. The thoughts going through her mind surprised even her. In a few days, she could leave and never look back. She could leave the guilt behind her, too.

She decided to go to the kitchen and meet with some of her relatives and friends that she had not seen in years. It was somewhat relaxing to her and if nothing else, it would satisfy her guilty conscience to be doing something that she should have done since she had arrived. She had just walked through the backdoor and stepped into the mud room when Patrick and Ava arrived. She watched them get out of the old farm truck through the screened back door. She had always been jealous of Ava's beauty, but watching Patrick assist her in getting out of the truck and grabbing her arm and escorting her toward the house sent her emotions into overdrive. Could this be jealousy, too? She knew she and Patrick were not exactly meant for each other, but Ava had stolen attention from her for as long as she could remember. And there was something in the way they looked at each other and smiled. Patience could feel the attraction between them and she didn't like it. She walked outside to meet them.

"Ava, you look beautiful today," Patience said. "Doesn't she Patrick?"

As she spoke, she put her arm in Patrick's and pulled him close to her. A clear signal for Ava to understand that she owned him and she couldn't take him away.

"Yes, all of your sisters are beautiful," Patrick said not taking his eyes from Ava.

"Yes, well, Patrick, I thought you and I could sneak off this evening for a little alone time. There is a small lake on the outskirts of town. I remember going there and skipping stones across the water when I was a little girl. I think you might enjoy the view. Maybe I'll introduce you to the town I grew up in."

Patience rubbed her body closely to Patrick's in an attempt to make Ava jealous.

"Don't think so," Ava said.

"And just why not?" Patience asked and looked Ava up and down.

"Lake's dried up," Ava said and walked away toward the house unscathed by Patience's attempt to make her jealous.

"What exactly was that all about?" Patrick asked as he pushed Patience away.

"Something I've wanted to do all my life. That's what that was all about. I have a man that Ava can't have. That felt almost as good as hearing the will being read today."

"Why did you even come back, Patience? You returned here hoping time would have just stood still. It doesn't. Not for you. Not for me. Not for anybody. Things change and people change with them. How much do you really know about your family and the lives they have led since you left? And even if you know, how much do you care? Julia was right about you. You only care about yourself."

"Julia said that to you, did she?" Patience asked her husband insistently.

"She didn't have to."

"It wouldn't matter if she did. We will be going back to our different world in a few days, and all of this will be behind us. I have some bags in the car, do you think you could get them?"

"My former boss called me today. They offered me my old job back."

"That's wonderful! I hope they offered you an increase in salary. With the money from the will and both of our salaries, we will be able to afford a prominent address in D.C."

Patience began to walk away only to have Patrick walk briskly past her almost knocking her down. As he passed her he said, "Don't be so sure of yourself, Patience. And, by the way, get your own damn bags!"

At first, Patience didn't know how to react to how Patrick responded to her. She felt he should feel the same way she did. That the money would mean a new life for them both. But then, she felt the strange sensation that a fire was brewing in her stomach. She recognized it. It was jealousy. The deep seeded jealousy that no amount of money could buy away and bragging couldn't resolve. Then, she remembered what Alvin had mentioned about the old barn and while she continued to let the jealousy burn, she turned curious and let his words smolder in her thoughts.

She hadn't been in the old barn in years. It was never her thing to hang out in a nasty barn where the animals lived. Some older men were gathering now and were pulling up an old table to play checkers. She saw nothing that would indicate anything swaying from innocence in anyone's behavior there. More people were making their pilgrimage to the cooker for freshly fried fish with hot sauce. Patience reluctantly approached the barn being careful not to touch the decaying doors with her recently done manicured nails. The old building reeked of damp, musty smelling hay. She stood at the barn's entry but saw nothing indicative of an illegal liquor still. She couldn't bring herself to go inside. There was really only one way to find out. She would have to ask someone who kept hanging around the barn if there was moonshine there to be had. She searched the crowd for a familiar face. She found one. Gerald, a cousin she knew from her childhood.

"Hey, Gerald. Good to see you here," Patience said as she walked up to him.

"Oh, my goodness, Patience, is that you?"

"Sure is. Look, Gerald, I was just wondering if you would happen to know where a girl could get a drink around here."

Gerald stepped back and looked at her, rubbed his chin and asked, "You? You want a drink? I didn't figure you for a beer drinking kinda girl."

"Actually, I had quite a tough morning and was looking for something a little stronger than beer. Would you know where I might get my hands on something like that?" Patience asked as she was looking around the barn.

"Well, what exactly do you have in mind?" Gerald asked, probing her.

"Oh, I don't know. I heard that somebody around here might have some of that white lightning. You know what I mean. Something with a kick to it."

"Come on now, girl, you can't just show up here asking for something like that," Gerald said with a smile.

"I can pay you for it," Patience said with smiling eyes.

"Well, I don't have any, but why don't you go and ask your Uncle Franklin?"

"Uncle Franklin? You sure?"

"That's where I get mine from," Gerald informed her.

"Have you seen him today?"

"He's around. He usually stays close to the old barn. It'll cost you though, and you'll have to bring your own bottle."

"Bring my own bottle? Why's that?"

"Crazy old man probably pours it straight from the still," Gerald said with a vibrant chuckle.

"How much does he charge?"

"Depends on how big your bottle is."

"Let's say a pint bottle," Patience said getting frustrated.

"I guess probably about fifteen."

"Dollars?" Patience questioned with surprise.

"Sure. No family discounts in the business."

"Where's the still?"

Gerald stood back and looked at her like she was crazy and responded, "You don't know?"

"Is it on this property?"

Gerald laughed and said, "One just never knows. It sure would be a good cover for one though, don't you think?"

"I wouldn't know, but I think you know more than what you are letting on."

"No man gives out those kind of secrets. Besides, he's your uncle."

"That ole fool is not my uncle."

"That's between you and him. Do you want it or not?"

"Yeah, I'll be back with a bottle."

Gerald smiled at her and said, "You know where to find me."

"You can count on me finding you," Patience said with a purpose in her tone.

Patience continued to work the crowds of people knowing that she would ultimately have to venture inside the barn itself. She hugged relatives she had not seen in years and spoke to friends that she had not seen since her childhood. She took in a deep breath as if it were the last one she would get in a long time like you do when you get ready to dive into deep water. She exhaled and worked up the nerve to walk inside the old barn. The stench of hay brought back her childhood as she entered and she looked for signs of a still. She had no clue as to what she was looking for when she noticed a copper object stashed in the corner of the barn that was unfamiliar to her. She smelled something burning like a campfire does when you get it ready to make crisp marshmallows. The strongest thing she had ever had to drink in her life was wine so she had no earthly concept as to what moonshine even tasted like, much less, how to investigate how to manufacture it. But what she saw was enough to make her suspicions rise. Enough to continue her quest. After all, she had heard enough of Appalachia to know that moonshine was made in copper pots and she did see a copper something or other in the corner of the barn. That, and not to mention, she was about to purchase some actual moonshine as soon as she was able to return with a bottle to put it in. She was convinced she was onto something.

Patience started walking back to the house and pulled out her cell phone. She called her office in Washington to find out more information.

"Hello, Sylvie, this is Patience Snow."

"Hello, Patience, I thought you were out of town."

"I am out of D.C., Sylvie. Hey, can you connect me with Robert, down in Alcohol, Tobacco, and Firearms?"

"Robert isn't in right now. Took some leave time before he lost it. He checks in though, I can have him call you when I hear from him."

"Yeah, that would be good, Sylvie. You have my cell number?"

"I'm sure I do. I'll let him know when I hear from him."

"Does he call in everyday?" Patience asked, hopeful he did.

"Seems to."

"Okay, just have him call me ASAP."

"Will do."

There were no good-byes. Just business as usual. Patience knew Robert to be a good man and a better investigator. He would have the answers she needed.

While she waited for him to call, which could be a day or so, Patience would just play nice and enjoy her family as best she could. She wandered up to the kitchen to look for a bottle for the hooch. She wondered how much money Uncle Franklin made on distilling illegal whiskey. It would have to be a lot for a pint to cost fifteen dollars. When she got to the house, she noticed that all of her sisters had arrived back to the farm. She prepared to go in and face the firing squad.

The kitchen was crowded and the crowd didn't seem to be thinning out. Patience decided to confront her sisters and feel them out to find out how they felt about the findings of the will. She found them in the parlor sipping coffee and iced tea. She wandered in and sat down on the sofa. Her intention was to simply stay quiet and listen to what her sisters had to say. Surprisingly, they only made small talk. They didn't seem to be at all angry about being left out of Mamie's will. Patience was beyond speechless. Elisabeth excused herself and left the parlor. Patience scooted over to be closer to the conversation.

"I hope this weather holds up. We have had some beautiful days recently," Gertie said and sipped her coffee.

"Always seems it be rainin' at fun'rels," Julia added and sat down her glass.

"You know you're right on that, Julia, seems like it does rain. I can't think of a single funeral that I have ever been to that it hasn't rained. Odd, isn't it? Gertie said and sat back and thought about it.

"Mamie probably would say it was because the angels cried for the people who lost their loved ones," I added.

"Girl," Julia said as she looked at me, "ya betta go up and get yo'self some sleep. Gonna be anotha long day startin' in the mo'ning."

"I really do need to sleep. I think I will go up and get some rest. My second wind has just about finished blowing."

When I left, the only sisters in the parlor were Gertie, Ava, Patience, and Julia. I was about to mount the stairs when Gertie's grandson, Roland came running in from outside yelling for Gertie.

"G'ma! G'ma! You better come quick. It's Auntie Elisabeth. Down at the barn," Roland said, nearly out of breath.

"Come here, boy, what do you mean? What happened to your Aunt Elisabeth?"

"Nothin' happened to her, G'ma. She's fine. It's the men down at the barn. She's slappin' 'em good upside they neck," Roland said with his big brown eyes glowing.

"Oh, my heavens. Is she playing that game you told us about that they play at your school?"

"Yeah, G'ma and she's winnin' and beatin' 'em up pretty good. Uncle Franklin is cryin'."

"Franklin's down there, too?" Gertie asked.

"Yes, ma'am. They all down at the old barn."

I knew what game Roland was talking about. I knew we should have never let Elisabeth hear about it. And, if I knew Elisabeth, she had probably changed the rules a little and there would be money involved. Julia would have to handle this one, though. My eyes were about to close and I continued up the steps. I could hear my pillow calling my name.

Gertie went running down to the old barn to see what was going on. Julia went to the kitchen and watched through the window over the sink. Ava and Patience went with her to see the action.

"I jus' don' know what we goin' be doin' with that woman," Julia said as though she was amused about the whole thing.

"I think it is just terrible for a woman to behave that way. Hanging around down at that barn with all those men drinking liquor," Patience said.

"I guess it be a good thin' nobody asked you what you think," Julia responded to Patience's judgmental attitude.

"Well, I have been waiting for your anger to come out about the will," Patience said shaking her head.

"Ain't nobody angry 'bout the will. Who be angry?" Julia flew back at Patience. "Besides the judge gave me a letter from Mamie she wrote jus' fo' me. We got all we wanted. The farm. Elisabeth will take care of her and Gertie with anythin' she got."

"So, you're not angry with being left out of Mamie's life insurance policy?" Patience asked.

"Nope. Not even a litta bit. Got eva'thin' I wanted. The house. The farm. The way I figger it, it was worth not gettin' money if it gets rid of you. We ain't ever spoke of it, but we all know whatcha come home for. Now that ya got it, ya can go."

Patience was intrigued that being put out of Mamie's life insurance didn't bother her sisters. Her curiosity made her ask, "But Elisabeth was in the life insurance policy?"

"Yeah. So? Maybe Mamie was thinkin' Elisabeth would take care of her and Gertie. They always have took care of each otha," Julia answered.

"I suppose you're right. What about the letter from Mamie the judge gave you? What did it say?"

"That's pers'nal. Nuttin' for you to be worryin' about," Julie replied and looked up as she heard some arguing at the back door.

"Elisabeth, you cannot be left alone for even a second. Why must you always fight or get into an argument with everyone?" Gertie asked Elisabeth.

"I ain't been in no fight, Gertie," Elisabeth said, defending herself.

"Well, you certainly could have fooled me. Those two men didn't fall on the ground by themselves."

"They coulda. You know Gerald can't hold his liquor, Gertie."

"Elisabeth, you were slapping them on the neck and they were getting irritated with you for doing it."

"Well, they slapped my neck, too, Gertie. Looka here."

266

Elisabeth held her head to the side, and we saw where her neck was slightly red.

"Well, what started all of this down at the barn anyway?" Gertie asked insistently.

"We was jus' playin' around," Elisabeth responded.

"Nuh uh, G'ma," Roland interjected. "They was pickin' on Aunt Elisabeth."

"See there, Gertie. They was pickin' on me. Ask Roland, you grandbaby. He be tellin' ya."

"So, what happened, Roland?" Gertie asked him.

"They was all standin' 'round talkin' and one of 'em said somethin' not nice to Auntie Elisabeth," Roland explained.

"What did they say to her, Roland?" Gertie asked prodding him forward.

"I dunno if I should say it, G'ma. I don't wanna get into no trouble."

"It is okay, Roland," Gertie reassured him, "you can say it this one time."

"Well, after Aunt Elisabeth smacked cousin Gerald on the neck, a man down there said...he said..."

"Go ahead, Roland, I gave you permission to say it," Gertie told him.

"Well, he said that Aunt Elisabeth was uglier than a sack full of assholes."

After Roland finally blurted it out, he rushed to stand behind Gertie to stay safe from Elisabeth. The whole crowd in the kitchen started to laugh and they became so rowdy that I awoke from what was already a restless sleep. My body was so exhausted that I couldn't sleep. It was odd really to feel that way, but none the less true. I decided to go downstairs and join the rest of the gathered mourners.

Julia filled me in on what happened. Gertie was very upset that anyone would say something so ugly with children around to hear it. Elisabeth was angry that people laughed. Ava wandered around cleaning up dirty dishes and dirty paper napkins seemingly untouched by any of it, and Patience pulled Roland aside to talk to him.

"Roland, were any of the men down at the barn drinking when all of this was going on?" Patience asked him.

"Yeah, they was."

"Well, what were they drinking? Was it from a bottle?"

"I'm not sure. It looked like it was water, but it smelled terr'ble. Didn't see no bottles. They was drinkin' from jars. Like the ones Aunt Julia and G'ma put jelly in," Roland explained.

"You didn't drink any of that stuff, did you Roland?"

"No way. G'ma tear my butt up. Auntie Elisabeth had some of it. She said it made her chest burn goin' down."

"I see. Thank you, Roland. You run along and play now and stay away from that old barn, okay?"

"Okay, Aunt Patience. I will."

Patience checked her cell phone to see if she had missed any calls. She hadn't. She focused on how she could find out more about whether or not illegal whiskey was being manufactured on the farm. She came to the conclusion that she might as well find a bottle and buy some for herself. She scoped out the kitchen for canning jars.

She looked through the cabinets until she was interrupted.

"Whatcha' lookin' fo', Patience?" Julia asked her.

"Oh, nothing important. Just one of those jars, you know like you can food in. Just a small one."

"What you need a canning jar fo'?" Elisabeth asked her curiously.

"It's not that I need one exactly. Someone I work for asked me to bring her one back from the south. A souveneir type of thing, you know what I mean?"

"I ain't got me nary a idea why anybody would want a cannin' jar for a gift. 'Sides that, ain't ya got nary un up yonder where you live?"

"No, Elisabeth, we don't do much canning where I live. We wouldn't know where to start."

"I see," Elisabeth said and looked at her with distrust.

"Well, I don't see. Sounds like gravy to me." Julia said to Patience.

"Folks up north use them as decorative decanters. They put beads and things in them to look at, Julia. It's just something they do. So, do you have any that you could spare?"

"Got lots of 'em. Look ova under the drink table. Might find a case or two unda there."

I was listening to the conversation and something wasn't right about it. Julia knew it and we exchanged glances. She motioned her head in Patience's direction and I knew to keep my eyes open. I nodded at Julia to let her know I understood.

Patience pulled out a jar and looked it over. She pulled out a lid and screwed it on the jar and held it up as though she had never seen one before. She admired it like it was a newly discovered bounty and made it her own. She tucked the jar under her arm and started for the door.

"Julia," I asked, "what is up with Patience and the jar?"

"I ain't got a clue, but I think we betta watch her. How's 'bout you step outside and see if she puts that jar in her car? Iffin' she don't, let me know what she doin' with it."

I nodded to the affirmative.

The food still poured into the farm from grieving friends and family. Some were repeat mourners who were close to the family and others were people we weren't even sure we knew. They just came to eat. As long as they were respectful, we didn't mind. Actually, we were glad they came to help us clear out the masses of mounting food. Minus the fish, most things were brimming over the top. We had to make sure everyone took a plate home. Sometimes

271

two. But the fish supply was always dwindling. We had some white men who had been fishing drop in because they saw a line of cars headed to our farm. They decided to follow suit and drove right in with everyone else with their boat in tow. No clue as to who they were, but we traded their fish for all the food they could eat. I don't think they realized that we got the better deal. They ate heartily and we were glad of it. The trade restocked our fish supply. And we sent them home with enough food to eat for a week.

Patience did not put the jar in her car. She still held it under her arm and strolled down to the old barn where the commotion had taken place between Elisabeth and some of the younger cousins. I was bewildered to understand what kind of mission she could possibly be on, but I followed her mingling throughout the crowd as I did so she could not figure out what I was up to. I found Jonathon outside talking and visiting with friends. Most of them were his customers. Some voicing complaints and others praising his work. He handled both professionally. I managed to pull him aside and make him my cohort in the plot to follow Patience and learn what she was up to.

I was never quite sure if Patience ever knew what Mamie did while we were growing up. My guess was that she didn't have a clue. What appeared now to be of interest to her was something to do in the old barn. Jonathon agreed to keep an eye on her. He went one way and I went the other. In a few moments, Julia came out to get an update.

"I takin' it she didn't put that jar in the car?"

"No, Julia, she didn't. She has some fascination with the old barn, though. I found Jonathon and he is staking her out. I thought he would be less obvious than I would be. She would get suspicious if she saw me around her too much."

"Uh huh. That was good thinkin'. Let Jonathon watch her. I gotta check the tobacco barn. Come on. Let's go see what we got cookin'."

Julia and I both wandered our way to the tobacco barn. We always kept the front locked, especially with all of the people coming around for Mamie's home going. We entered the back through the kitchen. The same way we did with Patrick, except this time we locked the front kitchen door before we headed to the secret door in the back.

The first thing we did was check the temperature. It was ninety-one degrees and we looked at one another and without words agreed that was a perfect setting. We checked our bud and found it to be remarkably well. The fans were functioning well in all of the stalls. Our bumper crop was doing exceptionally well. We smiled as we touched the buds knowing we would have a great harvest. These hot house tomatoes were going to be extremely fine. Since we were alone and would not likely be interrupted, I took the opportunity to talk to Julia about Mamie's will.

"Julia?"

"Yeah."

"Did you find anything out of line with the will reading today?"

"Sho' did."

"Julia, Mamie would never have left all of that to Patience and Elisabeth."

"I know that. Judge and me was talkin' 'bout that. He smelled hisself a rat in all of it."

"Did the rat have a name? Maybe, Alvin?" I asked.

"Eh, he thinks Alvin is a turd an' all, but he couldn't even figger 'im to do somethin' like changin' a will. Lessin' he got hisself somethin' outta it. Judge did gimme a letta Mamie left fo' me."

"Oh, yeah. Is it something anyone else should know about?"

"Well, I been thinkin' on it. She talks 'bout how she wants the farm to stay runnin' and then says somethin' 'bout buried treasure."

"What did she mean by that?"

"I ain't got no clue, litta 'un. I neva heard her talk 'bout no buried treasure."

"Julia, would you mind if I read the letter? Maybe having a second set of eyes have a look might help. We can put our heads together and try to see what she meant."

"I guess that'd be okay. I give it ta ya tonight."

"Sounds good. Worth a try anyway."

As we were getting ready to once again check the temperature, we heard a very loud pounding on what sounded like the kitchen door. We quickly secured the barn and went to see what or who was causing the interruption. It was Jonathon.

"Whatcha bangin' on the do' so loud fo'?" Julia asked him.

"Well, I tried to knock normally, but you must not have heard me," Jonathon replied to her a little frustrated.

"So, whatcha want?"

"To tell you about your sister."

"Oh, God, which one?"

"The one you told me to follow."

"Patience? So what is she up to? Did ya find out anythin'?"

"Yeah. She was down at the old barn trying to buy some moonshine."

"Get outta here! Patience?"

"Well, did she get some?"

"She sure did. Saw her buy it myself. Saw her try a drink of it, too."

"What happened?"

"It damned near killed her. Gerald told her to watch out. She damn near dropped the jar as she fell down to the ground. If Gerald hadn't caught it, she would have dropped it and wasted the whole jar."

"Uh huh, and that woulda been a real waste."

"Sure enough," Jonathon said with widened eyes, "it was premium shine."

"Who sold it to her?"

"That crazy Gerald and Uncle Franklin set up some gallon jugs in the old barn and have been selling shine outta there."

Julia was angry. I wasn't pleased and knew we had to get to the bottom of it. We didn't need the attention it could bring to us. We had too much at stake. Somebody come snooping for illegal whiskey would be one thing. If they continued to look and found the tobacco barn, that would be quite another.

"What did Patience do after she caught her breath?" Julia asked Jonathon.

"She paid him the money she owed him, took the jar, screwed on the lid and walked away with it."

"Now what in the hell is she goin' be doin' with moonshine? She don't even drink."

"Maybe that's the souvenir she intends to take back to her friend in D.C.," I said sarcastically.

"No," Julia said, "she is up to somethin'. I guess getting' the money from the will won't be all she's awantin' to get."

"What do you think she wants, Julia?" I asked.

"Revenge," Julia said and started to walk toward the front of the barn."

Jonathon, Julia, and I locked the kitchen store and started up the hill to the house. Something caught our eye. Ava and Patrick were standing side by side looking up at the trees. Ava was smiling and when Patrick looked at her, it was hard for him to look away. It was warming to us in a way. But we couldn't let ourselves forget that Patrick was married to Patience. We couldn't let Patrick and Ava forget it either. Then, it suddenly happened. Patrick kissed her. All three of us who were watching held our breath. For more than one reason. First, we were fearful of how Ava would respond considering her past. Would the kiss push back on all of the work we had done to bring her back around from her abusive relationship with Adrian? Second, what would Patience's reaction be if she found out. We were unsure and kept walking to address that at a later time. We were, at the moment, more concerned with why Patience wanted moonshine.

Patience made her purchase of a pint size jar of hooch, reluctantly giving Gerald fifteen dollars for something she thought was a deplorable habit. She carried the jar in a brown paper bag and secured it underneath her arm as not to be visible to anyone in the crowded yard. She ventured to her car and placed the jar, bag and all, underneath the driver's side front seat. She shut the car door, locked it, and then, tested the door to ensure it was locked. She was satisfied. She had found something she could bring Julia down with and perhaps, put a star on her lapel in her department at her job. The recognition she thought she so well deserved. Now, if only Robert would call her back so she could give him the full rundown. She would continue to be cordial and wait.

Jonathon and Julia held hands as we continued to stroll through the people gathered on the lawn. The tables were full and the grill was cooking away at full steam ahead with Ernie at the helm. Among all of the people, we found Pastor Washington and confirmed that he recalled Mamie's wishes that her funeral be held more sooner than later. She did not want a large mourning period. He told us he understood and explained that since it would be such an enormous affair that we should consider holding it at the Cookham Baptist Church. They had a much larger church and would therefore, hold what he expected to be an unusually large crowd. We agreed, and he said he would confirm the use of the facility with the church elders. We could not foresee a problem. As much as we regretted the service itself, we longed for the day that we could move forward and have time to find a somber few moments for ourselves to grieve Mamie's passing. We craved quiet and solitude and needed a more regimented day.

"You know," Julia said to me after Pastor Washington strolled away, "we got us a harvest comin' up soon. Mamie's last."

"I know. I noticed the red hair on the buds. It has to be done."

Jonathon squeezed Julia's hand and said, "I can help with that, ya know."

"Oh, I'm countin' on it," Julia responded with a smile.

He kissed her gently on the lips, and we continued on our quest to seek out Patience. When we reached the house, we finally saw her. She was sitting at a picnic table speaking with some of the guests. As she spoke, we noticed that she kept looking at her cell phone and frowning each time she had to put it back in her pocket. We sat down on the opposing side of her.

"Where have you all been?" she asked us.

"Just checking things out. What have you been up to?" I asked her.

"Much of the same. Talking. Catching up with all the family. You know how it is. Hey, have you seen Patrick?"

The three of us looked at one another and finally Jonathon answered, "Uh, I saw him on the other side of the house. I think he must have been taking some drinks to somebody. He was carrying some."

"You mean he was getting Ava a drink?" Patience asked. "Just so all of you know, I'm not blind. I see the attraction between the two of them. But that's all right. He knows where home is."

"He knows where home is. He jus' don't like what's there when he arrives," Julia said to Patience with a less than genuine smile.

"It would make you happy to see me miserable, wouldn't it, Julia?"

"I think you have always been miserable. Period."

Patience stood up and straightened her pants. She slipped her shoes back on her feet and started to walk away, but then turned and said directly to Julia, "I won't be miserable much longer, my sweet sister."

After she left, Julia turned to me. "She's up ta somethin'. We might wanna get that harvest cut tonight. Don't wanna take no chances with Mamie's last crop."

I agreed. Jonathon would leave for a few hours and check on his business. When he returned, he would pick up Gertie and bring her back to the farm. Elisabeth would be asleep and so would Gertie's grandchildren. Ava would assist and maybe, just maybe, Patrick would be a helping hand tonight in the harvest, too. But I needed sleep, so I headed up to my room to rest in order to be of use that night.

Before I closed my eyes, I read the letter Mamie had left for Julia. Mamie had always had an odd way of getting her points across. It was as though her words were encrypted. I loved that it was handwritten. It flooded me with warmth. In her letter, she told Julia, "Don't always keep your eyes on the roots of the plants unseen. Make sure you tend to the roots of the ones in full sight."

I didn't understand what the words meant, but I knew they had to hold some kind of meaning that we would stumble across. Mamie always said, "The proper food at the proper time." I folded the letter back carefully and put it back in its linen envelope and secured it beneath my pillow. I slept, and this time, it was a peaceful sleep.

Boil That Cabbage Down

From the experience we gained, mostly from trial and error, we knew that marijuana was not the most fragrant plant species. Its aroma was distinctive to most, known by many, and repulsive to all. Cooking it was no different. But, over the years, we learned to adapt. You know how you tour a paper mill and at the first scent, you want to gag at the smell, but once it's time to leave, you barely notice the horrid odor? It was the same with marijuana. Except the making of paper didn't make you giddy from the fumes or aroma. Just like any other crop, the harvest of weed had a process. You might say we had it down to a science.

We grew a lot of vegetables on the farm. Some crops did fairly well and others not so well. But we had a large variety of most any garden vegetable anyone had the need or desire for. A vegetable that we always grew in large quantities was cabbage. It would not be unusual for us to plant two hundred plants and we had two growing seasons for it. The crop we had recently harvested was planted in mid-February. We fostered the cabbage well for it to serve its purpose. We nurtured it. Almost as well as we did the marijuana. Julia and Mamie had always been particular about it. The rows were two and a half feet apart with the plants being twelve inches apart. Admittedly, our fall season of cabbage far exceeded our spring crop in flavor and vibrancy, but nonetheless, the spring crop served its purpose.

The spring cabbage was edible, but we weren't going for flavor. We needed the stench of the cooking cabbage to outweigh the smell of our marijuana harvest. Julia lit a fire under the large iron pot which put most of the ones who saw it in mind of a witches' cauldron. The water we added to it earlier would soon begin to boil and would let us know it was time to add the cabbage. When cabbage begins to boil, it fills the air with a not so pleasant smell. The cabbage gave us cover. We stirred the cabbage with what looked like a boat oar. For what little we knew of boating, it very well could have been. We would take turns stirring the pot. Figuratively speaking. The true harvest was taking place inside the barn and simultaneously, in the kitchen.

The majority of the guests had left for the night and Ernie finally got to stop cooking fish. What few guests remained, were forced out with the smell of boiling cabbage. With the farm to ourselves, we tended our crops. Jonathon did most of the laborious work by cutting down the stalks. It was our process to cut down the entire plant and then, review it carefully to snip off all of the buds it had produced. We gingerly cut the buds from the plant with enough stem on them to make sure we would have an end to clothes pin to a long wire we had stretched across the barn. As a matter of fact, we had several wires stretched across the barn and they would soon be full of marijuana hanging upside down to dry.

Each of us had a pair of strong sewing shears to clip the buds. It was not exactly rocket science, but it took a lot of patience to not miss any of the valuable commodity we had lying out across the tobacco barn floor. However, after tonight, this would clear out much of the supply of what we had growing. The rest of it was not ready to harvest and was in various growing stages. It was how we kept a continuous supply.

Julia and I left the barn to stir the cabbage we had boiling outside. We had masks on to escape the fumes. The boiling cabbage would also help to cover up the smell of making butter. Normally, we would make the actual butter ourselves, but with time restraints and with so many things going on, we purchased what seemed like tons of butter from the grocery store to mix with our marijuana. It was odd to work in almost silence. The motions became second nature to us and talking was unnecessary. With all of us concentrating on the job at hand, our work would be done in three hours. The clean-up would be fast. What leaves we didn't put to use would be hauled to the woods adjoining our farm. It would be combined with other farm debris and made into mulch. We would then use the mulch, mixed with coconut coir and nutrients to grow more weed. The cycle was endless.

"So, did ya read the letta Mamie left me?" Julia asked me.

"Sure did. Hit my heart to see Mamie's handwriting."

"What do ya think she meant by all that?"

"I haven't had much time to think it through, but I don't doubt the unseen plants she referred to was what we are doing right now. Maybe, it was Mamie's way to tell us to not forget to stop and smell the flowers. The ones Ava keeps cutting and sitting pretty in the house."

"Could be. Was strange soundin' to me."

"You know, the only plants that Mamie ever really loved, other than the marijuana, were the flowers she had growing around the house. She tended those flowers like they were her children. Never would let us play near them. Built that rock wall around her flower beds. I'll have to think on it. I remember how she would talk to them like they were her best friends."

"Well," Julia said as she wiped her forehead, "if you figger it out, make sho' ya let me know."

285

I laughed and went back into the kitchen. Julia went all the way through to the barn and made sure things were getting wrapped up for that session of the harvesting process. I went into the kitchen to prepare to make the butter. Sitting in the floor beside me were three huge containers of cured buds ready to be ground and mixed in the fatty butter.

This was the smelliest part of the process. And it was a little more meticulous than just clipping the buds off to dry. The butter had to be warmed carefully for it not to caramelize. We had three large cooking pots for this. Julia came back in to join me. We would need Gertie, too. We would each watch the butter melt.

This was tedious, but we had done it often before and were quite experienced at it. Julia began to blend the cured bud in the industrial sized blender, readying it for the melted butter. We steadily worked. Julia poured the blended marijuana into each of the pots containing the melted butter. At first, the smell was intense, but as it cooked down, it became more tolerable. We had the exhaust fans going full blast above the stove and the stench from the boiling cabbage aided in covering the smell of the marijuana. All was going well and we worked in sequence and silence. If it were not for the fans pulling out the fumes, the kitchen would be silent. But when the loud knock came against the kitchen door, we were all thrown into a state of panic.

Jonathon hit the lights and all became dark. The knock scared all of us and we jumped with a gasp. Julia left her work and went to see who was at the door. She turned on the outside light. The cabbage still boiled and the light from the fire and the small porch light was all we needed to recognize the figure standing at the door.

286

"Whatcha doin' comin' down here scarin' the hell outta us?" Julia asked with her mask covering her face.

"You asked me earlier to consider helping you with what you are doing tonight. I looked for Ava. She wasn't in the house. I saw the fire down here and processed that all of you would be down here."

"Where is Patience?" Gertie asked.

"Oh, she's asleep. I left a television on downstairs in case she woke up."

"I sure hope she's a sound sleeper," I said.

"She takes medication to make her sleep. You're safe there."

"So, ya decide to help us, did ya?" Julia asked Patrick.

"I thought I would come and check it out," he responded and held his nose. "I don't know what smells worse, the marijuana or whatever you have cooking outside. What is that?"

"Cabbage. Stinks, doesn't it?" Gertie said and handed him a mask.

"Yes, ma'am. It surely does. So, what can I do to help?"

Jonathan, feeling a little more reassured about Patrick being in the kitchen, turned on the kitchen light.

"You jus' about scared the shit out of all of us," Jonathon said to Patrick.

"I'm sorry. I didn't mean to do that. But I should have known better. Considering what is going on down here and all."

Ava pulled down her mask and smiled at Patrick.

"Well, too bad, you missed helping me cut down the stalks and carrying the waste to the woods," Jonathon said.

"Yeah, I had to wait to make sure Patience was asleep," Patrick said and smiled back at Ava.

Jonathon looked at Patrick, then at Ava, and then, at Julia. He raised his eyebrows as if to ask if she realized what was going on between them.

Julia smiled and shrugged her shoulders. Jonathon knew what that meant. Julia would not interfere with Ava and Patrick being smitten with one another regardless of how he felt about it. Jonathon was old school. No man messes with another woman when he was married, especially when his new found attraction was the wife's sister. There would be nothing good to come if it. Jonathon knew it and Julia new it, too. The rivalry Julia had with Patience outweighed the concern she had for Ava. Jonathon was worried for Ava. He had known Julia and Patience for a long time and understood both their strengths and weaknesses.

Patrick broke the tension and said, "There are a lot of plants out in front of the barn. What are those?"

"Tomatoes," Gertie replied. "We grow those in the barn, too, sometimes. Makes an interesting combination, don't you think?"

"I guess I quite honestly wouldn't know. I've never really ever been on a farm before," Patrick responded with a slight blush in his cheeks.

The silence was broken again by a ringing cell phone. Everyone checked their pockets. Gertie jumped at thinking something had happened to one of her grandchildren. My phone screen was blank. It was Julia's cell phone that was ringing and we were all confused as to who would be calling us this late. Or this early, it was nearing one in the morning.

Gertie, Ava, and I continued to stir the ground marijuana into the butter to release the potency of the pot into the butter. We stopped dead in our tracks when we heard Julia answer the phone with, "Sheriff?"

Instinctively, Jonathon turned off the kitchen light only to turn it back on, then hitting himself for being so ignorant. But when he looked and saw Patrick lying on the floor with his head covered, he felt like the smartest man in the world.

"What in the hell are you doin' on the floor?" Jonathon asked Patrick.

Patrick rolled over and sat up in the floor and answered, "You don't see where we are and what is surrounding us? Then, the sheriff calls Julia. Don't stand there and tell me you aren't scared. Being in here is enough to make anyone jumpy."

Julia began waving her hand for Jonathon and Patrick to stop talking so she could hear the sheriff. They stopped talking and started trying to listen, too.

"Yeah. Yeah. But what's that gots to do with me?" Julia said into the phone.

"I understand that, sheriff, but things such as that goes on all the time at fun'rels. Never knowed there to not be drinkin' goin' on. But, I ain't had no liquor in me."

"Say what?"

We could only hear one side of the conversation and that was Julia's. We stared intensely at her and tried to patiently wait for her to hang up so she could tell us why the sheriff would be calling her at this time of the morning.

All the while we continued to stir the butter and waited for it to turn a greenish hue.

"Well, sheriff, I reckon me comin' down there is goin' be the only way to straighten all this out. Ya say the agent said he was informed from some kind of anonymous tip. Beats the hell outta me who would say such a thin'. I guess I be seein' ya shortly."

Julia ended the call and dropped her phone into her shirt pocket. She checked the ghee and stirred it a little with a large wooden spoon. A frustrated Jonathon reached for the spoon and pulled it from her hand.

"You goin' a take a phone call like that and not tell us what in the world is goin' on. Are you crazy or something? What did the sheriff want?" Jonathon asked.

A tired Julia sat back on a kitchen stool and had a perplexing look on her face. She looked at each one of us individually and then at all of us as a whole. Then she spoke.

"I ain't sure I know how to say this. The sheriff said he's needin' me to come in fo' questionin'. Somebody done gone and tol' him we gots a still out here on the farm makin' and sellin' moonshine liquor."

"Oh, that's just crazy," Patrick blurted out, "this isn't liquor, this is weed."

We all looked at him. Jonathon looked as though he wanted to take a swing at him.

"Well, step aside Sherlock Holmes, Patrick has entered the building. Brotha, don't you get this? If somebody turned in some report about a moonshine still, how long do you think it would take them to find what's in this barn?" Jonathon said to Patrick.

"You are right," Patrick said to Jonathon, "I didn't think about that."

Julia took in a deep breath and told everyone to calm down. Jonathon and Patrick nodded at each other and made amends. Me, Gertie, and Ava kept stirring the butter. It would soon be time to start straining it to remove all of any leftover stems and pieces of leaves.

I tapped my wooden spoon on the side of the pan I was stirring so as not to lose any butter and pulled down the mask from my face. I turned to Julia and asked, "Did the sheriff say where exactly someone told him the still was on the farm?"

"He jus' mentioned somethin' about the barn."

"Oh, Lord Jesus!" Patrick yelled out. "We're going to get arrested. I just know it! I just know it!"

This time, Jonathon didn't hold back. He reached over and slapped Patrick. Ava ran to him and gently touched his face.

"Now, I done tol' y'all to calm down. Nuttin' goin' to get solved by hittin' each otha. Howeva much you'd like to," Julia said with agitation in her voice. "Now we can all see, there is mo' than one barn on the farm here. We know nobody been in this one 'cept for us. We been had it locked up the whole time. What about the ol' barn? Anybody see anythin' unus'al down there?"

"Not unusual for us. Bunch of the older men were down there drinking. Of course, Elisabeth was down there drinking, too, but she wouldn't have reported a still being in the old barn. She would want to keep that running herself," Gertie answered.

"Patience," Ava said softly.

"What was that, Ava?" Gertie asked.

"Patience was down there. Talking to cousin Gerald."

"Well, there you go, Julia. We all know that Gerald and your Uncle Franklin cook and make shine," Jonathon said busting into the conversation. "Those two fools have a place down in the woods now behind my grandmama's house. Big shots walking around town like everybody don't know what they doin'."

293

"Judge not, lest ye be judged, Jonathon," Gertie reminded him.

"Yes, ma'am. But you ladies ain't out hustling your weed on the street to just anybody who wants to buy it to get high," Jonathon added.

"No, Jonathon, we are more reserved. We take it to nursing homes where people are dying," Gertie said, bouncing back at him.

"You know what I meant, Gertie. Just the other day, I caught Gerald selling booze to a kid right over there on Greenbriar Street close to my shop."

"Well, no you didn't," Julia said.

"Sure enough did, Julia."

"Ya say somethin' to 'im?"

"I punched him, took the booze, and busted the bottle against a rock."

"Well, good fo' you, but seein' what we do, we don' need to make enemies in the fam'ly."

"Julia," Patrick interrupted, "Aren't you forgetting that you already have one?"

"Who, Patience? She and me has always been enemies. I don't think even she'd come up wit' somethin' this stupid."

"Don't underestimate her, Julia. Patience hates to be overlooked and something like this is right up her alley. She has been looking for a way to get a promotion at her job. She has been skipped over twice in the past year."

"How'd somethin' like this get her a betta job?" Julia asked.

"It would gain recognition for her. If she would turn in her own family, she would turn in anybody."

"I don't like it, Julia. I don't like it at all. Patience is cunning and has always looked out for herself. Even though she gets a large portion of Mamie's life insurance, it's not enough. She wants to take you down and destroy the rest of us with you," I said with my words resonating with everyone else standing in the barn's kitchen.

"Well, I tol' the sheriff I'd go down and talk to 'im. He'll be 'specting' me. The butta is ready to sift and poured inta the containers. Afta it cools, jus' put it inta the fridge. I think y'all can handle the res' a this without me."

"Julia, you can't go by yourself," Gertie said to her.

"Sho' can. Asides that, y'all goin' ta be a hand short without me. I'll be back afta I get this mess straightened out. Takin' the truck. Jonathon, you get Gertie home, ya hear?"

Julia removed her mask and her apron and after we heard the truck start, we knew she was gone. We all had a worried look on our face. We continued to work in silence.

I finally broke the silence and said, "Look, I really don't have a good feeling about all of this. Out of all the years we been doing this, we have never been questioned. Something is not right and I don't know about the rest of you, but I feel it."

"I feel it," Ava added.

"Me, too," Gertie agreed. "Jonathon, I believe I'll being staying at the farm until Julia gets home. Elisabeth will watch the children."

"I know Julia usually makes all of the decisions, but this time, I am going to make one. I think you all know what has to be done. We have to empty the barn," I said.

"We can't destroy Mamie's last crop. Julia will be heart broken," Jonathon said.

"Her heart will heal. If an outsider walks in this barn, we'll all be taken away," Gertie said with a voice of reason. "We have school contracts and if the news gets their hands on something like this, we'll be accused of feeding marijuana to children."

"She's right," I said. "We need a plan, and I think I have one."

Jailbirds Can't Fly

Julia pulled the farm truck into the back of the courthouse in Cookham. The sheriff's office was located on the bottom floor of the town's only majestic government structure. Not realizing what was waiting for her, Julia entered the solid wooden door and her hand on the door knob caught her eye. She had green butter underneath her fingernails. She thought it best to go to the bathroom and wash her hands. She quickly zipped in and walked to the sink. The soap container was empty, but the water was hot enough to wash away any residue of the ghee, or marijuana butter. She was glad the paper towel dispenser was full, unlike the soap dispenser. She was rubbing her hands together when she looked up and saw a familiar face.

"Alvin?" Julia asked with surprise.

"Yes," Alvin responded.

Glancing at the bathroom door to make sure it still had the universally accepted image of a female on it, Julia asked, "Alvin, why you in the women's toilet?"

"Well, Miss Julia, you must not have observed, the men's restroom is closed for cleaning."

"Oh. I see. Well, whatchoo doin' down her so early in the mornin' fo'?"

"Handling the judge's business, as usual. What brings you down here at this hour, Miss Julia?"

"Somethin' tells me you already know somethin' 'bout why I'm here."

"And what would give you that idea?"

"A litta birdie tol' me."

"Well," Alvin said with a snarky tone, "it could be that you will soon find out that some birds don't fly."

"Maybe not, Alvin. Maybe not."

Alvin washed his hands and walked out the bathroom door without saying anything else to Julia. Julia continued to dry her hands when she caught a glimpse of herself in the mirror. She never considered herself an attractive woman, but she could never be considered unattractive either. Her hair was in long braids and her teeth were as perfect and white as the pearl earrings she wore in her ears. She turned to leave when she noticed that there was a briefcase sitting beside the sink. As elaborate as it looked, she knew it had to be Alvin's. She picked it up and took it out into the hallway to see if she could see Alvin to return it to him. He was standing beside the water cooler.

"Hey, Alvin, ya forgot ya purse," Julia said as she passed Alvin and continued to walk. She pushed the briefcase into his chest and he flinched as he felt the sharpness of its ends.

"Oh, thank you so much. Miss Julia," he called out to her as she was entering the sheriff's office. "I hope you have a most pleasant morning."

Somehow Julia knew that his words were not sincere. Julia scanned the office for the sheriff. She found his dispatcher behind the desk and leaned across it with her hands relaxed at her sides. Her hair was still braided on both sides of her head and as always, her hair glistened. She still donned her grandfather's fedora upon her head, but reached and pushed it back before she asked where the sheriff was.

"Oh, hello, Julia. The sheriff has been waiting on you," his dispatcher said. "I'll just tell him you're here."

"Thank ya."

Julia strummed her fingers on the counter while she waited on the sheriff to come out of his office. She didn't have to wait long before he came out and waved her to come in with a large cup of coffee in his hand.

"Have a seat, Julia. Right there'd be fine," he said pointing to a chair across from his desk.

"Okay, thanks."

"Can I get you some coffee? I don't know how I could keep my job without caffeine."

"'Preciate it, but nah. I'm good," Julia said and sat back into the chair.

"Well, I guess you are probably wondering why I would call you at such an odd hour."

"Well, sheriff, I'd be lyin' if I said I wasn't curious 'bout that."

"I just need you to know, Julia, that there is really no doubt in my mind that the accusations made by this caller are completely unfounded."

"Sheriff, ya know as well as anybody that we don't cook no shine out at the farm."

"I know that, Julia, but you understand that I have to check out a call whether I believe it or not."

"Oh, I understand that," Julia said, still relaxed in her chair.

"But, Julia, I have to tell you that I have a little pressure coming down on me on this one."

"I don't understand. Ya know I ain't inta liquor. Ya said ya didn't believe whoever is spreadin' all this."

"And, I, myself, personally don't believe it, but we've got a federal agent in town from the Alcohol, Tobacco, and Firearms who is out for blood. He is convinced that you and your family are in the business of selling moonshine."

"Can't ya reason wit' 'im?" Julia asked.

"No, I don't think I can. He said his informant is rock solid."

"Sheriff, I ain't gotta tell you that they is a lot more at risk here."

"I know, Julia. I know. I don't believe my own mama would be getting through her chemotherapy if it weren't for you."

The sheriff began to rub his head to exemplify his stress and concern over the situation he had on his hands.

"Sheriff, did this ATF man say who tol' 'im 'bout all this nonsense?"

"He won't tell me. Just said it was a local man."

"A man, huh?" Julia said. "Sheriff, I think that man is Alvin. Run inta 'im this mo'ning in the woman's bathroom. Figgered it kinda odd his bein' here at this time of day."

"The women's bathroom?"

"Yeah, he said the men's was bein' cleaned up."

"The men's restroom wasn't being cleaned this morning. I don't know why that little freak was here."

"Where is the ATF man?"

"He's in the next office over. I told him I wanted to have a word with you first."

"Then, now ya know why Alvin was here fo'. He jus' tryin' ta start somethin' with the ATF to earn hisself some brownie points."

"But why? What would Alvin have to gain by starting a vicious lie?"

"I ain't sho' 'bout that, sheriff. I guess we'll find out soon enough."

It was then that a stranger walked into the sheriff's office. He set a leather bag that looked like a briefcase on the sheriff's desk and took a seat beside of Julia. He held out his hand to introduce himself.

"Good morning, you must be Julia. I have been hearing a lot of good things about you. You are a very well respected person in this town. By the way, I am Robert Milan. I work for the..."

"ATF," Julia said, finishing his sentence, but kept her hands in her lap.

The agent put his unaccepted hand down and opened his briefcase. His voice was gentle, but his demeanor was stiff; his moves were calculative.

"Miss Nesbitt, we don't want to waste any more time than we have to. I think the sheriff has probably already told you that someone has given us a fairly good lead that brings us to believe that either you or you and your family are distilling and distributing illegal liquor out on your family farm."

"That's what I been hearin'."

"Is there anything you'd like to say about the things I just said?"

"Not really," Julia answered. "Maybe jus' that the person who said somethin' like that's got shit for brains."

"Do you understand that we have a witness that says they saw illegal whiskey being sold on your farm?"

"Well, Mr. Milan..."

"Please, call me Robert," the agent interrupted Julia to say.

"Well, Mr. Milan, I can't sit here and say that somebody ain't ever sol' no shine while they was on the farm. I can tell ya that not me or my sisters ever made none or sol' it on the farm or ever had nothin' ta do wit' it. Elisabeth drinks sometimes, but she wouldn't know how ta start makin' it. I'm thinkin' ya need ta go and have a betta talk with the one who's lied to ya."

"So, I can be safe in saying that you deny any accusations of any illegal distilling of liquor on your property?" the agent asked Julia.

"I'm tellin' ya that we don't cook it or sell it on the farm. If that's what ya jus' said, then that's what I'm sayin'."

"All right, then. Sheriff, put her in a holding cell while we wait on the warrant."

"What warrant?" Julia asked.

"Search warrant," replied Agent Milan. "We would like for you to be our guest while we wait on it to arrive. It shouldn't take but an hour or so. I'm sure the sheriff will attend to your needs."

"ATF or not, I don't have anything to hold her on, and I'm not putting Julia in a cell."

"Then, sheriff, cuff her to a chair. I don't care as long as she can't tip off her family."

"With all due respect, you are tipping the scales of justice on this. You don't have any authority in this state. Not to mention, you don't have any proof. You have hearsay."

"I'm taking authority, sheriff. If you don't like it, then I can put you in a cell myself," Agent Milan said to the sheriff. "Since the two of you seem to be so chummy, I think that might be in the best interests to all involved anyway. I'm not convinced that you wouldn't tip the family off yourself, sheriff."

"You can think anything you want, but I have been on that farm many times. In every building on it. There is no illegal distillery on the property. But if you want to make a fool out of yourself by putting me in a cell, then go ahead. Any person in this town can tell you and will be proud to speak of the fine reputation of Julia and her sisters."

"Sheriff, I am placing you under arrest for interfering with a federal investigation," the agent said and within minutes the sheriff was behind bars with Julia handcuffed to a radiator outside of his cell.

"Agent Milan," the sheriff said, "Julia was going to go over and check on her sister after she left here this morning. Her sister doesn't live on the farm and is going to get mighty worried if Julia doesn't stop in. You think you could drop by and tell her Julia is tied up over here at the jail and will be by later. Poor little thing is ailing and hardly able to get around. Broke her hand recently. She just lives a couple of streets over. Could you at least do that?"

Agent Milan twisted his face not wanting to comply with the sheriff's request, but looked at Julia who was looking at him with puppy dog eyes. Finally, he agreed and wrote down Elisabeth's address.

"I'll drop by, but this better not be a set up," Agent Milan said to the sheriff.

"They're just two sisters living together. Just as mild mannered as your mama. They are going to appreciate you doing this so much."

Agent Milan took the address and directions to Gertie and Elisabeth's house, left the office and got into his car, then headed to the home that Gertie and Elisabeth shared.

"Sheriff," Julia said.

"Yeah?"

"Elisabeth might jus' kill that man."

"Yeah, I know. But I won't tell if you don't."

There was a sadness that came over the room where Julia sat with her hand in a strong cuff attached to the radiator. The sheriff looked at her and felt her pain.

"It will be okay, Julia."

"No, sheriff, I don't think it will. My sisters, 'cept for Elisabeth and Patience, will go ta jail for growing and distributing marijuana. The man I'm in love with is probably going to go down with them. I'm already in jail or might as well be. Patrick is with them. They are not goin' ta know what hit 'em. Patience walks away free and clear and I'm believin' she set this whole thin' in motion. Mamie sho' would be prouda me. Gonna lose the farm and the business."

"Well, you'll all be in good company in jail, I'm one of your best customers. I can see the lot of us on CNN now," the sheriff said.

"Sheriff, nobody'll eva know that. I ain't tellin'. Not nary a person's business. You was jus' helpin' yo' mama."

309

Agent Milan got out of his car and stepped up on the front porch of 131 Marion Street. He checked the house numbers to make sure his visit wouldn't awaken the wrong person. He wrestled with why he was doing this. He could have let a marked car handle it, but he knew that he was jeopardizing his job by making the call on taking over the case from local authorities. He put his trust in Patience for giving him the tip of the still and she was willing to go so far as to report her own family, how could he go wrong? And, the judge's grandson making the call to him and being prepared to be an eyewitness of the selling of illegal moonshine was another reason to move forward. He stepped up to the door and knocked on it. Gently at first, but then harder when he got no response. Finally, he heard movement from inside.

"Auntie Elisabeth! Auntie Elisabeth! You gotta get up. There's a man down at the front door. G'ma must be over at the farm. Auntie Elisabeth! Wake up!" Roland said as he shook Elisabeth awake.

"What's amatta wit' ya? Whatcha doin' in ma house, ya litta shit?"

"Auntie Elisabeth, they is a man at the front door. And it looks like he's gotta gun."

"A gun! I know they betta not be no strange man at my do' carryin' no gun. Reach me ma purse, Roland!"

"You gonna cut him, Auntie Elisabeth?"

Elisabeth reached into her purse and pulled out her weapon.

"No, I ain't gonna cut 'im. I'm gonna shoot his sorry ass! Now ya go back in ya side of the house and get all the chil'ren unda the bed. Hurry up now. We got us a crime in progress here."

"You want me to call 911?"

"Hell, nah! Jus' go on and do what I tol' ya to now 'fore I light a fire unda yo' ass. Now git!"

Roland ran as if he really was on fire. He sped down Elisabeth's steps and quickly ran through the connecting door to his grandma's house and then, quickly up the steps to his sibling's rooms. He coaxed them under the bed even though they were partially asleep. Carefully, he went to the bedroom windows and lifted the one window that overlooked the front of the house so he could listen to any conversations that might take place. With Elisabeth at home, Roland felt more comfortable and safe than he would have with the police being there. Keeping his head low, he placed his ear to the crack in the window.

There was another knock on the door. Elisabeth heard it this time and looked at clock on her wall. Three A.M. Still in her nightgown and long, heavier robe, she made her way to the door without turning on any lights. She peered out the peep hole she had installed on the door, but could see nothing other than the silhouette of a man standing on the front porch. She flipped on the lights and unlocked the deadbolt on the door. Her gun was in the pocket of her robe, locked and loaded.

311

"Who out there?" Elisabeth asked.

"I am Agent Milan."

"I don't know nobody named Agent. Whatchoo doin' here at ma house this time o' the mo'ning?"

"Ma'am could you just open the door so we could talk?"

"You fixin' ta be cold, dead, and stinkin' afore I open ma do' this early in the mo'ning fo' anybody I don't know who they is."

"I explained who I am, ma'am."

"And I done tol' ya I ain't know nobody wit' yo' name."

"Ma'am the sheriff asked me to come over and check on you. Your sister, Julia, was supposed to come by, but she got held up at the courthouse."

"The sheriff, huh? If he bein' so worried 'bout me, why he not come his own self?"

"Look, lady, I don't know. I was just told you were old and injured and the sheriff needed me to come over and check on you," Agent Milan said getting more frustrated by the second. He, by now, was standing with his left hand up on the wall beside the front door leaning his body upon the side of the house with his head down.

Elisabeth cracked the door and by the time Agent Milan looked up, she had her gun pointing directly into his face.

"Oh, my God! Lady, are you crazy?"

"No, and I ain't old neither. Now ya betta talk real slow and tells me where ma sista, Julia, be at."

"Sh-Sh-She be, I mean, she is over at the jail with the sheriff."

"Goin' ta be needin' ya ta put yo' hands up ova ya head. Then, I is gonna be openin' this do' and ya goin' ta come in and sit down."

"W-wait. Just hold on there. I don't think it would be a good idea to come inside," Agent Milan said to Elisabeth.

Elisabeth pulled the hammer back on her revolver until it made a click. It was pointed right between the eyes of the agent. Elisabeth's gun and the agent's face were up close and personal. So close, in fact, that the agent appeared cross-eyed as he hadn't the nerve to take his eyes from the end of the gun.

"But, then again, maybe I could come in for just a minute or so to make sure you are okay."

"Git those hands up ova yo' head!" Elisabeth barked out loudly.

Agent Milan quickly obeyed.

"Roland! Git down here. Fetch me a rope! Ya hear me?"

Roland shortly appeared with widened eyes and said, "You gonna shoot him, Auntie Elisabeth?"

"Only iffin' I gots to. Where's tha' rope?"

"We ain't got no rope," Roland responded.

"Well, go get me some of that new clothes line I jus' bought and brin' it in here ta me."

"Okay, Auntie Elisabeth."

Agent Milan was still focusing on the point of Elisabeth's gun. He wasn't sure, but he thought he wet himself, but it could have just been sweat. This was not what he was expecting his day to turn out like. He thought of his wife and children and how he hoped he would get to see them again. He had to gain control of the situation.

"Ma'am, you are making a really big mistake. You could get into a lot of trouble holding a gun on a federal officer."

"Roland! I need me that clothes line today!"

"What are you going to do with clothes line?" Agent Milan asked.

"I gonna hog tie yo' ass up. Breakin' inta my house like ya did. Ya picked the wrong house to break inta today," Elisabeth told him.

"What do you mean? I never broke into your house! That's just crazy!"

Elisabeth touched the gun to Agent Milan head and said between gritted teeth, "How's tha' agin?"

"I meant to say that I broke into your house and I should never have done that."

"Well, ya can be damn skippy ya won't be doin' it no mo'. I's gonna haul yo' ass inta the jail."

Agent Milan gave a sigh of relief to know she wasn't going to shoot him. At least, not at the moment.

"Here, Roland, hol' this gun on the man. If he moves, shoot 'im!"

"Oh, Jesus, don't give that kid a gun!"

"Shut up! Roland can't hol' a gun as good as me. He might slip up and shoot yo' ass."

With one good hand, Elisabeth took the clothes line and wrapped up the agent as tightly as she could. Two hands would have been better, but her broken hand kept her from making it as tight as she wanted it. She continued to wrap until he could barely walk. What the clothes line lacked in tautness, it made up for in mass. His hands were straight down by his side and his gun, which he always carried was pinned to his side in its holster. Fortunately for Elisabeth, he left his keys in his car.

"Come on, Roland. We caught us a crim'nal and he got ta be taken down to the jail. Gettin' 'im down the steps goin' ta be tricky. Hold tha' gun steady now, boy."

"Auntie Elisabeth, I don't believe he's gonna be able to walk down those steps. He'll break his neck."

"Well, he ain't got no choice in tha matta. He's goin' ta jail."

Elisabeth leaned the agent against her and made him jump down the steps and waddle to the car. Roland held the gun, but its heaviness made his hands a bit shaky and his aim shifted from where Elisabeth wanted him to point the gun. Finally making it to the agent's car, Elisabeth opened the back door and pushed the agent forward and let him fall head first into the back seat. His legs were barely bendable so she had to use her good hand to shove the rest of his body in so she could shut the door. It would forever be a mystery as to how all of the neighbors slept through the calls for help the agent administered in the still darkness of that early morning. To no avail. Elisabeth got into the driver's side of the agent's car and managed to start it. She had Roland position himself on his knees in the front seat facing the back of the car. In that way, he could hold the gun on the agent while Elisabeth made her way to the courthouse to claim her citizen's arrest. She smiled broadly while driving with her captive safely in the back seat regardless of how disappointed she was that the car had no sirens or flashing blue lights.

"Auntie Elisabeth, you need to slow down. You gonna make me fall over. This here gun is heavy," Roland said to Elisabeth as she sped up the road.

"Jus' hang on, Roland, and keep ya hands tight ta that gun. We be almost to the courthouse."

"I'ma holding on as best I can, but you going so fast that I keep bouncing up and down. And G'ma gonna be mad you made me hold this here gun, Auntie Elisabeth."

"Boy, lemme worry 'bout Gertie. Ya thinkin' she'd want ta let some stran'ga jus' break inta the house?"

"No, ma'am," Roland responded.

Elisabeth took a sharp right and headed straight to the sheriff's office. She thought she had driven well considering she had a broken right hand. She slammed on the brakes and turned in to park. She had pretended that the speed bump she crossed before turning wasn't there forcing herself and Roland to lift up out of their seats and bump the top of the car. The agent, lying in the back seat, rolled into the floorboard and moaned in pain. When she stopped she saw Julia's truck parked outside the sheriff's back door.

"Look here. Julia's truck down here. Wonda wha' in the worl' she be doin' down here?" Elisabeth said out loud as if it was a thought inside her head.

Roland rubbed the top of his head and looked back at the agent who had rolled face down in the floor.

"Auntie Elisabeth, I think you killed that man. I don't hear him screaming anymore."

"He ain't dead, Roland. He prob'ly jus' fakin' bein' asleep. Now run inside and fetch yo' Aunt Julia and the sheriff. Go'ne now and hurry up back here."

Roland, still in his pajamas, scampered through the same heavy wooden door that Julia had entered a couple of hours earlier. He ran down the office and rushed past the sheriff's door and had to turn around and go back. When he entered, there was no one at the front desk and he began to look around for the sheriff. Confused with there being no one there, he called out for Julia.

Julia sat straight up in her chair and the sheriff stood up in his cell.

"Sheriff, that sounded like Roland. Nah, couldn't be. It's four o'clock in the mo'ning."

"Auntie Julia! Where are you?"

"Oh, damn, that is Roland. What he doin' here? Roland! In here! Folla my voice!"

Roland peeked around the corner where the jail cells were, feeling a little timid of who he might find. He had never seen a real jail before. Then, he smiled when he found Julia and rushed over to her.

"Aunt Julia, Aunt Elisabeth done caught a burglar and she brought him down for the sheriff to arrest."

Suddenly, Roland did a double take and realized Julia was handcuffed to the radiator and the sheriff was in a cell.

"Itta be okay, Roland. Go get Aunt Elisabeth and tell her me and the sheriff needs her in here to help us."

"She can't, Aunt Julia."

"Sho' she can. Just find her and tell her to come in here."

"But, she can't."

"Why can't she, Roland?" the sheriff asked him.

"Cause sheriff, she's holding a gun on the man she caught trying to break into the house," Roland answered.

"Who broke inta the house, Roland?" Julia asked.

"Some man named Agent. Auntie Elisabeth says she ain't never seen him before. Got him tied up in the back of his car and holding a gun on him."

"Well, damn, where did your Aunt Elisabeth get a gun? Did she take it from this guy?" the sheriff asked.

"No, sir, Auntie Elisabeth would never do anything bad like stealin'. She just took it outta her purse."

Julia readjusted herself in the straight back wooden chair the agent had put her in before he handcuffed her to the radiator. She was tired and most uncomfortable, but her adrenaline was now running on high.

"Listen, Roland. We gotta have yo' Auntie Elisabeth ta come in here right now. Tell her ain't no reason to worry about that man in the back seat. Tell her we need her to come in here and get me and the sheriff outta jail. Ya hear me, Roland? Tell her we in serious trouble, okay? Now, get out there and brin' her to us."

Roland nodded his head to let Julia know he understood. Soon afterward, he was off, again, to find Elisabeth. When he reached the back door where Elisabeth had parked the car, he was in for another surprise. Surrounding Agent's car were several other cars with strange men he didn't recognize. They had Elisabeth in handcuffs and they had let the burglar free. He was standing up straight and didn't have the clothes line around him any longer. He was angry enough to shoot Elisabeth, but he wouldn't dare do it with all of the other men there. Roland jumped behind the wooden door as they all marched in and walked straight to the sheriff's office. Auntie Elisabeth was saying words that he had never her say before. He would store them away for future reference.

Julia and the sheriff heard the ruckus coming up the hallway and heard Agent Robert Milan arguing with Elisabeth.

"Watch out fo' my hand, ya nasty summabitch. Ya know I hurt it and ya come ta ma house harrassin' me."

"Are you kidding me, lady? How can you say I was harassing you? You pointed a gun at my head and wanted to hog tie me after you forced me into your house. You are one crazy ole bat. And, you had a kid hold the gun on me while you put me in the back of my car. Look at me! I've pissed myself!"

"Yeah, an' ya startin' ta smell, too. I ain't neva seed a growed man piss hisself. Won't ya ask ya buddies ta go fetch a clean pair o' drawls?"

The men brought in to assist Agent Milan in searching the farm for an illegal distillery had to either turn around completely or cover their face in order not to laugh at the situation. Two men found it necessary to step out into the hallway and let out a howl of laughter. Elisabeth sat motionless without even cracking a smile.

"Hey! Do you think you can let me out of my own jail now?" came the request from the sheriff. "I'll try my best to hold my bladder!"

"You locked up the sheriff?" one of Milan's men asked him.

"Yes, I did. I was told that the sheriff and the sisters were close knit and I felt that to be a problem. As a matter of fact, I think he knew exactly what he was doing when he sent me over to this one's house," Milan said while pointing at Elisabeth.

"Well, I think it will be safe to let him out now," the man said.

"Oh, all right, let them out," Milan said.

"Them? How many do you have in there? The whole town?"

"No, of course not. Just the sheriff and one of the sisters," Agent Milan responded.

"Ya put one a' my sistas in jail? Ya no good bastard. Ya betta be glad ya took ma purse," Elisabeth said to Agent Milan.

Still handcuffed, Elisabeth sat at the table and Agent Milan stood over her. He leaned down to put his face in hers.

"I just might put your crazy ass in jail," Milan said to Elisabeth.

Elisabeth squinted her eyes at Milan and in one quick move forced her upper body back and gave a full thrust forward and had her head butt right into

Milan's. It sent him backwards where he landed against the counter in excruciating pain. Elisabeth, unscathed, regained her former composure as Agent Milan grabbed his head and fell to his knees blurting out expletives.

One of his fellow agents looked down at him and said, "Ooh, that's going to leave a mark."

"Oh, shut up! Go get the sheriff and see if the search warrant has gotten here!" Milan barked out, still in pain.

"Sure thing. Do you want the sister, too?"

"Yeah, if we have the search warrant. Damn if my head doesn't feel as if it was hit by a sledge hammer," Milan said as he tried to shake off the pain.

"Iffin' I had me a sledge hamma, ya wouldn't still be talkin'. Shouda shot ya when I had me the chance," Elisabeth said to Milan. "Wha' y'all tryin' ta search anyway. Ya already cased ma house. Betta hope nothin' comes up missin'."

Agent Milan slowly rose to his feet, still feeling a little shaky. He was careful not to get near Elisabeth. Julia and the sheriff entered the room. Julia was still cuffed, but the sheriff was free and pretty ticked off to have had his office taken over by what he considered to be an unlawful means.

Julia sat down beside of Elisabeth and the sheriff went behind the counter to check the fax. The search warrant was there. He handed it to Agent Milan.

"I don't know what kind of strings you pulled to get this, but you have your warrant," the sheriff told Milan.

"Well, that's marvelous. It looks like we can head on out to the farm and bust up an illegal still operation."

"A still!" Elisabeth yelled out. On the farm? Jus' a bunch of mo' foolishness, I say."

"Well, we'll see what you say after the search," Agent Milan said to Elisabeth. "You men ready to head out?"

"Sure, whenever you are," one of the men said to Milan.

The men were dressed in tactical gear. They wore camouflage suits with a large insignia on the back with large letters defining them as the ATF. Some of the men wore holstered guns and four others carried rifles in their arms. Their boots were military fashion. On the say so from Agent Milan, they headed off into battle with Julia, the sheriff, and Elisabeth in tow. Julia and Elisabeth were still in handcuffs, now though, they were cuffed with their hands in front of them. The sheriff was allowed to go without restraint, although they refused to allow him to carry his weapon.

Julia and Elisabeth sat in the car with Agent Milan. He tried to get Julia to talk as she had been very quiet while being at the station.

"Julia, all of this could go a lot easier if you would just give up what you know. A judge would go a lot easier on you if you just confess to owning a still. Easier on your sisters, too."

"Don' listen to nuttin' tha' fool gots to say. That bump on tha' head he took got 'im talkin' fool's talk."

Julia didn't say a word, but her mind was racing. She looked down at her cuffed hands and realized that they may never come off of her. For so many years, Mamie had gotten by with what now might be coming to an end. When those barn doors opened, the entire enterprise would be exposed for what it was. Mamie's last crop would go up in smoke.

"You're sweating, Julia. Are you feeling the pressure of what a jail might be like? You should be," Agent Milan said trying to feel her out.

The water on Julia's face was not what the agent thought. She had sweat rolling down her back from the plastic seats in the car, but the wetness on her face was not caused from sweat. Those were tears. Tears that held her fear and failure. Tears that could not be wiped away with the gentle stroke to the face. She remembered Mamie. Mamie had always told her to rely on her faith. Her faith would pull her through her darkest hour and sorrow. Julia figured this would have to be one of those times. She bowed her head and prayed harder than she had ever prayed in her life. It would take the grace of God and His performing some kind of miracle to get her through what lay in front of her in the next few minutes. She turned her head to stare out of the window, but felt that there was nothing for her to see.

The four vehicles pulled off the highway and turned to approach Mamie's farm. At four-thirty in the morning, everything should have been quiet, but things appeared to be out of the normal. Willie and Jake, the two farm hands were working the fields. Patrick and Jonathon were sitting on the back porch steps drinking coffee. They looked tired, but were rejuvenated when they saw the cars pull up. Agent Milan stepped out with two of his men. He left Julia and Elisabeth in the car. The sheriff walked over with Milan and the men from the ATF.

"Morning, sheriff," Jonathon said, "What brings you out this way so early in the morning? Is that Julia and Elisabeth in the car over there?"

"Yeah, Jonathon, that's them in the car. These here men are from the ATF. The Alcohol, Tobacco, and…"

"I know what it stands for, sheriff," Jonathon said, "but I don't know what they are doing here."

"We are here to search the place. If we could just round everyone up, we could get started," Agent Milan interjected.

"What exactly do you mean by rounding everybody up?" Patrick asked the men.

"Just what I said. Everybody on the premises as of right now needs to be put together. Let's just call it a meeting of the minds, okay?"

"I don't have a problem with it. Do you Jonathon?"

"Where is everybody?" Agent Milan asked.

"Nah. I'm good with it. Ava and her sister should be right inside in the house kitchen. I believe Gertie is down at the store kitchen or in the barn. Patience is still asleep. Willie and Jake are in the fields. And, you have Julia and Elisabeth over in the car. I believe that's it. Well, there's me and Patrick and we are right here. Can I get you gentlemen some coffee or a drink or something?"

"No, we have our own," one agent answered.

"I will certainly take a cup of coffee, Jonathon," the sheriff said, "I have been up all night. Could sure use it."

The request from the sheriff got a scornful look from Agent Milan for the sheriff breaking protocol. The sheriff knew it would anger Milan to accept a drink from a person subject to be searched. That was probably why he asked for it.

"If it's okay for me to move, I'll be happy to get the sheriff a cup of coffee," Patrick offered.

"The sheriff can wait, but thanks anyway," Agent Milan said. "Why don't we all head into the house so we can get everyone together. Sheriff, can I trust you to escort Miss Julia and Miss Elisabeth into the house?"

"Certainly, Agent Milan. Do you want me to get a set of handcuffs for all of these people or are you just going to keep these two in chains?"

"Stop being a smart ass, they can be released from the handcuffs now. Well, maybe that one with the broken hand should be restrained," Agent Milan said as he rubbed his throbbing head.

"I tell you what, Agent Milan, I'll protect you if she tries to hurt you, okay?" the sheriff said with a chuckle.

"Oh, shut up! I still think you set me up," Milan said to the sheriff.

"I figured a man from the ATF could handle a woman, especially one with a broken hand," the sheriff fired back at Milan as he walked to the car to retrieve Elisabeth and Julia.

"Gather up everybody on the premises, guys. Even the field hands. Check for people in all these buildings, and let's get this party started," Milan said, barking out orders like a drill sergeant.

329

And, so we gathered. I was with Ava and Gertie in the kitchen. Patience was awakened and brought down to sit at the kitchen table. Jonathon and Patrick were put in the parlor with Willie and Jake, the two farm hands who looked bewildered to be taken from their work. It was not the average day when men dressed in combat uniforms invaded your home. Those of us gathered in the kitchen and the parlor were startled, but relaxed. Julia and Elisabeth were brought into the kitchen still wearing the handcuffs. The sheriff had no key to unlock them. Julia looked at me and I smiled at her. So happy to see that she was here. In our home where she belonged. I knew she would be worried. We all were to some extent, but Julia did not know what we did, and she could not read our minds.

Jonathon and Patrick, along with Jake and Willie, were brought into the kitchen. We were all herded together in order for Agent Milan to explain to us why he and his men were there. He gave his key to the sheriff to unlock the handcuffs from Julia and Elisabeth. She rubbed her hand that had been cuffed. She appeared to be in pain, but she still managed to cuss like a sailor. She still had on her nightgown and large robe with deep pockets.

"Ladies and gentlemen, my name is Agent Robert Milan with the ATF. I am here with a search warrant to take a look around for, what has been reported to me, an illegal liquor distillery. We didn't bring a bunch of attorneys with us to interpret what all the legal jargon means, but we are going to leave it here on the table for all of you to take a gander at while we take a look around. One of my men will be present with you at all times. If you need something, ask us, and we will try to accommodate your needs."

"I gots me a question," Elisabeth said, raising her hand.

"Yeah, what is it?" asked Agent Milan.

"Are we gonna get to whoop yo' ass when y'all don' fin' no liquor still?"

"Sure, lady, you can whip my ass if I don't find anything illegal on this property," Agent Milan responded.

"That ain't what I axed ya. Ya said ya was here ta look fo' a still with illegal whiskey. Iffin' ya don' fin' none, I say we should get ta whoop ya ass."

"Okay, you ole crazy bat, it's a deal!" Agent Milan angrily said to Elisabeth.

"I done tol' you I wasn't ol' and ain't crazy neither."

"Calm down, Elisabeth. All of this nonsense will be over soon and these men can be on their way to wherever that might be," Gertie said to Elisabeth trying to comfort her.

"Well, I'ma hopin' it be straight back to hell, sista," Elisabeth said loudly as for Agent Milan to hear her.

"Right straight back to the fiery pits o' hell for eter'nal damanation. The lake of fire itself. Jus' burn, baby, burn," Elisabeth shouted in order to show her disgust for Agent Milan.

"Is she a minister or something?" Milan asked, trying to aggravate Elisabeth.

"No, she probably just missed her medicine. She has a broken hand and it is likely to be bothering her," Gertie explained. "If you would be so kind as to allow me to get her medicine for her, we would be ever so grateful, and I think it might calm her down."

"Oh, absolutely! Give her whatever you need to give her to get that mouth of hers shut." Agent Milan told Gertie.

Gertie opened the cabinet and took down Elisabeth's medicine the doctor had prescribed for her when she was in the ER for her broken hand. She opened the bottle and took out the prescribed dosage. She went to the sink and got a freshly washed glass and poured Elisabeth a glass of iced tea.

"Gertie," Julia said, "I'm thinkin' them pills needs ta be taken with food. Ya know, so not ta get her stomach upset. I believe they is some brownies in the white covered container that is Elisabeth's favorite. Should be a couple left."

Gertie knew about what brownies Julia spoke of. Those were some of the judge's special brownies. She looked at Julia with a puzzled look and asked, "You sure that her taking those special brownies would be okay, Julia?"

"I think so. Some food on her belly might be good fo' her."

Julia's eyes were telling Gertie to give Elisabeth the brownies. Those two brownies were the only thing in the house that contained any remnants of what they had grown in the barn. Julia knew their strength would not hurt Elisabeth. It would also destroy evidence.

"Just a minute. I need to take a look in that refrigerator before you open it," Milan advised Gertie.

"Certainly. Would you mind reaching me that white container while you're in there?" Gertie asked the agent.

Agent Milan picked up the container and opened it to ensure there were no weapons inside. Satisfied, he handed the container back to Gertie. She, then, placed the brownies on a plate.

"Those look very tasty," Milan said to Gertie.

"Oh, they are, would you like one?" Gertie asked and held the plate close to the agent's face.

Julia and the ones who knew what those brownies contained almost fell off their chair. Julia put her hand to her face and felt no relief from her anxiety until Agent Milan refused Gertie's offer. She set the plate in front of Elisabeth along with a glass of tea and her medicine. Elisabeth gladly took the medication and was grateful for the brownies. She devoured them and asked Julia if she had baked them.

"Uh, no. No, it musta been Sister Gist or one of the other ladies from the church that brung 'em. Jus' eat 'em up. They'll make ya feel betta."

"Hope they not put none of that there wil' parsley in 'em that you and Gertie been experimentin' with. Mamie always told us tha' wild parsley was a healin' 'erb. Always tasted bitta ta me. Neva cared too much fo' it ma'self. These be delicious. Goin' have ta tell Sister Gist she done a good job."

"You can tell her next time you see her, Elisabeth," Gertie said as she rubbed her back.

Patience was the only one who did not appear to be at all stressed at what was happening. She sat stolidly in her chair and had very little to say. Maybe, that was the lawyer in her or maybe, it was because she knew it was going to happen. We weren't sure. The fact that Patrick had sat next to Ava didn't seem to bother her either. Patrick laid his hand on his leg and Ava laid hers on her leg and their hands touched. Perhaps that went unnoticed to the rest of us, but Ava and Patrick felt a warm sensation just from being close to one another. Julia kept her eye on Patience. Patience could feel the icy stare, but refused to look back at Julia. Julia knew. And Patience knew she did.

Suddenly, there was a tap on the kitchen door. Agent Milan stepped up to answer the door. His body jumped to find a large female at the door who was large enough to be an effective defensive end on any football program. It was Bulldog Gist. Elisabeth saw her and was glad she dropped by.

"Speak o' the devil and up he pops. I's jus' talkin' 'bout you, Sista Gist. Ya out did yo'self on them brownies. They was good eatin'."

"Elisabeth, I ain't made no brownies. Who is all these white boys hangin' 'round here? Saw 'em lookin' through everythin' outside."

"Come on ova and pulls yo'self up a seat. Don' worry 'bout them fools. They say they come here lookin' fo' a whiskey still."

"Shut yo' mouth, a still? On Mamie Nesbitt's farm. That ain't neva goin' ta happen. That's crazy white folks, fo' ya. Elisabeth, ya got any mo' of them brownies? I could use a bite or two o' somethin'."

"Sorry, Bulldog, I eats 'em all up. Come on ova here and sit yo'self down."

"Elisabeth, I is sittin' down right 'chere aside ya."

"Well, good. Glad ya came by ta see us."

Bulldog looked over at Gertie and pointed at Elisabeth. "She all right, Gertie?"

"She's fine. Took some pain medicine. For her hand, you know," Gertie answered.

About that time, there was another tap on the kitchen door. Agent Milan looked frustrated and said, "What the hell is this?"

"It's our Mamie's home going, ya stupid bastard," Elisabeth yelled out to him.

This time it was one of the men who was out surveying the property. He huddled with Agent Milan in the corner of the kitchen to explain what he had found. They spoke lowly as so we could not hear, but by the shrugging of the agent's shoulders and his head moving from side to side, we interpreted that they had found nothing that was illegal. Agent Milan touched the man's shoulders and walked over to us sitting at the table.

"How many acres does this property consist of?" he asked all of us.

"Pert near thirty, give or take a foot or two," Julia answered.

"All right, then. My men have searched around the house and some of the out buildings. We still have a few places to search. We would like for Miss Julia and Miss Gertie to accompany us. An agent will stay with the rest of you while we take a look around."

Julia and Gertie stood up and walked slowly between Agent Milan and his other man. Julia still could not be positive of what the agents might find.

Gertie grabbed her arm tightly as though she felt uncomfortable being held prisoner.

"This way ladies," Agent Milan directed.

He headed towards the old barn. The smell was still as bad as it was when Patience was there. It didn't bother Gertie or Julia. It smelled like home and was familiar to them.

"What is inside of this building?" Agent Milan asked the two women.

"Hay, horse shit, pig shit, chicken shit. Ol' junk, mos'ly," Julia answered.

"We had a report that someone was distilling liquor in this old barn," Agent Milan stated.

"Must have been a long time ago. I think my granddaddy did make liquor at one time here on the farm. But, my goodness, that had to be before any of us was born. Mamie moved most of his still out to the flower beds and planted flowers in it. It was a pretty thing when it was all shined up," Gertie explained to him.

"What was it made of?" Agent Milan asked Gertie.

"Shined like a new penny. Copper, I guess it was. I thought there was a piece still in this old barn. Not sure. Why don't you send your men in to look?"

"Don't worry. We will check it all out," Milan retorted. "What is it that is in that huge barn down the way there?"

"Oh, that's the kitchen where we bake the goods we sell from the farm. And the big red building is the new barn," Gertie answered proudly.

"Let's take a walk down there if you don't mind," Agent Milan requested.

Julia and Gertie gave each other a soulful glance and walked slowly behind the agent.

"You keep it locked, I see. The other agent here will go and get the keys for the place. We will just stay here and wait on him."

It didn't take the agent long to get the keys. He was almost out of breath when he returned with a large key ring that must have held twenty keys. Julia recognized them as hers.

"I believe these to be your keys, Miss Julia. Would you do us the honor of unlocking the door to the barn?"

Julia hesitated to take the keys. She did not want to open the barn door to expose what could ruin her life as well as so many others. Gertie grabbed the keys and unlocked the large locks on the front of the barn. More of the men who had been searching the woods surrounding the farm had approached to enter the barn. Julia closed her eyes and Agent Milan pushed her inside.

Julia gasped and then took in a large deep breath. The weed was gone. All of it. Every last plant had been erased except for what lie on the center table underneath the large lights that magnified the white walls.

"Well, just what do we have here? This is quite an operation you ladies have got here. Whatever would this be that you are growing?" Agent Milan asked.

"Tomatoes, hydroponic tomatoes," Gertie said to the agent.

"Huh?" exclaimed the agent in an unexpected voice. This is not tomatoes!"

"Well, what did you think it was?" Gertie asked him.

"Marijuana! Damn it! This is marijuana!" the agent screamed.

"Marijuana? Agent, marijuana is illegal. What you see in here is tomatoes. We grow them. Mamie taught us how."

"Hey, Agent Milan, look over here at this. This is definitely not tomatoes on this table," one of his men said.

They walked over to the table and picked up a plant and held it out to Gertie.

"Well, you caught me on this one," Gertie told them. "This is definitely not a tomato. This is Texas hibiscus. In two growing seasons, it will have the prettiest flower on it. I think these will be white with a crimson red star right in the center. Can't leave them in here in the heat and lights too long. They like a lot of water and the shade. Here, Agent Milan, take one to your wife. She's sure to love it."

"All right. Let's get to the kitchen," Agent Milan instructed.

"Milan," one of the agent's said, "we checked it. It's clean. We've got nothing here. It's just a farm."

Agent Milan was infuriated with himself and those who he let betray him into wasting his time and all the trouble he was going to be in with his superiors. He stomped the ground with his leg and it must have hit too hard. He walked back to the top of the hill with a limp and a throbbing headache to boot. He walked straight to his car and drove off. He would have a lot to answer for.

The rest of the men packed their things and apologized to all of the people for the inconvenience. Julia told them to go. She was done with the entire situation. What she really wanted was to find out where in the world all of the marijuana had disappeared to. She also wanted to sit and figure out why she felt as though the weight of the world had been lifted off of her shoulders.

The Shoulders of Atlas

It was seven in the morning and Julia sat on the kitchen steps with a coffee cup in her hand, holding it close to her mouth; thinking as she rubbed the rim of the cup to her lip. Willie and Jake were back at their jobs in the field. Elisabeth had succumbed to the potency of the marijuana baked in the brownies and was snoring loudly on the couch inside. The rest of us were dressed to receive visitors, but sat on sofas and chairs with our heads bowed in sleep. Jonathon came outside and sat down close to Julia.

"Why aren't you asleep, Julia?" he asked her.

"I don' know. I 'spose I should be."

"Come upstairs and let me tuck you in."

"In a litta bit. I jus' want ta look at the farm for a while. I want ta breathe the air and stare at the clouds."

"Are you okay?"

"I guess I'm good. I'm not in jail so I 'spose maybe I am relieved 'bout that. I've looked out ova these fields all my life, but today they look diff'rent."

"How's that?" Jonathon asked her and put his arm around her.

"Don' ya think it's odd that I ain't asked ya 'bout the marijuana?"

"Yeah, it crossed my mind some. Why haven't ya?"

"I think part of me is glad ta not have it here and part of me feels guilty fo' feelin' that way."

Both Jonathon and Julia turned their head to see Ernie pull up in his truck with his grill to get the food started for the day. Julia shook her head.

"Look at ole Ernie. Do ya think he eva gets tired of cookin' fish for when people die? Me and Ernie got a lot in common. Evabody depends on us for somethin'. I wanna jus' depend on somebody else fo' a change," Julia said and laid her head on Jonathon's shoulder.

"Julia, I wouldn't feel so sorry for Ernie. I bet he pulls down over a thousand dollars a week easy. Cash money. Gets to eat everybody else's fish and all their food all the time. Drives a better truck than you do."

"Damn," Julia said, "I need ta get me a fish fryer."

"No, what you need to get is a vacation. You need to get away from this farm for a while. Maybe, on a honeymoon or something like that. It would sure answer the problems I have with some windshields."

"Now, that's not funny," Julia said as she laughed.

"Come down here with me. I wanna show you something," Jonathon said to Julia.

Jonathon pulled her up and wrapped his arm around her waist and they started walking toward the tobacco barn. They heard the house phone ring and someone yelled for Patience, telling her Judge Holcombe was on the phone for her. Julia didn't care. She just wanted to escape.

Jonathon opened the barn door and they walked inside. It was warm inside the barn and Julia began to wonder how in the world they removed all of the marijuana.

"Okay, ya have me curious, how'd all of y'all clear out the barn?"

"You can thank your little sister for that. Well, for knowing that something was wrong and that we had to clear out the barn."

How'd she know?" Julia asked.

"She said she had a feeling. I guess we all felt a little uncomfortable and knew something was out of whack for the sheriff to call you down to his office at such an odd time. Maybe that wasn't an accident he did that."

"Ya mean he tipped me off?"

"Possibly. I couldn't say that for sure, but he could have waited and just come out here with the agents."

"Yeah, I guess he could've at that."

"The one you really need to thank is Roland."

"Roland?" Julia asked. "Oh my goodness, where is Roland. So much goin' on I forgot all 'bout him."

"He's fine. He called Gertie from the police station. Gertie's neighbor went and picked him up and kept the kids at their house. But he told Gertie all about the man coming to the house and his adventures with Elisabeth."

"I haven't even heard all that yet. But what about all the weed? I don't see it 'round anywhere here?"

"You remember those tomatoes you just bought and had sitting outside of the barn?"

"Yeah, I jus' bought 'em."

"Yeah, well, you remember all that weed we just hung up to dry?"

"Yeah."

"We had to take all of it down. Got some stakes from the shed and rolled the hanging weed around the stakes and hauled it over to my grandmama's house. She's got that big barn that she don't use anymore. Then, we took all the seedlings and put those in my shop. I'm just glad they didn't go into the kitchen freezer and pay close attention to the butter. We didn't really have a place to store that except in the freezer. We didn't want to ruin Mamie's last crop."

"Well, mister, y'all did real good. Y'all did betta than I coulda done myself. Proud of ya. You all saved my life."

Julia wrapped her arms around Jonathon's neck and fell into him. He welcomed holding her up and could have stood there forever, but he knew it would never last. It never did. He had asked her to marry him so many times and she always had an excuse not to. He had no reason to think this would turn out any differently. He let go of her and started to walk away.

"Jonathon?"

"Yeah, Julia?" he said as he turned back toward her.

"Marry me?" Julia asked him.

Jonathon looked puzzled and wanted to pinch himself. He looked at her as though he was waiting on the punch line to a joke. Then, he realized from the look on her face, she might not be joking.

"Well, I don't know if I can, Julia. You know, I have got so many things I have to do. I got my business to run and I got my grandmother to take care of and who will clean my house and the do the shopping and..."

"Oh, shut up and marry me!"

"Will you wear my ring?" Jonathon asked her.

"Do you have it with ya?"

"Check my pocket," Jonathon told her.

"Oh, I'm not fallin' fo' that now!"

"Not my pants pocket, Julia. My shirt pocket."

"You got a ring with ya?"

"I've carried that ring around with me for five years hoping you would someday say you would be my wife."

Julia ran her hands across his chest and pulled a worn red velvet box from his shirt pocket and opened the ring box.

"Oh, wow, this is beautiful. Put it on my hand before I change my mind."

"My intentions were to get on one knee and ask you the proper way, but I'm afraid you will change your mind, so give me that hand."

Jonathon put the ring on her finger and Julia looked down at her hand.

"It feels right, ya know. It jus' feels right."

"Come on, let's go give your family some good news. They probably could use it."

Half way back to the house, Jonathon picked Julia up and carried her. He couldn't believe that she was wearing his ring, now her ring. Their ring. When they stepped into the kitchen, everyone glared at Julia's hand. At first, they were afraid to say anything, but Julia finally told them it was official. She and Jonathon were engaged. We gathered around her and took turns looking at the ring. We were so glad that it finally happened. The men congratulated

Jonathon with hugs and handshakes. Julia looked around and noticed someone missing from the crowd.

"Where is Patience?" Julia asked into the crowd.

"She got a phone call from Judge Holcombe. He wanted her to come down to his office. She mentioned something about the will. She didn't seem concerned," Gertie explained.

"Julia, the funeral home called, too. They said you might want to come down there. Actually, they asked for the family," Gertie told her.

"Did they tell ya what it was all about?" Julia asked.

"No, not much. Just that we should get down there."

"Oh, Lord, what can go wrong now?" Julia said wiping her forehead. "All right, I guess we betta load up and head down there."

Julia rode with Jonathon. I drove Elisabeth's car with Gertie and Elisabeth. Patrick drove Ava in the farm truck. We left the house in the charge of the church members we trusted and knew could handle the crowds of visitors.

We pulled up to the funeral parlor and exited the various vehicles. Everyone kept their eye on Patrick and Ava. We shook our heads not knowing quite what to think of the two of them. We were happy in one way, but sister to sister rivalry never ended pleasantly, especially with Patrick being married to Patience.

We walked inside and went into the office. The secretary was the only one in at the time, but she was familiar with why the family was called in. Julia spoke for the family.

"What's the problem, Ruby?"

"Well, Julia, there's some conflict with the burial expenses. Mamie had everything picked out, and we understand that the will was read and everything was distributed. However, we haven't received any payment from that yet. The cost of the funeral is quite expensive and we will have to have a large portion of it placed down and well, with your good name, I am sure we can work out arrangements.

"I understand, Ruby. Y'all can't work fo' free. How much are we required to put down?"

"Well, Julia, the final cost is well over fifteen thousand dollars. How much can you afford to put down?" Ruby asked. "And, please understand that when the life insurance policy goes through, you will get this money back. I hope this doesn't put the family in a bad way, but I have to know how much you can pay today."

A timid voice came out of nowhere and said, "All of it."

We all looked around and found that it was Ava that had said we would pay the cost in full.

Gertie took her by the arm and said, "Ava, maybe you must have misunderstood. They need to know how much we could all put down to pay for the full fifteen thousand dollars."

"I understand, Gertie. I'd like to pay it all," Ava said quietly, almost in a whisper.

"Ava, you ain't got that kinda money," Julia said to her.

Ava stepped up to the window where Ruby sat. She put her purse on the counter and opened it. Then, she pulled out a wad of money. She counted out fifteen thousand dollars. We all stood in awe as we watched her put all of that money on the counter. We looked at each other and were dumbfounded.

"Ava, where did you get that kind of money?" Gertie asked her.

"Grew it," Ava answered.

"No, Ava, seriously, where did you get all of that money?" Patrick asked her.

"I told you. I grew it."

Ava continued her business and made sure the balance of the funeral was paid in full. She signed where Ruby told her to and closed her purse and acted as though she was the only one in the room. She started to walk out of the building with the rest of the family trailing behind her with bewildered faces.

"Patrick," Julia said to him, "I think Ava needs ta be ridin' back with me and Jonathon.

"Sure, Julia," Patrick told her.

Patience drove to Judge Holcombe's office a little concerned about why he would be calling her. She pulled up on Main Street and parked the car. She got out and straightened her skirt, rubbing out the wrinkles trying to make herself look presentable. She opened the front door and walked in expecting to be greeted by Alvin. She was more than surprised to see Alvin's desk vacant. It looked as though no one had ever used it. It was a bare desk with a plain wooden chair waiting for someone to occupy it.

The judge's door was open and she could see that he was there. His head was bent downward looking over documents. She tapped lightly on the glass panel of the door and was greeted with a warm smile from Judge Holcombe.

"Patience, come in. Have a seat. Can I get you something to drink?" the judge asked her.

"Uh, no, your honor, I am fine, thank you. Here, my sister, Gertie, asked if I could bring this package to you. She said something about brownies."

"Oh, wonderful. Make sure you thank Gertie for me. I'm not usually in my office this time of the morning, but I did manage to make coffee. Are you sure I can't get you some?"

"I'm sure. Thank you, though. If you don't mind me asking. I noticed that Alvin's desk looked as though it had been completely evacuated. Is he no longer working here?"

"No, Patience, I had to let him go."

"I see. I thought with him being your grandson and all, he might want to stay in Cookham and take over your law office, I mean, maybe become a partner or something like that."

"No, I don't think I could allow that. Somehow or another Alvin got it in his head that he could move to Washington and make a name for himself. I told him how difficult that could be, but he was determined to go. I suppose you know what Washington is like. Perhaps, maybe I should have had you speak to him, but that is all water under the bridge now."

"Yes, I suppose so. Judge Holcombe, why did you want to see me today?"

"Patience, your grandmother and I were very good friends. I knew all about her life and she knew about mine. All she ever wanted for her granddaughters was for each of them to be happy and successful in whatever they chose to do with their lives. She was proud of you. She thought you were successful as an attorney in Washington. Maybe she didn't realize."

"What do you mean?" Patience asked and shifted in her seat.

"I ran a credit check on you, Patience."

"I beg your pardon. Why would you ever do anything like that?"

"I know the will that we read with the family was not accurate," Judge Holcombe said and leaned back in his leather chair. Mamie wanted the life insurance money to be split between all of the sisters, except for you. But I think you already knew that didn't you? Before you convinced Alvin to change it?"

"I don't know what Alvin told you, but I absolutely never told him to change anything in the will!"

"No, not technically. But you did ask him to give me the wrong one which had you in the will, didn't you?"

"No, of course not." Patience began to sweat. "Judge Holcombe, you know me. I have never touched Mamie's will. I am just without words as to why you would accuse me…"

Patience stopped talking when the judge reached into his desk drawer and pulled out a tape. The same tape that Alvin had recorded the day she had come in to see him.

The judge laid the tape on his desk and once again leaned back in his chair. He looked at Patience with an almost sympathetic look.

"Are you sure that's what you want to stick to?"

"Judge, what are your intentions in regard to the tape?"

"Patience, you could lose your license for this. Actually, you could go to jail. Alvin should go to, but you gave him good advice in just saying that he made a mistake."

"Have you told my sisters?"

"Most of them know."

"And I suppose they want me disbarred and stuck back here on the farm?"

"Quite the contrary. They want you to leave and not return. They want you to keep the money and just go. Pretty good sisters, I would say. But if you keep the money, you cannot ever hold any claim to the farm or the house. And, you will also call off any searches you might have planned for any illegal activity you allege going on at the farm."

"Julia agreed to all of this?"

"Julia, Ava..."

"Of course, Ava would, she just considers the money a down payment for my husband."

"You can always decline their terms, Patience. You could trade the money for your family."

"Are they going to allow me to attend Mamie's funeral?"

"Yes, but you are to leave as soon as it's over."

"Then, I suppose I will agree to what they want."

"You understand that you will lose your family after this?"

"I have Patrick. He and I will go back to Washington and move forward from there."

"That, of course, is up to him and you, too, I suppose. However, there is one stipulation that I will put into all of this."

"And what is that?" Patience asked.

"Alvin needs a ride to D.C."

Patience hung her head and pondered the decision she had before her. She had not been to this town in years and she would surely not miss it. Mamie was gone and with her went everything she had left here. Still, the idea of family had to mean something. People asked her about her family. If she took the offer, there would be nothing she would have to say. She would only have Patrick and they didn't exactly have a relationship to speak of. Just as she had not seen Mamie in years, she knew she was there if she needed her. It was a hard decision to make. They weren't much, but they were her family. She could tell the judge she had changed her mind and the whole thing with the will truly had been a mistake. She lifted her head and looked Judge Holcombe in the eyes.

"Tell Alvin to be packed and ready to leave town as soon as the funeral is over tomorrow."

"I have some papers for you to sign."

"What happens to the tape?" Patience asked.

"I'll hold onto that. I will see that it is properly taken care of."

Patience gathered her purse, signed the documents, and walked out of the office. She didn't look back.

The Madder Hatters

Pastor Washington came through with arranging to have Mamie's funeral at the local Baptist Church instead of our own church that was much too small to hold the expected overflow of people. As Cookham was a small town, we all knew everybody anyway. We felt at home there.

The family sat in the front of the church. Elisabeth and Gertie sat side by side. Stunning to us all, Roosevelt Hendrix sat on the other side of Gertie. He was, after all, still her husband and over the years, grew to have a deep respect for Mamie and Mamie for him. Roosevelt knew he should be fine as long as he kept out of Elisabeth's line of fire which he had no intentions of crossing.

Jonathon sat by Julia and they held hands like they were in high school. Everyone commented on their engagement and were happy they were finally making it official. I sat beside of Julia with Ava and Patrick, in that order, beside me down the pew. Patience sat on the other side of Patrick. She was with us, but remained so far away. She was not one of us now. I had only four sisters. In a sense, it felt that we were burying two family members that day.

The church was filling to capacity. We received condolences from family and friends and returned their attendance with pleasantries and smiles that thanked them for being there. We had seen most of them out at the farm during Mamie's week long visitation period where we shared plates of fish and grits and so many other foods that we still felt stuffed to the gills.

After the past several days that we had endured, today felt almost relaxing to us. We were calmer and more accepting that we could survive without Mamie holding us together. We could now rely on each other for everyday sisterly advice with Mamie's memory set securely and forever in our minds. She had taught us well and we would survive as long as we held tightly onto the lessons she taught us. Not to mention, the money she had left us.

The drive home from the funeral parlor after watching Ava pay all that cash for Mamie's final expenses proved to be quite productive for us. Julia coaxed Ava into explaining where she got the fifteen thousand dollars that she shocked all of us with when she pulled it out of her purse. The flower beds turned into money trees. Ava had known that the coffee cans underneath the flowers she so loved to tend and keep looking picturesque were filled with thousands of dollars. She had stumbled across them while transplanting new flowers from pots to the flowerbed ground. I imagine that was her and Mamie's little secret that Ava had kept quite well. It also explained the note that Mamie had left for Julia in the event Ava really did keep the secret about where the money lay hidden. Jonathon and Julia had found about thirty cans as of the day of Mamie's funeral totaling over five hundred thousand dollars. There were still more cans to be found, but we would discover how much later. Today was a tribute to Mamie, and we owed her a fine tribute.

As I usually did, I turned to survey the crowd and was astonished at the carnival like atmosphere on display in the church. The hatters had returned with large elaborate adornments on their heads. Today it was not the black women who strutted with pride wearing a vibrant array of designer hats, it was the white women. Some much more elaborate than others, but odd they all were. I nudged Julia to look at the parade. Amy Rogers must have been proud of herself for putting all of these hats together. Some of them would put the black ladies to shame. They kept touching them and adjusting them to their heads in order to bring attention to themselves. That, however, was unnecessary, not a soul in the place could miss them. Their hats were as hideous as those worn by the black folks. Mrs. Tisdale's hat looked as though she had taken down her bedroom curtains and wrapped them around her hat. When we saw the hooks on her hat, we no longer had to be convinced that was exactly what she had done. Hat decorating would become Cookham's new fashion trend and newest competitive field. My sisters and I would not be entering that competition.

Alvin, however, appeared to have already gotten into the spirit of the upcoming rivalry. He was there and on his head was his typical top hat, but today with a zebra print with a red carnation adorning the hat band. The disgust on Patience's face made Julia and I chuckle, now knowing that he would be traveling to Washington with her.

Gertie and Elisabeth chatted in whispers to themselves. One of our distant relatives, Dominica held a rosary in her hand. Elisabeth thought the young cousin had broken her necklace, but with an injured hand herself, would be unable to assist her in fixing it. She asked Gertie if she could go and help her fix her beautiful black pearl beaded necklace that appeared to Elisabeth to have a cross as a medallion on it.

"That is not a necklace, Elisabeth. It is a rosary," Gertie explained to her.

"A what?" Elisabeth asked.

"It is a chain of beads that Catholic people pray with. Each bead represents a prayer."

"I ain't neva heard of no such thang."

"Just don't make a big deal out of it, Elisabeth. Her beliefs are different from ours, but she is a lovely girl."

"Well, all I can says is that I got Jesus in ma heart and don't need no beads to be prayin' to the Lord. Hallelujah! Now that's what I be talkin' 'bout."

"Calm down, now Elisabeth. We are at Mamie's funeral and there's not going to be an altar call this morning. You understand me?" Gertie asked to make sure Elisabeth understood.

"Well, now ya know how it be when the spirit hits me, sista, I gots to move wit' it."

Elisabeth began to voluntarily shake her body to demonstrate how she could move.

"I understand, Elisabeth, but today is a solemn occasion and we aren't going to be dancing today. Now I want you to sit still and stop moving around so much so you won't hurt your hand. Here, rest in on my arm."

"I'm gonna res' it up fo' now, Gertie, but I jus' have gots ta tell ya I ain't feelin' no comfort within' that girl, cousin or no, holdin' 'em pagan beads in here now."

"Elisabeth, that is her religion and we are not going to judge her for worshiping the Lord the way she chooses. Just don't look her way and focus on the service. Look at all of the wonderful people who came to see Mamie off for her home going. Isn't that a beautiful thing?"

"Sho' be, Gertie, 'ceptin' for all them ugly hats they be wearin'. Table cloths and sheets on they head. Drainin' ma spirit outta me."

"Well, then, keep on looking at them," Gertie said as she rubbed Elisabeth's arm. "Mamie certainly did get a lot of flowers, didn't she Elisabeth? She would have loved to have had all of these in her garden. Mamie sure loved her flowers."

"Ya know what, Gertie?"

"What's that, Elisabeth?"

"I ain't neva gots my gun back from tha' gov'ment man."

"Oh, Elisabeth, this is really not the time to think about things like that."

"Jus' lettin' ya know I gots it on ma mind."

Gertie began to rub Elisabeth's arm a little firmer. She couldn't tell Elisabeth that she knew exactly where the gun was. Elisabeth was one person who did not need to have anything of the sort around her. It would stay where it was buried. Right in the flower bed where the Julia had dug up so many of the coffee cans. Jonathon had removed all of the bullets and wrapped the gun in an old burlap sack. We said a little prayer that evening and that was for Elisabeth to never find or ever want a gun again. We put the gun in the ground and filled the hole in with dirt and then placed a pile of rocks on top of it. Jonathon and Patrick gave the gun its last rites and rolled a large stone over the ground it was buried in to mark the spot. We were all relieved that it would not be in her possession again. We gave Ava the chore to make the large rock part of the scenery with planted flowers and vines to cover it. She gladly agreed with a smile.

Suddenly, we heard a commotion coming from the back of the church. We couldn't see, but we all turned in that direction and found ourselves bobbing and weaving to see above and around the women's hats. Seemed that a man was screaming.

"Oh, Lord have mercy. Ann, she done tore off my bandages from ma face with that big ole hat she be wearin'. Somethin' on it done near poked out ma eye! Lord, help me, death caused by a hat."

Amy Rogers then appeared with a hat larger than any of us had ever seen. It looked like an entire village could take shelter underneath it, and it had more lights on it than Main Street at Christmas. She could barely keep her balance from the volume of decorations she had on the hat. We just supposed that she would have to outdo everyone else at the funeral to advertise her fashion accessory business. We had to laugh when the church elders asked her to park her hat outside. It was a first for any of them to ask a female to remove their hat. The black women smiled as she had to retreat in disgrace.

We all had a good chuckle over that. I thought that I had even seen Patience crack a smile, but I guess she had her mind on other things.

The choir gathered on the stage behind where Mamie's coffin sat. It was closed. Somehow that made it easier for us. Part of us could imagine that she was not inside and was still back at the farm. Except for Patience, we all held hands and became one as a family.

The choir sang and much to Elisabeth's joy, Pastor Washington did not give the eulogy. He was broken up over Mamie's death himself and was suffering from a case of laryngitis. Reverend McCallister preached Mamie's funeral service and it was a peaceful message. We felt soothed and melancholy at its conclusion. Then, it was time for the coffin to be opened and visitors would walk by the open casket and speak to the family sitting on the front row of the church as they passed. Since the church was packed, this would take over an hour to accomplish barring any breakdowns or emotional outbursts. That did not happen. So many people respected Mamie that they let love fill their hearts and their concern was for us.

Judge Holcombe was one of the first people to come by. He had a difficult time walking so we each went to him for hugs and to accept his condolences. He had tears streaming down his face which made us tear up, too. Julia took a tissue and wiped his face and assured him that everything was going to be okay and thanked him for all he had done for us and for being such a wonderful friend to Mamie.

He nodded and said little. He took hold of his young wife's hand and proceeded to his car where he would be in the funeral processional to Mamie's gravesite to attend her graveside service. The final farewell. Many others passed and we shared personal exchanges of hugs and thoughts. After the final person walked out of the church, we gathered our belongings and made our way to the family car to lead the funeral processional to the grave site. We exited through a separate side door where a limo awaited us.

If the rest of the day could go along as smoothly as the funeral itself had, we would be a very happy family. Unfortunately, things did not usually run on that smoothly of a course.

The Processional

Patience managed to be the first one to get out the side door of the church. As Patrick walked by her, she grabbed his arm and pulled him closely to her,

"Patrick, I don't think we should ride in the family car with the rest of them," Patience said with her head lowered.

"And, just why is that, Judas? Maybe because you sold them out for a few pieces of silver?"

"Patrick, in just a few minutes, we will be out of Cookham and back to our lives in Washington. I will go back to my job and you have your old job waiting on you. We don't belong here. We are better than this town. Mamie was the only reason I came back at all."

"Yeah, right, don't forget about the silver, Patience. Don't kid yourself and don't lie to me. You came for the money."

"Look, Patrick, let's not argue right here. Not today. Just ride with me in our car to the cemetery. We can talk about everything else later. Please. I had the funeral director put our car right behind the church van. Please, just do not make a scene here, just do this. I am begging you."

"Because I respect your family, I will ride with you, Patience. But you shouldn't get accustomed to having your way with me. Just remind me later to send my mother a sympathy card."

"What in the world for?"

"To express how sorry I am for not knowing you were a bitch a lot sooner than she did."

Patrick and Patience got into their car. Patience decided to drive. Patrick looked in the back and noticed that their luggage was in the SUV.

"Patience, what are all of our things doing in the car?"

"I thought we would leave from the graveside service. We have a long way to travel and I thought we could get an early start. Besides, I know you must be anxious to get back," Patience said as she looked in the rearview mirror to check her mascara.

Patrick leaned against the passenger's side mirror and slumped on his arm lying against it. He caught a glimpse of Ava and managed to give a weak wave in her direction.

"Ava is beautiful. You're not the first one to fall for her, Patrick. You won't be the last. She would just use you up and toss you aside just like she's done all the rest. She's like a siren without the song."

"You obviously don't know her at all, Patience."

"I know her well enough. You'll get over her, Patrick. Everybody does."

Patrick felt tears welling up in his eyes. He wanted to be in the car with Ava.

There seemed to have been a mix-up with the funeral planning. All of us with a guest would never have comfortably fit in one limo. We had ordered two, but only one was parked outside. We would make do. We did not want to make the guests who were already in processional order wait for another family car to arrive. We decided to let Elisabeth and Gertie ride in the family car with Franklin and Ann. There was room for a couple of others, but Julia and Jonathon decided to follow in Jonathon's truck. I rode with them. Ava, finally accepting that Patrick was going to ride with Patience got into the family car with Gertie and Elisabeth. Roosevelt rode in the family car, but chose to ride up front with the driver. He knew the best thing between himself and Elisabeth was distance.

The director knocked on the family car window and asked if there was space for one more in the car. Gertie told him that they would make room for someone to fit. It was our cousin, Dominica.

"Oh, nah, it be that damn pagan wantin' in here. Don' let 'er in, Gertie. She tryin' ta be puttin' a spell or somethin' on us," Elisabeth said voicing her objections.

"No, she won't, Elisabeth. She's family and you should respect her."

Dominica got into the car and thanked everyone for allowing her to ride. After a full hour of getting everyone in a car and lining all the cars in formation, we finally started moving very slowly to the cemetery. For all of the time that we put into the funeral processional, we probably could have walked the five miles to the cemetery where Mamie was to be buried which was on the ground behind our home church. We were about to lay Mamie to rest in one of the very graves that we considered in our youths to be a murderous villain's hiding spot. I wondered if my sisters had thought of that.

The drive was slow and mournful. Even Elisabeth and Franklin sat still for the ride without arguing amongst themselves. That was most likely because Elisabeth kept her eye on Dominica who was still holding her rosary with her head bent down moving the beads through her fingers. Elisabeth refused to turn her head in the event Dominica said something she would have to sling her purse at her for. Gertie was careful to keep her eye on Elisabeth's purse even though she had remembered to remove the razor from it the night before. Elisabeth was spry for her age and Gertie never knew what to expect from her.

What had started out a very clear day, suddenly became overcast. Large drops of rain begin to fall on the windshields and highway. I don't think I had ever been to a funeral when it hadn't rained. Mamie would have called them teardrops. They began to fall heavier to the ground. The sloshing sound of the windshield wipers had a rhythmic pattern to their back and forth movement.

We had moved only about two miles before we came to a four way stop in the road. We all saw the car coming towards the family car, but could do nothing to slow it down. The rain on the roads mixed with the oil had made the roads like ice. We sat motionless in our seats as we watched the speeding car hit the family limo that carried our sisters. As Julia and I screamed out for Gertie and Elisabeth, Patrick called out for Ava. There was nothing we could do except run to the limousine which was now turned on its top spinning in the middle of the road.

"Hail Mary! Full of Grace!" Dominica kept screaming while she ran her beads though her hands and fingers.

Elisabeth had been tossed almost on top of Dominica and looked at her like she was looking at an escapee from a mental institution. Dominica continued to call on Mother Mary. Elisabeth did what she thought was right and slapped Dominica a hard slap to the face that Dominica was sure to never forget. Confused as to why Dominica was calling on Mary, Elisabeth made the effort to set the record straight and said with a determined voice, "Mary! Mary? Jus' who in tha hell is Mary? Girl, in times like this, ya need a man! You betta call on Jesus!"

Dominica began to cry and hold her face where Elisabeth slapped her.

"Elisabeth! Move over and get away from that girl before you kill her!" Gertie yelled out to her.

"I can't, Gertie! Got somethin' on the toppa me."

It was Uncle Franklin. His face bloodied by some broken glass. Ann, shook her head and said, "Franklin, you jus' bound and determined to put out one of your eyes."

By this time, the car stopped spinning on its top and everyone began to collect their bearings. The church van that was lined up right behind the family car had rammed into the back of the limo and as people started making their way free, they began to lie down in the middle of the road screaming that they thought their backs were broken. We made our way to find Elisabeth, Gertie, and Ava. Ambulances had already been dispatched to the scene along with the town's two fire trucks.

Patrick reached the car first and managed to pull Ava free from the wreckage. He caressed her face and assured her she was fine, but would need to see a doctor to make sure. He put her securely in my arms and went in to get Gertie and Elisabeth out of the damaged car. Elisabeth managed to come out of a side window with a few minor scratches, but Gertie was unable to move one of her legs. She thought it was broken. They thought it would be better to wait for an ambulance and the firemen to get there before they tried to move her. As we sat there huddled together, Patience sat alone in her vehicle.

Cookham had not seen this large of a disaster in a long time. Everyone was accounted for. Roosevelt stayed with Gertie to keep her calm until more help had arrived. All of a sudden, we noticed that something was missing. The hearse carrying Mamie's body. It was nowhere to be seen. After we had collected ourselves and thought about it, we couldn't remember the hearse stopping after the accident. Could it be possible that the hearse had continued driving to its destination without even having noticed that the accident had occurred? On that day, we couldn't rule anything out. We wondered if the driver was at the cemetery waiting on us.

Patience had maneuvered her car around the mess in the road and screamed for Patrick to come over to her.

"What, Patience?" Patrick demanded.

"I am going to go on ahead to the burial. Why don't you go with me and we can leave from there. I can visit Mamie's grave, say good-bye, and put things to rest."

"Are you kidding me, Patience? Gertie isn't even out of the wrecked car yet? Are you just going to leave and not know what happened or if she's okay?"

"It's better this way, Patrick. Now get in the car."

"No, I can't do that. These people need us to be here."

"They don't need me and they don't need you. You are married to me, Patrick, not them," Patience said pointing to us gathered in the road.

"We should stay, Patience."

"You should get in the car before I make a scene bigger than the one that is out here right now!" Patience said beginning to get loud.

Patrick shuffled his feet and really did not want to cause more stress for the sisters than they already had going on. He walked to the passenger's side of the car and got in. He rode off with Patience with his head hanging low thinking that would disallow anyone to be able to see him leave. He didn't look back.

It was becoming obvious to us that Mamie's graveside service would not take place that day. We could hear sirens and then more sirens coming toward us. They managed to get Gertie out of the family limo and stabilized. Roosevelt offered to ride in the ambulance with her to the hospital. Elisabeth pushed him back and told him she would be the one riding with Gertie. Julia made her way to the funeral director and told him that she would like for Mamie to go ahead and be put into the ground with a service to be held on a later date. Maybe, even tomorrow depending on how things went with Gertie. He understood and phoned ahead to his men at the gravesite to carry out the family's wishes.

Afterwards, we sisters piled into Jonathon's truck and made our way to the hospital. When we arrived, the ER looked like Grand Central Station. I was becoming a little too familiar with this hospital. A lot more familiar than I ever wanted to be.

We looked like Moses trying to part the waters among all of the people blocking us from Gertie. Fortunately, we heard Elisabeth in what sounded like an argument with someone. It just so happened that someone was Uncle Franklin. We weren't exactly what anyone could call surprised.

"Oh, why don' ya shut yo' trap, Franklin. They ain't nothin' wrong wit' ya anyways. Gertie here be the sick one. Ya ole greedy bas'tard," Elisabeth was telling Uncle Franklin as we pulled back the curtain to see Gertie lying in the hospital bed.

"Oh, Gertie!" Ava exclaimed when she saw Gertie in the bed.

"It's all right, darling. We are just waiting for the x-ray to come back. The doctor will be here soon. Don't you be worrying yourself," Gertie said, comforting Ava.

"Has the doctor already been in here?" Jonathon asked.

"Oh, yeah, he sho' has. I had to go and fetch 'im," Elisabeth told us.

"What she means is that she pulled him in here against his will, taking him from another patient," Gertie added.

"He be ova there wit' Franklin. Y'all know he ain't got nothin' wrong wit' 'im. Jus' fakin' ta get some insurance monies. I ain't worried 'bout tha' ole fool."

"I can hear ya ova there, 'Lisabeth, runnin' that mouth as us'ule," Franklin argued.

"How are you feeling, Gertie?" I asked as I leaned over her and kissed her forehead.

"Not too bad, darling. They gave me a shot of something so I feel relaxed. They need to give Elisabeth something to calm her down."

"Ya got that right, Gertie," Uncle Franklin added.

"Min' ya own bis'ness, Franklin an' keep ya'self outta ourn," Elisabeth yelled backed at him through the curtain.

Julia stood back and just shook her head. She wrapped one of her arms around Ava and laid her head on Jonathon's arm. If it had not been for his strength, she may not have made it through the ordeal of the last week. She loved him, and she didn't have to ask herself if she was sure.

The nurse came in to check on Gertie and found her to be comfortable and relaxed. We were still waiting for the doctor to come and advise us concerning the x-rays. The nurse assured us that it should only be a few minutes.

Jonathon stepped outside of the hospital cubicle and closed the curtain. He followed the nurse and asked, "Pardon me, ma'am, could I just ask a question?"

"Certainly, Jonathon, and don't call me ma'am, you make me seem older than I feel," the nurse replied.

"Well, I was just wondering, does the hospital have a chapel in it?"

"Sure, at the end of the hall. But, Jonathon, I'm not a doctor, but I really don't think Gertie is anywhere near what you might be thinking."

"Oh, no, no, no. That had never crossed my mind. I was actually wondering, too, if there might be a minister on call."

"Well, with all of the chaos we have going on today, I wouldn't be surprised if there was one on every corner of the hospital, Jonathon. Why do you need to know, if you don't mind me asking?"

"Yeah, Jonathon, what is going on that you need a chapel and a minister?" I asked him stepping up from behind him.

"Well," he said, "I thought that since I have most of the family already assembled and I have a chapel, then if I could get a minister, I might have a bride ready to marry me."

"But, today? Now? Here?" I asked.

"Why not?" Jonathon asked. "If I wait, she might change her mind. And I can't live through that again."

"Well, does she know what your plans are?" the nurse asked. "I have always thought that letting the bride in on the plans was a good idea."

"You would have to ask me that, wouldn't you? Looks like I am going to have to ask her. Well, here goes."

Jonathon stepped back inside the cubicle and took Julia's hand. Gertie could see that there was a light in his eye. She smiled and looked at Julia.

"Julia, if we can find a minister, I want you to marry me right here at the hospital. There, I said it and I hope you don't say you won't because I think it is the right thing to do. I love you, Julia."

"Jonathon, that's just crazy. Gertie is sick. We can't get married now."

"Just why can't you?" Gertie asked.

"Well, because, we're just not ready for a wedding," Julia responded.

"I don't see why not. It's not like we would have to send out invitations. Julia, you told me you didn't want a large wedding with all of the thrills. You don't want the white dress. You wanted to keep it as simple as possible."

"Jonathon, we don't have a license to get married," Julia said looking for reasons to not take the plunge.

"Are you serious? We have several. Do you even know how many times we planned to get married and you always backed out?"

"Come on, Julia. Let's have a wedding! We have a few cuts and bruises, but we would have something going on with one of us regardless of when a wedding was planned," I told her.

"I don't know," Julia said wrestling with the idea. "We ain't got no minister. And Gertie is sick. I can't get married with Gertie not there."

"Okay, here is the deal. If we find a minister or somebody to perform the ceremony and Gertie is able to make it, then will you marry me right here and right now?" Jonathon asked.

"Yes, she will," Gertie answered.

"Yep, I agree, too, she will," I said.

"Do it, Julia," Ava added.

"Ya betta marry that guy fo' he turns 'round and walks outtta here."

The curtain opened and it was the nurse Jonathon had asked about the chapel. She had a large smile on her face.

"I couldn't find a minister, but I did find somebody willing to marry you that I am sure could make it legal," she told us.

Judge Holcombe stepped into the cubicle with the use of a cane. He looked at Julia and asked, "Will I do?"

"He's perfect, Julia!" Jonathon said in excitement.

"Oh, I don't know," Julia said turning the engagement ring around on her finger. "What would Mamie thinka all this?"

"She would be happy," Judge Holcombe said to Julia as he gently placed his hand on her shoulder. "I can honestly say that this would be one union she would actually be happy about."

We all agreed. He had a point on that. Mamie was never too keen on who her granddaughters had picked to marry, but she liked Jonathon.

The ER was filling with excitement over the news of a wedding. Some of the hospital staff was preparing the chapel with flowers. For an impromptu event, it looked rather nice, even if Julia had to admit it.

Gertie's leg was not broken. It was severely bruised and she would need bed rest for a week or so with physician follow-up, but it was not broken. She was allowed to attend the wedding in a wheelchair. We all stood by Julia looking like characters from the Battle Hymn of the Republic. Uncle Franklin, still looking like a mummy was present with his wife, Ann, who had her head bandaged from a cut she took to the head. Ava had a few cuts, but nothing serious. She wore only a few bandages. And there was Elisabeth posing in the wedding photograph with her ever present middle finger flying high in the air for all to see. There were not many people who had a morgue technician take their wedding portraits. But regardless of everything, we loved all of it. We loved every memory we had made. That broken circle was finally coming a little closer to forming a bond.

Ava smiled through her sadness of Patrick not being present. She tried hard not to let it show, but we could all see her sadness through her smiles. Gertie pushed her wheelchair over to her and reminded her to never give up hope. True love never runs smooth.

It was time for Julia to throw her bouquet that had been put together by the hospital flower and gift shop. It was made of yellow roses and lavender irises. Mamie's favorite colors. Julia turned her back and the bouquet took to the air and slow motion set into play. The flowers must have turned a hundred times before they hit the hands of the recipient. Ava smiled when they fell into her arms. Not a single man present didn't wish he could be the one walking down the aisle with Ava, but Ava had her mind on only one man and knew she would never have him.

Over the ER intercom, the nuptials were announced and everybody was invited out to the farm for a grand reception. That, of course, would consist of the mounds of food that was leftover from Mamie's home going. Ernie would start up the grill and there would be a continuation of the fish fry that never seemed to end. The only thing the family asked was that the reception be held in about two hours giving the family time to make it home and prepare. In all honesty, they really needed time to relax and take a breath. They also wanted to stop by the graveyard and visit Mamie's grave. They would still hold a service there, but none of us would sleep that night not knowing that Mamie was laid to rest with our not being present.

The funeral director was still there and had the roses that each of us were to put on Mamie's grave during the service. We each took a rose and put it on Mamie's plot. There was a single red rose already lying on the freshly covered grave. We were told that Patience had placed it there. Julia wanted to clear it away, but realized that even Patience could pay homage to death. We took turns at placing our roses on Mamie's final resting place. We made our peace and headed for home.

Before we left Ava approached the men filling in the grave and asked them if Patience had been alone when she visited the grave. They told her that she was at the grave alone but they thought there was a man in the car waiting for her. They added that she wasn't there long. With tears ready to fill her eyes, Ava thanked them and got into the truck. Gertie and Elisabeth were still riding in an ambulance to accommodate Gertie's leg. We finally pulled up to the farm full of excitement and grief.

"Julia," Jonathon asked, "have you given any thought as to where we are going to live?"

"Sure, at the farm," Julia responded.

"But I have a house, we could live there."

"We could, or you could. But I'm livin' at the farm."

"But what about my house?"

"Sell it."

"But what if I don't want to sell it?"

"Then, rent it out."

"I don't want no strangers living in my house."

"Now, you see, this is exactly why we should notta rushed inta marryin'," Julia said to him.

"Rushed? I've been trying to get you to marry me for five years. If you call that rushing, then I sure hope you never decide to slow down."

"Well, I'ma livin' at the farm. You can decide where ya wanna stay later."

"Julia, you are so stubborn," Jonathon told her.

"Uh huh, and I'ma still goin' ta live at the farm."

We knew Jonathon would be living at the farm, too. He would not let real estate destroy all of the work he had put into getting Julia to marry him. They would do well together. We would all do well together.

We finally pulled up into the yard and Elisabeth and Gertie were already there. Elisabeth would need help getting Gertie up the steps and into the house. They must not have had a key to the house or the ambulance driver would have helped them in. Jonathon got out and offered to help. Gertie thought she could walk up the steps into the mudroom, but we wouldn't let her. We managed to convince her to allow us to lift her inside.

I reached for the doorknob and noticed the door wasn't locked and I panicked.

"Hey, did we lock the door when we left this morning?" I asked.

"We always lock the door," Julia said.

"I think I hear something moving in the house." I said in a whisper.

"Gertie, gimme ma purse. Might have ta be some cuttin'," Elisabeth said as she reach out her hand to receive the purse.

"Should we call the sheriff?" I asked.

"Let's not over react. Let me check it out," Jonathon said.

"I go in yonda wit' ya. Ya might be needin' some backup."

"Not with that razor, Elisabeth, you could slip up and cut me. I don't want to be on the receiving end of that," Jonathon told her.

"I jus' tote it and pull it out iffin' I have ta."

"No, Elisabeth, you stay right here with me," Gertie demanded without mentioning she had removed the razor from Elisabeth's purse.

Jonathon went inside and followed the noise. He soon realized that someone was in the shower. He slipped back out the door.

"What is it Jonathon? Is somebody in the house?" Gertie asked.

"It's either that or someone left the shower on," Jonathon said mystified.

"Are you saying that someone is in our house taking a shower?" I asked.

"That's what I'm saying," Jonathon responded.

"Do ya think Patience mighta come back?" Julia asked.

"Her car isn't here. The only car here is Elisabeth's and ours," Jonathon reasoned.

"Be quiet!" Jonathon said and held his finger to his lips. "I think I heard the water shut off."

"I jus' want evabody ta know tha' iffin' I had me my gun, I could shoot whoever broke inta the house."

"Elisabeth! Stop talking about shooting people. We just left a hospital and I don't want to go back anytime soon," Gertie scolded.

"Jus' lettin' y'all know."

"We should call the sheriff. We need to report this," I reasoned.

"Go ahead, but nobody breaks into a house and takes a shower," Jonathon said rubbing his forehead. "I'm going back in there. It could be a family member and we could be getting worked up over nothing."

"Okay, but be careful, Jonathon. I don' wanna lose my husban' the same day I got 'im."

"Hey," I said, "is that the washing machine running?"

"Sounds like it," Gertie answered.

Jonathon crept through the mudroom and peeked around the corner to see an odd looking man sitting at the kitchen table wearing a woman's bathrobe. The man's head was bent down and Jonathon couldn't see his face. Then, Jonathon busted out in laughter.

"Where in the world did you get that robe?" Jonathon asked still laughing. "And how did you get into the house?" he asked with his voice growing a little more serious.

"Patience didn't take the news too well that I wasn't going back to Washington with her and threw my luggage out on the highway. With all of this rain, everything I owned got muddy and I was soaked so I took a shower and this was the only thing I could find to put on."

"Well, you just sit there a minute. I think we have someone who will be happy to see you."

Jonathon went outside and grabbed Ava's hand and pulled her reluctantly in the house. The rest of us looked at each other wondering if Jonathon was delirious. We gently got Gertie's wheelchair up the back steps and managed to push her into the kitchen where we saw Ava with Patrick in her arms.

They had the look between them that Mamie always called the look of love. A look that said more than words ever could. We were all full of questions.

"Where is Patience?" Gertie asked.

"On her way back to Washington, I suppose. She was so angry when she threw me and all of my luggage out of the car, she wasn't exactly telling me what her immediate plans were."

"But the man at the graveyard said you were in the car with Patience," Jonathon said.

"No, that wasn't me. That must have been Alvin. Patience told me she had to give him a ride up to D.C. Something about him starting over up there and helping him learn the ropes of Washington. Best wishes to him with that."

"Well, how did you get back to the farm?" I asked him.

"Oh, that. Remember the friend I made earlier in the week, Buck? He saw me on the side of the road and helped me pick up my things. He offered me a place to stay for today, but I wanted to get back here," Patrick said looking at Ava. "He kind of, sort of, helped me get into the house, too."

"Well, that explains the washing machine running," I said.

"Yes, I hope that's all right. I'm pretty refined at doing laundry. Patience never did the wash."

"Some thin's neva change," Julia interjected.

"Your job. What about that?" Ava asked timidly.

"I told them I wasn't interested. I really don't want to go back to Washington. I thought I might find a position here. In Cookham. Perhaps at the bank. I am a CPA and accustomed to handling money."

"Well, I don't know about the rest of the sisters, but I think we could use somebody with some knowledge about money right here on the farm," Gertie said.

"That's a good idea, Gertie. Not to mention, a responsible person who knows how to keep their mouth shut," I added.

"Oh, I can do that!" Patrick proclaimed and jumped with excitement exposing more than he intended to when he jumped.

"My. My. My," Gertie said, getting a bird's eye view of Patrick's exposed front.

Embarrassed, he quickly closed his robe and apologized.

"No need ta be apologizin' fo' that. Hell, most men'd be proud," Elisabeth told him.

"Sister," Gertie said to Elisabeth, "we have missed out on so much in our lives."

"Ain't it the truth, sista? Ain't it the truth?" Elisabeth responded fanning herself.

"Okay, now. Patrick you should know that Julia is a married woman now."

"Well, congratulations! But, when? Where?"

"At the hospital just today. It's a long story. I'm sure you will see the photographs."

We all laughed and heard the buzzer on the dryer go off.

"That should be my clothes. Just let me slip in there and get them," Patrick said, happy to get out of an embarrassing moment.

"Patience never had much sense. She is one foolish woman to let him go, but Ava I am sure glad things are looking up for you," Gertie said to Ava.

Ava smiled and waited for Patrick to return, this time fully dressed. He returned in khaki pants and a blue button up oxford shirt. He looked very nice and you could see it in Ava's eyes.

"Oh, I am going to need a place to live," Patrick mentioned. I feel a little uncomfortable about being married to one of your sister's and loving another one. Patience did tell me that she would be filing for divorce on Monday. I told her I would sign with no hesitation. I told her I didn't want any of her money. She could have everything."

"You won't need it," Ava said, still smiling.

"Hey, I got a house," Jonathon said.

"Are you interested in renting it out?" Patrick asked.

Jonathon frowned at Julia and said, "I guess I'm going to have to if I want to keep it…"

"…And if he wants ta see his wife," Julia added.

"We can work all of that out later. We have a wedding reception any minute now and there will probably be a lot of people here. Ernie already has the fish going," Jonathon said.

"Hey, what about a cake?" Gertie asked.

"How's be 'bout some mo' of 'em brownies y'all give me the other day? Best ones eva had," Elisabeth said.

"We don't have any more of those, Elisabeth. Those were special ones," Gertie said.

"Need ta make some mo' of 'em. Had a odd tastes ta 'em. But afta 'bout twenty minutes, I don' really 'member much. Need ta fin' out who made 'em."

"We will, sister. We will, but I think we should make a toast amongst ourselves before we get flooded with people," Gertie said.

I went to get Mamie's crystal and a bottle of grape juice. I poured each of us a half a glass and we tipped the glasses together and enjoyed hearing the tingling of the crystal.

Each person toasted to something they were thankful for. Jonathon went first.

"I am thankful for my new bride, and that I will hopefully not ever need to replace the windshield in my truck ever again."

"I am thankful tha' I finally got the nerve ta get married and I got rid of Patience," Julia said.

"I second that," Patrick said, "and I am thankful for second chances."

"I'm thankful for flowers," Ava said quietly.

"As are we all," Jonathon added.

"I'ma be grateful fo' health for all o' us and the new gun I'ma gonna get," Elisabeth said and raised her glass very high in the air.

It was my turn and I held up my glass and said, "I'm thankful for family and all of the happiness that mine has brought to my life."

Gertie was last and had put thought into what she was about to say. "I am grateful for Mamie, who held this family together through whatever happened and," she paused, "I will be eternally grateful for Wild Parsley. The one thing that has done more for us than anyone will ever know."